Adolescent Literacy

Adolescent Literacy

Integrating the Sciences of Reading and Writing in Grades 4–12

Shea Kerkhoff

BLOOMSBURY ACADEMIC
NEW YORK • LONDON • OXFORD • NEW DELHI • SYDNEY

BLOOMSBURY ACADEMIC
Bloomsbury Publishing Inc, 1359 Broadway, New York, NY 10018, USA
Bloomsbury Publishing Plc, 50 Bedford Square, London, WC1B 3DP, UK
Bloomsbury Publishing Ireland, 29 Earlsfort Terrace, Dublin 2, D02 AY28, Ireland

BLOOMSBURY, BLOOMSBURY ACADEMIC and the Diana logo are
trademarks of Bloomsbury Publishing Plc

First published in the United States of America 2026

Library of Congress Cataloging in Publication Data is available

ISBN: HB: 979-8-7651-4451-0
          PB: 979-8-7651-4452-7
          ePDF: 979-8-7651-5131-0
          eBook: 979-8-7651-5130-3

Typeset by Integra Software Services Pvt. Ltd.
Printed and bound in the United States of America

For product safety related questions contact productsafety@bloomsbury.com.

To find out more about our authors and books visit www.bloomsbury.com
and sign up for our newsletters.

For my dad, who showed me that reading is a way to understand the world—even if, at the time, I teased him for lying on the floor and reading encyclopedias for fun. And who always encouraged my love of writing.

Table of Contents

Acknowledgments

This book is the synthesis of the interesting research and bright ideas of my education community. Thank you to all of you who have shared your experiences and brilliance with me. A special thank you to:

Katherine O'Daniels for her wisdom and deep understanding of evidence-based literacy instruction.

CJ Jones, whose thoughtful feedback and organizational skills are next level.

My spouse Ben, my sounding board, word detective, and true love.

My son Gavin for his creative ideas and insightful adolescent perspective.

Nathan Davidson and the team at Bloomsbury for believing in this book.

The National Writing Project, Missouri Writing Project Network, and my local site Gateway Writing Project for supporting me in continuing to grow as an educator.

And a very special thank you to the educators who opened the door to their classrooms and let us take a peek at their Tried and True strategies. My gratitude goes to Tracy Brosch, Diana Hammond, Michele Hicks, Bryan Gaskill, Jordan Kerkhoff, Lynne Petersen, Marsha Tyson, Julie Sheerman, Veronica Walsh, Exley Warren, Sharon Wright, Ben Vessa, and the Show Me Literacies Collaborative.

Introduction

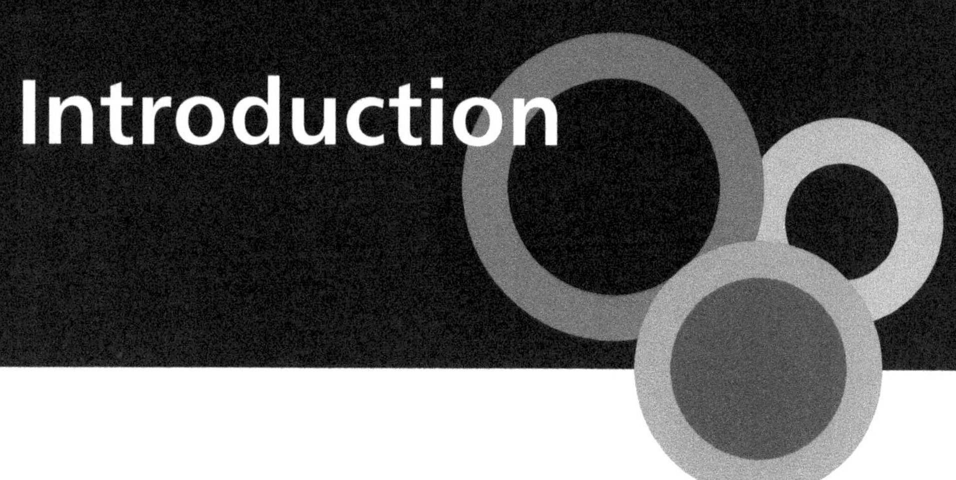

Back in the day, I was a runner. Not a *just-in-case-I'm-being-chased* kind of runner, but the kind who laced up my shoes four times a week and reserved Saturday mornings for long, sweaty miles while the rest of the world was still in pajamas.

Here's the thing about running: it gets in your head. The minute I conquered a 5K, I thought, *Well, why not a 10K?* Then I survived the 10K, and suddenly I was Googling half-marathon training plans like I was training for the Olympics. There's something kind of magical about it—feeling your legs get stronger, your lungs work like a well-oiled machine, and finishing a run with the self-righteous glow of someone who *chose* this level of suffering. It's weirdly addicting.

But then … life. Work, kids, laundry that somehow multiplies like rabbits. And suddenly my sneakers were collecting dust and my long run was a long *walk* to the fridge. After a few months off, I hadn't lost everything—I could still shuffle through a 5K without complete humiliation—but that half-marathon? Yeah, not happening without some serious couch-to-trail redemption. Running taught me that progress sticks … but only if you keep showing up.

I think literacy and running have a lot in common. We're making strides with literacy in early childhood, and we're off to a great start. But, if we don't continue hitting the pavement in grades 4–12, we risk losing the progress we've made.

Urgent Need for Adolescent Literacy

Literacy learning never stops. Early childhood education is an exciting time as children learn how to read and use written language to share their experiences.

But, learning to read and write does not stop there. Throughout our lifetime, we continue to become better readers—learning new words, making deeper connections, drawing accurate conclusions—and better writers—using more precise language, organizing our thoughts for better coherence, adapting our communication style depending on our audience. This makes the upper-grade levels just as important for supporting literacy as the early grades.

It is no secret that as children progress through school, they encounter more complex texts. The basic reading skills learned in early elementary are not enough to meet the reading, writing, and language demands found in the upper grades. Without continued literacy instruction many adolescents are left without the support they need to be successful. All too often we hear students say, "I can read it, but I don't get it" (Tovani, 2023, p. 4). As texts stairstep in complexity from grade level to grade level, the skills needed to read them advance step-by-step. The job of teachers in grades 4 through 12 is to help students approach grade-level texts strategically, think critically, and express their thoughts effectively to others. These advanced literacy skills do not magically appear, they take time, effort, and practice to develop. As teachers, we can cultivate the maturing of our students' literacy skills, knowledge, and attitudes so that they blossom to their full potential. Our hope is that they will become lifelong readers and writers and live a fruitful life.

Unpacking the Title

Let's take a closer look at the book title for a second: *Adolescent Literacy: Integrating the Sciences of Reading and Writing in Grades 4–12*. I crammed a lot into it, so it's probably worth slowing down and unpacking what it's really saying. Unpacking text refers to making meaning from a longer text by taking it one phrase at a time. The first phrase in the title is "Adolescent Literacy." People define the age range that adolescent literacy refers to differently because children reach the developmental stage at different ages. Regarding teaching, we generally think about literacy as progressing from early literacy in primary grades to adolescent literacy in upper grades. Although some people classify adolescent literacy as reserved for secondary grades, I see some children who are ready for advanced literacy learning beginning in grade 4. I also see many similarities in evidence-based practices for teaching literacy across the 4–12 grade band, although the complexity of text and maturity of topics evolve, of course. For these reasons, in this book, adolescent literacy refers to advanced reading, writing, and sense-making in grades 4–12.

The next phrase is "Integrating the Sciences of Reading and Writing." Although much of the focus in headlines and legislation is on the Science of Reading for foundational skills in the primary grades, we know from previous experience and from the research that what makes the biggest difference in student literacy outcomes is BOTH a strong foundation of literacy AND comprehensive literacy in elementary and secondary grades (Kamil et al., 2008; Shanahan, 2025). This book builds upon the national conversation around foundational skills to provide an understanding of scientific research-based literacy instruction in grades 4–12. This book integrates cognitive perspectives that dominate Science of Reading conversations with sociocultural, affective, and critical research perspectives on literacy. As such, I use the plural sciences to denote these multiple research-based perspectives.

Research shows that integrating reading and writing instruction is not only efficient but also highly effective (Fisher et al., 2016; Graham et al., 2025). Rather than focusing specifically on reading or specifically on writing, this book approaches teaching literacy in a more integrated way, with strategies in each chapter that incorporate reading, writing, speaking, listening, viewing, and composing.

That last phrase "In Grades 4–12" is not to suggest that teaching fourth graders is the same as teaching high school seniors, nor to suggest that all fourth-grade children have reached adolescence. However, as a teacher, it's important to know where students are coming from and where they are going in order to meet them where they are and guide them to the next level.

Overview of the Book

The rest of this book is divided into two sections. The first section introduces theories and models of literacy teaching and learning. Having a solid theoretical foundation will enable you to understand the "why" behind the strategies and lesson plan components that you come across in this book and in curricular resources.

Teaching reading and writing cannot be decontextualized from the "why." Quite the opposite! Research shows that teaching literacy should be an orchestrated act (Duke et al., 2018) of motivational, managerial, curricular, environmental, and instructional practices that make learning responsive, meaningful, and culturally relevant.

The learning you gain from this book will help you strengthen your professional identity as a teacher, literacy professional, and education advocate. Throughout this book, you will build your knowledge of reading, writing, and literacy instruction. As you implement this knowledge in your teaching practice, you will encounter challenges, both on a personal level and a systemic level. In each chapter, we will look at how teachers continuously improve through self-reflection and commitment to lifelong learning. And, we look at how teachers take up reflective practice to continuously grow and create positive change in their community.

The second section showcases instructional strategies, literacy strategies, and lesson plan ideas for each of the major components of adolescent literacy instruction: word recognition, fluency, vocabulary, comprehension, writing, digital literacy, motivation, and assessment.

Section One: Theories and Models of Literacy

- Chapter 1: A Comprehensive View of Literacy
- Chapter 2: Diving into the Science of Reading
- Chapter 3: Shining a Light on the Science of Writing
- Chapter 4: Comparing Content Area and Disciplinary Literacy

Section Two: The Teaching of Reading and Writing

- Chapter 5: Informing Instruction Through Literacy Assessment
- Chapter 6: Motivating and Engaging Learners in Literacy
- Chapter 7: Boosting Word Recognition and Fluency
- Chapter 8: Building Vocabulary and Knowledge
- Chapter 9: Making Meaning through Text
- Chapter 10: Communicating Meaning through Text
- Chapter 11: Digging Into Digital Literacy

The chapters do not have to be read in numerical order. Choose the order that makes the most sense to you and meets your needs. The chapters are described in more detail below with objectives for each that align to the International Literacy Association's (2018) Standards for the Preparation of Literacy Professionals.

Chapter 1: A Comprehensive View of Literacy

In this chapter, we look at literacy expansively to include reading, writing, speaking, listening, viewing, and visually representing from multiple disciplines and for multiple purposes. We explore definitions of literacy from different theoretical perspectives and research philosophies as we construct a working definition that fits our practice as literacy educators. This chapter is meant to help you think intentionally about how you define literacy and strengthen your knowledge of literacy as an educator. In this chapter, you will:

- Explore multiple definitions and perspectives of literacy.
- Understand that literacy develops across a lifetime and evolves as society evolves.
- Recognize how our social and cultural experiences affect our literacy practices.
- Synthesize ideas to articulate your own working definition of literacy.

Chapter 2: Diving into the Science of Reading

This chapter dives into research-based models of reading, including what is commonly referred to as the Science of Reading. We discuss the foundations of reading and the multiple interactive components of reading development. The chapter provides an overview of the following components: phonological awareness, phonics, fluency, vocabulary, comprehension, background knowledge, and executive function. We consider how to apply these components from reading research in our classroom in order to effectively teach reading. In this chapter, you will:

- Gain knowledge about research-based models of reading.
- Understand what the active view of reading entails.
- Identify reading components and how the components relate.
- Evaluate instructional materials to develop foundational reading skills.

Chapter 3: Shining a Light on the Science of Writing

Chapter 3 explains the research base on the teaching of writing and describes research-based models of writing. The chapter also provides an overview of processes, knowledge, affective needs, and executive functions involved in composing and communicating ideas. We then consider research-based practices for teaching writing. You will:

- Identify the cognitive processes associated with producing written text.
- Outline how social and affective components interact with cognitive components of writing.
- Understand how writing influences reading development.
- Understand how gradual release of responsibility supports students in using writing strategies.

Chapter 4: Comparing Content Area and Disciplinary Literacy

This chapter compares and contrasts ways of reading, writing, and thinking across the content areas of English language arts, science, social studies, mathematics, health, physical education, music, arts, and career and technical education. Through reading this chapter, you will be able to:

- Understand the difference between content area literacy and disciplinary literacy.
- Compare and contrast literacy practices in each discipline.
- Promote content learning through scaffolded reading instruction.
- Facilitate writing to enhance the learning of content in your discipline.

Chapter 5: Informing Instruction Through Literacy Assessment

This chapter explores best practices for teaching literacy, drawing from research on instructional design, learning science, and sociocognitive learning. This chapter describes different types of literacy assessment and tools used to identify students' literacy strengths and needs. We examine the use of assessment data to identify student profiles for differentiated instruction. We explore asset-based approaches to providing feedback on students' reading and writing development. Throughout this chapter, we invite you to consider how assessments position students in ways that impact their reading and writing identities. After reading, you will be able to:

- Build upon students' cultural and linguistic histories as a resource for literacy development.
- Interpret diagnostic, progress monitoring, and classroom assessment data to effectively guide student progress.
- Use assessment to inform and differentiate instruction.
- Identify the characteristics of students who have difficulty with language and reading comprehension.
- Provide asset-based feedback to promote growth.

Chapter 6: Motivating and Engaging Learners in Literacy

This chapter explains the relationship between motivation and literacy engagement. The chapter outlines eight principles, the 8 C's, that educators can implement in the classroom to foster students' motivation and engagement with literacy. The 8 C's are community, collaboration, control, consequence, confidence, challenge, constructing meaning, and culturally sustaining. After reading, you will be able to:

- Identify the 8 C's of literacy motivation.
- Evaluate texts for cultural and linguistic relevance.
- Empower students to see themselves as capable, confident readers and writers.

Chapter 7: Boosting Word Recognition and Fluency

This chapter explores how to support students with word recognition and fluency beyond the primary school years. We will explore the relationships between accuracy and decoding, rate and automatic word recognition, and prosody and comprehension. You will learn how to apply instructional practices to teach multisyllabic decoding and encoding to support students' fluent reading and writing. We explain how to design instruction that helps students develop independence in literacy over time by initially providing explicit guidance and then gradually releasing responsibility to students as they grow. After reading this chapter, you will be able to:

- Explain how automatic word recognition facilitates reading fluency and comprehension.
- Differentiate among the syllable types and articulate syllable division patterns to assist in decoding and encoding multisyllabic words.
- Explain how morphemic awareness and vocabulary knowledge support advanced decoding and encoding.
- Identify strategies to develop students' independent reading fluency.
- Understand how gradual release of responsibility supports students in using literacy strategies.

Chapter 8: Building Vocabulary and Knowledge

Chapter 8 explains the reciprocal nature of background knowledge and vocabulary with reading comprehension. Both are a requirement for and a product of understanding a text. In other words, we have to know enough of the words and concepts in a text to be able to comprehend it, and we gain knowledge and build our vocabulary as we encounter new words and concepts in texts also. You will learn strategies to build students' background knowledge and vocabulary to support reading comprehension and writing. After reading this chapter, you will be able to:

- Explain the centrality of background knowledge in reading comprehension as both a requirement for and a product of understanding a text.
- Select essential, valuable, and accessible vocabulary words for direct instruction from a text.
- Design evidence-based instruction to develop students' vocabulary knowledge and word learning strategies.
- Use before, during, and after reading strategies to support vocabulary and knowledge building.

Chapter 9: Making Meaning through Text

In this chapter, we focus on literacy as a meaning-making process. We will learn about what reading comprehension requires and how to effectively guide students' thinking and metacognition during reading. We share strategies for scaffolding students' reading comprehension through writing, talking, and visually representing main ideas. The chapter explains the organizational structures commonly used in academic texts and how to scaffold texts based on complexity. Through this chapter, you will be able to:

- Describe the comprehension strategies that skilled readers use to make meaning (e.g., questioning, summarizing, visualizing, monitoring understanding, and talking about texts).

- Scaffold reading experiences to help children understand, interpret, and evaluate what they read.

- Analyze instructional texts for structure, complexity, and cultural relevance in order to scaffold instruction.

Chapter 10: Communicating Meaning through Text

Chapter 10 describes strategies for writing, using an expanded view of writing and of text. We explore strategies to teach a recursive process of writing and to scaffold self-regulation during writing. We unpack traditional methods of teaching grammar and composition and advocate for equitable methods that focus on writers' agency to make decisions about communication based on audience and purpose. We explore strategies to support routine writing and the development of writer's craft. After reading, you will be able to:

- Identify strategies to scaffold self-regulation during the writing process.

- Identify strategies to support idea development, organization, word choice, sentence structure, and voice.

- Integrate routine writing and writing to learn across the curriculum.

- Foster student agency through writing for authentic audiences and purposes.

Chapter 11: Digging Into Digital Literacy

In this chapter, we explore the knowledge, skills, and attitudes that are needed to be digitally literate and a responsible global citizen in a digital age. We explore strategies for advancing students' online reading comprehension and inquiry-based research skills. We also explore strategies for supporting students' critical media literacy and multimodal digital composition to help them communicate effectively, responsibility, and safely online. We consider the role of AI in literacy teaching and learning. After reading this chapter, you will be able to:

- Support students' critical media literacy and use of digital tools and platforms to advocate for positive change.
- Consider the pros and cons of generative AI in the context of literacy instruction.
- Understand digital citizenship responsibilities and privacy concerns when communicating online.
- Scaffold each stage of online research from question development to publication, using digital tools and resources.

Overarching Objectives

The goal of this book is to synthesize the sociocognitive research on literacy education and offer strategies that are evidence-based and field-tested. Sociocognitive research looks at how learning happens through both social interaction and individual thinking. It combines the *social* (how we learn from others, like teachers, peers, and cultural communities) and the *cognitive* (how our minds process information). In the sociocognitive approach, learning is seen as something we do with others—not just inside our heads—within a larger sociocultural context.

Although the goal for the book is to be a full-scope resource, each chapter topic could be its own book. By keeping to a sociocognitive lens, each chapter is focused and detailed without feeling overwhelming, and the sociocognitive connections throughout the chapters provide coherence and depth for the reader helping them see how each part contributes to the bigger picture of adolescent literacy. This book isn't everything teachers should or could do to support adolescent literacy, but it's a good starting place.

Design Features

Each chapter includes a number of features that scaffold learning and model evidence-based literacy instruction.

- Invitations for reader engagement through Literacy Strategies at the beginning of each chapter to invite active reading and writing to learn. Readers can then teach from personal experience with the strategies in their own classrooms. Strategies are compiled in the Index of Strategies to make planning fast, flexible, and focused.

- Tried and True Strategy examples from real classrooms are embedded throughout each chapter. You will hear from teachers about how they have used evidence-based literacy instruction. The strategies from their classrooms are also compiled in the index.

- Preview Key Vocabulary at the beginning of each chapter alerts readers to essential vocabulary and key ideas before reading. The book marks vocabulary words in bold and defines them in the glossary.

- Multimodal explanations through narrative, figures, and multimedia QR codes to exemplify an expansive view of literacy and learning.

- Reflection and Discussion questions at the end of each chapter can be used by individual readers for deeper learning and by course instructors for instructional purposes.

- Index of Strategies provides one place to locate every literacy move in the book. From Alphaboxes to Zettelkasten Note-Taking, strategies are alphabetized to find the right strategy at a glance.

Final Thought

This book is for all preservice and in-service educators looking to support their students' literacy beyond the early years and to develop lifelong readers, writers, and learners.

References

Duke, N. K., Cervetti, G. N., & Wise, C. N. (2018). Learning from exemplary teachers of literacy. *The Reading Teacher*, *71*(4), 395–400.

Fisher, D., Hattie, J., & Frey, N. (2016). *Visible learning for literacy, grades K–12: Implementing the practices that work best to accelerate student learning*. SAGE Publications.

Graham, S., Cao, Y., Kim, Y. S. G., Lee, J., Tate, T., Collins, P., … & Olson, C. B. (2025). Effective writing instruction for students in grades 6 to 12: A best evidence meta-analysis. *Reading and Writing, 38*(4), 1–46.

International Literacy Association. (2018). *Standards for the preparation of literacy professionals 2017*. International Literacy Association.

Kamil, M. L., Borman, G. D., Dole, J., Kral, C. C., Salinger, T., & Torgesen, J. (2008). Improving adolescent literacy: Effective classroom and intervention practices. IES Practice Guide. NCEE 2008-4027. National Center for Education Evaluation and Regional Assistance.

Shanahan, T. (2025). A good start is not enough: Adolescent literacy instruction. https://www.shanahanonliteracy.com/publications/adolescent-literacy-instruction

Tovani, C. (2023). *Do I really need to teach reading?* Routledge.

A Comprehensive View of Literacy

1

Literacy is a critical skill needed to participate in our digitized, globalized world. Whether we are reading a ballot, a job application, a textbook, or a text message, literacy skills are required to successfully function in our society. Stop for a minute and think about all of the various purposes and methods of communication you use in a day. It is likely you sent a text message, looked something up online, and perhaps consumed news via a social media platform. Yet, methods of communication are constantly shifting. Some of the things we rely on today for communication will have evolved and be obsolete by the time today's children reach adulthood. Consider this, when I graduated high school in 1997:

- There were no smartphones or tablets.
- We didn't use email regularly.
- There was no Facebook, X, Instagram, Snapchat, LinkedIn, etc. Social media didn't exist.
- There was no Netflix, no YouTube, and no such thing as podcasts.
- WiFi was in its infancy, and Bluetooth didn't exist.
- Google had just been invented.

Today, because of rapid economic and social change, schools have to prepare students for jobs that have not yet been created, technologies that have not yet been invented, and problems that we don't yet know will arise. In this chapter, you will explore different definitions of literacy and how multiple perspectives come together to form a comprehensive view of literacy from birth through high school graduation. After considering different perspectives, you will create your own definition of literacy.

Literacy Strategy: Square, Circle, Triangle

As you read, annotate or take notes to actively think about what you are reading. You can use the Square, Circle, Triangle routine to guide your active reading. If you are annotating, put a box around the ideas that square with your thinking (e.g., what you agree with), a circle around ideas circling in your head (e.g., where you have questions), and a triangle next to important points (e.g., takeaways that you want to remember).

If you are taking notes, make three sections on your paper. Mark the first section with a square and write about what is squaring with you as you are reading. Mark the second section with a circle and capture questions circling in your head as you read. Mark the third section with a triangle, and list at least three points from the reading. See Figure 1.1.

Figure 1.1

Preview Key Vocabulary

cognitive function: mental processes involved in learning and comprehending

comprehension: making meaning of written, spoken, or viewed text

multimodal: made up of more than one mode: written, visual, and/or audio

social practices: actions based on the norms of the group

text: reading material that includes traditional print books as well as multimedia and digital sources, such as podcasts, videos, poetry, articles, and more

What Is Literacy?

In schools, literacy is often synonymous with a narrow set of reading and writing skills. However, it's a little more complex than that, especially when we consider the knowledge, skills, and attitudes needed to communicate successfully in the twenty-first century. As an educator, it's important to have a solid understanding of what you believe literacy means because your beliefs guide your practice. And, when working collaboratively, it's important to have a shared definition as a school or a district.

Check out these definitions of literacy by two international organizations. Notice how both organizations use a long list of verbs to describe the actions readers and writers take. And notice how they both talk about how literacy takes place within real-world contexts for authentic purposes.

As defined by the International Literacy Association (ILA, 2025),

Literacy is the ability to identify, understand, interpret, create, compute, and communicate using visual, audible, and digital materials across disciplines and in any context. The ability to read, write and communicate connects people to one another and empowers them to achieve things they never thought possible. Communication and connection are the basis of who we are and how we live together and interact with the world.

According to UNESCO (2007, p. 4),

Literacy is the ability to identify, understand, interpret, create, communicate and compute, using printed and written materials associated with varying contexts. Literacy involves a continuum of learning in enabling individuals to achieve their goals, to develop their knowledge and potential, and to participate fully in their community and wider society. This definition sees literacy as something that enables people to achieve their own goals and develop their potential. If this definition is applied to ethnolinguistic minority communities, the language(s) in which literacy is learned becomes an important issue. People's goals cannot always be reached, and potential developed, if only alien languages are used in literacy. Likewise, if members of ethnolinguistic communities are to participate fully in their community, they need literacy in the community language. On the other hand, to participate fully in the wider society, literacy in the language of the wider society is required. So, in the case of ethnolinguistic minority communities, this definition has biliteracy inherently written into it.

It's important to reflect on your definition of literacy, because how you conceptualize literacy will impact how you teach literacy in your classroom. Frankel and colleagues (2016) wrote a foundational article that offers implications for teaching based on their definition of literacy. They define literacy as "the process of using reading, writing, and oral language to extract, construct, integrate, and critique meaning through interaction and involvement with **multimodal texts** in the context of socially situated practices" (p. 7). The authors articulate four implications for teaching literacy, outlined in Table 1.1.

The definitions you engaged with in this section are expansive. They recognize multiple processes involved in literacy, multiple contexts, multiple disciplines, and multiple modalities. They help to illuminate the complexity of literacy teaching and learning. When we embrace expansive, complex understandings of literacy we are well on our way to envisioning a comprehensive view of literacy.

Perspectives of Literacy

When you hear the term "science" you may think of the *physical* sciences such as biology, chemistry, and physics. However, education is a *social* science, which includes academic disciplines focused on human behavior

---

Show Me Literacies Collaborative's Tried and True Strategy

Lesson Name: Creating a Shared Definition of Literacy

Context: Professional learning community of high school teachers in Missouri

Educators worked together to collaboratively craft a definition of literacy to guide teaching and learning in their school.

The world demands that a literate person applies a wide range of knowledge, skills, and attitudes toward learning.

Literacies are interconnected, everchanging, and adaptable.

Literacies cannot be separated from histories, narratives, life possibilities, and social trajectories of all individuals and groups.

Literacy changes as society and technology changes.

Literacy is a collection of communicative and sociocultural practices shared among communities.

Table 1.1 Implications for Teaching Literacy

Literacy is...	Belief	Implication
Integrated	Literacy involves productive (e.g., writing, speaking) as well as receptive (e.g., reading, listening) processes that are integrative.	Literacy should be taught in an integrated manner.
Social	Literacy happens in the context of social practices that are socially, culturally, and historically rooted.	Literacy should be taught in context.
Discipline specific	Literacy is strategic and discipline specific. In school settings, some of the key contexts in which literacy is enacted are the disciplines of science and social studies. Literacy processes vary across disciplinary contexts and are informed by the inquiry practices, ways of thinking, texts, and language of the discipline.	Literacy should be taught across content areas.
Multimodal	Modalities beyond written language bring unique complications and possibilities to the practice of literacy. For example, the meaning that comes from the layering of modes (e.g., text, image, sound) in a multimodal text may differ from the meaning that comes from simply reading the written words. As another example, the meaning that an individual constructs while navigating online from hyperlink to hyperlink compels us to rethink notions of what it means to make meaning in the context of digital literacy practices.	Literacy instruction should include multimodal and digital literacies.

in society, such as psychology, sociology, political science, anthropology, and economics. These are considered "sciences" because knowledge is built through systematic research, just as it is within the physical sciences. We have come to understand much of what we know about literacy teaching and learning through scientific study across many perspectives. Collectively, we can think of these perspectives as the "sciences" of literacy. Four perspectives are briefly introduced to support your comprehensive understanding of the field of literacy education.

Cognitive Perspectives on Literacy

Cognitive researchers investigate what happens in a person's mind. The terms "Science of Reading" or "Science of Writing" are commonly associated with cognitive research in literacy; however, it is important to remember that other perspectives of literacy also rely on systematic study (or "science"). Cognitive perspectives of literacy are primarily interested in the processes that take place within an individual's mind when they engage in literacy practices. Throughout preschool to secondary grades, students are building complex **cognitive functions**, or mental processes, related to literacy that teachers can support. The Reading for Understanding (Pearson et al., 2020) report outlines several cognitive functions that support **comprehension**:

> Listening and reading comprehension are associated with and may depend on an array of cognitive skills, such as the ability to activate information relevant to the situation described in a text (activate schema), to suppress irrelevant information (inhibitory control), to evaluate one's own ongoing understanding during reading (comprehension monitoring), to form connections within a text and between textual information and prior knowledge (inferencing), and to remember and follow sets of directions (an aspect of self-regulation). (p. 43)

Cartwright (2021) explains the cognitive functions happening during reading as the glue that holds reading together. There are many components that work together in order for a reader to decode and comprehend what they read. **Decoding** involves knowledge of how letters create words and translating print into speech. Reading comprehension is the ability to understand, interpret, and make sense of written text. It requires decoding and involves a higher-level cognitive process in which the reader actively engages with the **text** to extract meaning, infer information, and connect ideas. For example, a student can sound out the words *bypass* and *candid*, but may not know what they mean. Or, they may know what *bypass* means on the highway but not when referring to a surgery.

Effective reading comprehension entails understanding the context in which the text is written, including whether the text is talking about a highway or a surgery. The context also includes the social context that is useful in determining the intended message, such as the author's point of view or the time period of the writing. Because of the interactive nature of social context and cognitive processes, many reading researchers use the term *sociocognitive* to describe their perspective.

While reading involves decoding text and information processing, writing involves **encoding** text and communicating meaning through the writing process. Cognitive research on writing outlines the multiple components writers rely on to translate speech into text, called encoding, and the underlying process writers use to create a written product. As writing is often about communicating ideas to other people, the social context becomes entwined with the cognitive processes. Like reading, many writing researchers refer to their perspective as sociocognitive.

Affective Perspectives on Literacy

In addition to being capable readers and writers, teachers often tell me that they want their students to be confident writers or to love reading. Confidence and love refer to the affective. Affective dimensions of literacy include emotions, attitudes, and beliefs about reading, writing, and text.

Affect connected to literacy teaching and learning includes love, joy, and pleasure. After all, reading and writing for pleasure are part of the human experience. In Skerrett's (2016) case study research, she shows how youth enjoyed playing with language and found value in the artistic expression that writing provided them. Research on **motivation** shows that pleasure can lead to engaging more often in an activity, be it reading, writing, or non-literacy-related activities. However, emotions are not the only driver of motivation. The joy of reading is motivating, but so is learning something new. For example, a child may be very motivated to read a cookbook to learn how to bake or the instructions to learn how to play a popular game.

As teachers, supporting students' attitudes about literacy and beliefs about themselves can be just as important as their skills and strategies. In a TEDxTalk, Leigh Hall (2022) tells the story of a girl who was struggling with reading in school. When Hall asked her why she didn't use the reading strategies her teacher had just taught, the girl replied that if she used the strategies, the other students in the class would find out that she was struggling with the reading. She knew the cognitive strategies would help her, but she was not going to use them because of the affective dimensions at play.

According to the Reading for Understanding report, "A range of motivational factors, including those related to competence and expectancies, valuing of reading, achievement goals, and socially mediated aspects of motivation for reading ... were positively and significantly related to reading comprehension" (Pearson et al., 2020, p. 55). In other words, when students believe that they can succeed at the literacy task, value literacy and learning, and are within a supportive social environment, those affective dimensions allow for reading comprehension to happen. They may not directly cause comprehension, but lack of those affective factors can prevent the reading from ever taking place.

Sociocultural Perspectives on Literacy

Sociocultural researchers investigate how social and cultural identities and contexts impact language and literacy. Brian Street was a foundational scholar on the sociocultural perspective on literacy. His view underscored the importance of both a comprehensive and critical view of literacy. Street (2017) argued that traditionally, literacy was defined narrowly as being able to read and write words, which he calls autonomous literacy. Teaching from an autonomous literacy definition emphasizes the development of individual skills for independent reading and writing, often neglecting the broader sociocultural and political contexts of literacy.

In contrast, what he called ideological literacy is all about seeing how language, culture, and society are tightly connected when we talk about developing literacy skills. In this view, literacy isn't just about decoding words or putting sentences together—it's a **social practice** shaped by the world we live in. This sociocultural and political perspective reminds us that reading and writing always happen in a context. The way people use language, the kinds of texts they create, and even what counts as "good" literacy are all influenced by the social norms, values, and power structures around them.

Think about how a wedding announcement might look in the newspaper compared to one posted on Instagram. In the newspaper, the language is usually formal, with full names, details about family backgrounds, and a tone that follows long-standing traditions. On Instagram, the announcement might be a playful selfie with emojis, hashtags, and inside jokes. Both announce the same event, but the *language* and *format* shift because the social norms of print journalism value formality and tradition, while social media norms encourage casual, visual, and highly personal expression.

Sociocultural perspectives acknowledge that individuals use language and literacy in diverse ways depending on cultural backgrounds. Because language is an aspect of culture, they are interdependent. That makes it difficult to separate language and culture when thinking about identity. According to the Center for Advanced Research on Language Acquisition (2022), culture is the shared patterns of interactions, behaviors, and understandings that are learned through socialization. Examples of literacy and language practices that are culturally dependent include customary greetings, turn-taking in conversations, dialects, narrative structures, and argument structures.

To provide equitable education, teachers must identify and assess their behaviors and beliefs and make sure not to privilege their own culture's language and literacy over another's. In other words, teachers can honor both oral and written communication, value standard academic English alongside other dialects and languages, and provide authentic opportunities to use language in real-world contexts so that students can draw on their full range of literacy skills to make meaning.

When comprehensively considering the ways that people across cultures in today's societies communicate, literacy from a sociocultural view values the various ways equally, which can include:

- Written text—printed words.
- Visual elements—images, photographs, diagrams, charts, and other forms of visual representation.
- Auditory elements—sound, music, and spoken language.
- Gestural elements—body language, gestures, and physical movements.
- Spatial elements—the arrangement of elements on a page, screen, or physical space.
- Multimodal—Combining two or more of the above elements to create a cohesive message.

For example, multimodal writing might combine recorded spoken words, visual design of written text on slides, and background music to convey a message or tell a story. Multimodality reflects the evolving nature of communication in a digital age, where individuals have access to a wide range of modes, tools, and technologies to access information and express themselves (Kress, 2015).

Critical Perspectives on Literacy

Critical literacy examines literacy from a critical theory lens. Critical theory goes beyond the individual scale to investigate systems of power in society. Relating critical theory to literacy instruction, teachers consider the cultural,

Tried and True Strategy by Katherine O'Daniels

Lesson Name: Community Walk to Discover our Literacy Landscape

Context: Elementary class in Ferguson, Missouri

My co-teacher and I took our class of elementary students in Ferguson, Missouri on a Community Literacy Walk to explore the many ways people in our community communicate to each other. Students filed out of the classroom onto the sidewalk, writing notebooks in hand. As they encountered literacy, they would stop and take note, either copying the text or drawing a picture to represent what they saw. They saw political signs in neighbor's yards, newspapers for sale at a corner store, a mural at a laundromat, and multiple languages on an advertisement. When we returned to the classroom, we had a discussion about what they saw and what it meant to them.

social, and political systems surrounding literacy production inside and outside the classroom. This requires teachers to reflect on their identities, beliefs, biases, and privileges as to not replicate inequities in society in their classroom (Leland et al., 2020).

Teachers from a critical lens teach learners to analyze how language is constructed, helping them understand and challenge the power structures inherent in written texts. This viewpoint emphasizes a critical awareness of the ideological dimensions of literacy to empower learners in a complex and unequal world. In other words, critical literacy teaches students to "read the word and the world" (Freire & Macedo, 2005, p. i). Take a look at the Tried and True Strategy above to see what critical literacy can look like with students.

Literacy from Birth through Adolescence: A Comprehensive View

From the time we are born, we begin to develop ways to communicate our needs and feelings to others. Our communication skills develop into language and further develop into literacy. Throughout our lifetime, we continue to gain knowledge and skills that help us become better readers and writers. In fact, literacy is a lifelong journey.

Emergent and Early Literacy Stages

Emergent literacy refers to the earliest developmental period from birth to when children begin to discover the match between letters and spoken sounds. Some components occur before formal literacy instruction begins while others take shape as a result of instruction. View the slides to see the components of emergent literacy by scanning the QR code in Figure 1.2 or using this case-sensitive link (https://bit.ly/3vE4p4M).

Figure 1.2

Early literacy commonly refers to the developmental stage that often takes place from preschool to second grade. The early literacy stage is when research suggests formal instruction on the cognitive elements of reading, writing, speaking, listening, and language begins. Although explicit, systematic instruction is essential to build early literacy skills, children continue to develop literacy knowledge and skill through interactions with families, communities, and digital media outside of formal instruction.

Cognitive Perspectives on Early Literacy

During the beginning early literacy stage, learners develop increased sophistication with all elements of emergent literacy. For example, learners become increasingly proficient with segmenting, blending, and manipulating phonemes (the smallest unit of sound). In addition, they have a firm understanding of the alphabetic principle. That is, they understand that letters and sounds have systematic and predictable relationships. As a result, children develop the concept of word in text, or the ability to match spoken words to printed words by attending to known letters and sounds, as well as spaces between words. This is demonstrated as children track text by pointing to the words of a familiar text while following along with oral reading. The concept of word in text is reinforced through writing using print concepts like spacing and letter–sound correlation.

As children continue through the early literacy stage, they learn to read words and text without the support of memory, and they begin to write words and sentences that are readable to themselves and others. This is due to their growing ability to apply **phonics** to decode and encode words. Learners progress from *pre-alphabetic readers*, who are able to identify a few familiar words, nonalphabetic cues such as shape and color, to *partial-alphabetic readers*, who recognize some consonants, but do not yet have knowledge of vowels to fully sound out words, to *full alphabetic readers*, who know all consonants and vowels and are able to connect letters and sounds with meaning, a process known as orthographic mapping (Ehri, 2022). In addition, they move from being able to only represent obvious sounds while writing words to more accurate sound-by-sound matching to spell single-syllable words. They can also produce correct spellings of words in their sight vocabularies. Learners in this stage rely on phonetic (or temporary, invented) spelling to represent the sounds associated with more complex words.

Affective Perspectives on Early Literacy

Children who have regular exposure to reading and participate in discussions about books demonstrate better academic performance. Creating a classroom environment that promotes literacy experiences and interactions with texts across the curriculum and during choice time is essential to foster reading success in young students. Establishing a literacy-rich environment is a key factor in achieving this goal. Teachers can create an inviting reading space with comfortable reading chairs, floor pillows, and other amenities. Texts of a variety of **genres** (picture books, magazines, comics, etc.) should be easily accessible and organized by topic (sports, weather, etc.). Responsive texts that provide students with authentic representations of themselves are essential to building learning communities where children feel a sense of belonging. Student writing can be shared on bulletin boards or binders, as well as orally within their learning communities. And, classroom discussions and decor can illustrate joy in literacy.

Sociocultural Perspectives on Early Literacy

A family and community literacy lens recognizes the literacy practices that already exist among families in their homes and community as part of many everyday activities (Compton-Lilly et al., 2019). Shopping lists, jump rope rhymes, following recipes, telling stories, and reading the news are literacy activities that are typical parts of a family day. Rather than narrowing our definition of literacy to practices common in school, family, and community literacy encompasses and values the literacy skills that every child brings to the classroom.

Family and community literacy programs bring people in a community together around literacy and learning. Some programs may connect families and communities to school initiatives, and others may connect literacy to family and community events outside of school. Examples of how to enact family and community literacy in your classroom include: build your classroom library with culturally and linguistically diverse books, communicate to families through social media apps that allow for images and words, survey the school and community to learn about the languages spoken, reflect on your language and literacy history, support families to discuss their language and literacy practices, and invite family and community members to share their literacy practices with the class (Zapata & Laman, 2016).

Critical Perspectives on Early Literacy

Critical literacy in early childhood can be approached through reading picture books that represent diverse families and communities. Children can learn about the world through reading even as they are learning to read.

Consider this example from Spires, Kerkhoff, and Paul (2020):

> Marcus, a 4-year-old, is reading sight words. He loves Mo Willem's book *I Really Like Slop!* where a pig introduces the food of her culture, slop, to her elephant friend, who thinks it's disgusting. While Marcus is reading along and saying the words he knows aloud, he stops to ask his mother, "What is culture?" We know Marcus understands the explanation when he asks a friend from China visiting on Thanksgiving to describe the food in her culture. He is able to simultaneously learn to read and read to learn. (p. 12)

Picture books can teach children about different cultures and also bring counternarratives to children's attention. Counternarratives push back against negative stereotypes of groups of people by showing a variety of lived experiences. For example, in *The Paper Bag Princess* written by Robert Munsch (2010) and illustrated by Michael Martchenko, it is the princess who saves people rather than the princess being the one who needs to be rescued.

Another way that critical perspectives shape early literacy instruction is through fostering a community of learners where differences are valued and respected. Teachers can foster community by attending to and nurturing the whole child, not just the academic part. Teachers can also create an environment where students share about themselves, their feelings, and their thoughts. Students can learn, not just from the teacher, but from each other as well. In fact, teachers can learn as much from their students as they learn from us.

Intermediate Literacy Stage

We continue explicitly teaching reading and writing in intermediate grades because literacy develops over a lifetime. We may focus on learning to read in the early literacy stage, but we continue to learn reading skills and strategies in the intermediate stage and beyond. Learning to read never ends because we never stop growing as readers. Intermediate literacy builds on early literacy and requires more advanced literacy skills in order to read **multisyllabic** words and understand more complex text. Intermediate literacy typically occurs from around third to sixth grade; however, individual development varies from child to child within each phase of literacy development. As students progress through elementary school, they meet shifting demands on their literacy knowledge, skills, and dispositions. The emphasis on learning to read and write in earlier grades begins to shift to an emphasis on reading to learn and writing to learn in the content areas. However, the view that reading skills develop in two stages from learning to read (emergent and early literacy) to reading to learn (intermediate and adolescent literacy) sets up a false dichotomy. Even during the early stage when students are learning to read, they are still able to learn new concepts from the text. And, during the intermediate stage, students are still learning to become better readers by building their advanced skills. As such, the intermediate stage acts as a bridge between early literacy and adolescent literacy development.

Adolescent Literacy Stage

Adolescent literacy refers to the developmental period that often coincides with middle and high school. In early literacy, the main focus is on learning to read and write, which moves to reading and writing to build and apply knowledge in the intermediate stage. In the adolescent stage, the focus shifts to higher-order thinking where students analyze and evaluate the texts they are reading and create texts to communicate their ideas. We can shift from Bloom's taxonomy of thinking as a pyramid to an inverted pyramid in adolescent literacy (Spires et al., 2016), as displayed in Figure 1.3.

In other words, both lower-order and higher-order thinking should occur throughout one's education, but in secondary education, the focus and the majority of students' time should be spent analyzing, evaluating, and creating. Research suggests several components to consider during the development of literacy in adolescents. View the slides linked in the bit.ly or by following the QR code in Figure 1.4 for an overview (https://bit.ly/3vTa5b1).

When someone says that an adolescent can't read, they typically mean that an adolescent isn't comprehending what they read. The adolescent might be able to decode the words on the page, but when asked about what they just read, they reply with "I don't know." One barrier to comprehension could be not knowing what the words mean. For example, the short story "The Most Dangerous Game" by Richard Connell (1924) uses the phrases "the moss was lacerated; one patch of weeds was stained crimson" to describe what the main character finds upon arriving on the island. Without knowing what the words *lacerated* and *crimson* mean, the reader would miss the clues that something, or someone, had been killed. Therefore, a student may miss the foreshadowing, and the suspense, that makes the short story so captivating.

Cognitive Perspectives on Adolescent Literacy

Cognitive research also details how information processing and executive function relate to reading and writing. Information processing helps readers and writers take in, organize, make sense of, and remember information, which is essential for understanding texts and expressing ideas clearly. Executive function supports planning, focusing, and managing tasks, which are important for staying on task, organizing thoughts, and revising when reading and writing.

As students progress through school, literacy is more and more connected to content learning. This means that content area teachers share the responsibility for supporting literacy development. As students advance, the vocabulary they encounter will become even more technical

Figure 1.3 Inverted Bloom's Taxonomy.

Figure 1.4

and specialized. **Disciplinary literacy** refers to the discipline-specific technical language and specialized ways of communicating in an academic discipline, such as mathematics, history, or American literature. Content teachers can make the language and structures of their discipline explicit to adolescents to increase access to the content knowledge. For example, a science text might say *Felis catus* or a poem might say *feline friend*. Both refer to a cat, but the authors chose the different terminology because of a value of precision in science (referring to the domestic cat according to the taxonomy) and a value of the sound of the language in poetry (alliteration and rhythm in this case).

As for structure, scientific research articles are often written with a problem—solution organizational structure, for example. Narrative texts are often written in chronological order. As texts become more complex, they may integrate more than one structure or play with structure, such as using flashbacks that disrupt the chronological order of a story. For these reasons, it's important that teachers of adolescents continue to teach vocabulary and literacy strategies in order for students to make meaning through texts.

Affective Perspectives on Adolescent Literacy

Developmentally, adolescents are in need of more independence as they transition from children to adults. Providing choices can help fulfill this need for **autonomy**. Choices can include reading and writing about topics of interest to them, in a genre they enjoy, and at various complexity levels. Adolescence is also a time of identity development. Texts by and about people from diverse lived experiences can promote healthy identity development. Adolescents need to see representations of their cultures in texts and to read about different perspectives to broaden their understanding of the world beyond their local community.

Rudine Sims Bishop (2015) refers to this as giving students mirrors, windows, and sliding glass doors. Providing books that are mirrors allows youth to see themselves represented in the curriculum. Books that are windows broaden youths' horizons by providing windows to see other people's perspectives, and books that challenge youth to see others' perspectives and take action to change the world for the better are symbolized by the sliding glass doors. Additionally, previous research has shown that adolescents find lessons that require critical and creative thinking to be more engaging than lessons that only require memorization and recall (Guthrie, 2008; Lent, 2009). If adolescents are motivated to read, then they will persevere through the challenging complex texts they will encounter in secondary school.

If they are not motivated, even those with strong literacy skills may choose not to engage with a text.

Sociocultural Perspectives on Adolescent Literacy

Negative stereotypes about adolescents can affect how we interact with them. Sociocultural research on adolescence critiques neuroscience research that claims that all people ages 12 to 18 experience the same developmental stages and behave in the same way because of what parts of their brains are and are not developed. In actuality, youth across the world are very diverse in their interests and behaviors.

One negative stereotype about adolescents is that they do not read and write. In fact, research on youth literacies suggests that youth are reading and writing more than ever before. However, the type of reading and writing youth are participating in may not be the same literacies valued in school. This point is important for two reasons. First, this means that we can pay attention to the reading and writing that students are engaging in outside of school and tie those into the learning we want students to engage in inside of school to increase relevance and motivation. The second reason is related to digital literacy. The digital literacy that adolescents may be fluent in outside of school may not be the same digital literacies needed to be successful in school. This means that we need to teach and model the digital literacy practices that students will need to use in our class and not assume that they already know how to use technology for academic literacy purposes. Learn more about digital literacy in Chapter 11.

Another way that sociocultural perspectives inform adolescent literacy instruction is through our understanding of how readers make meaning through text. Readers have to read between the lines to make inferences and draw conclusions. Consider this text and read between the lines to figure out what is going on:

> *He plunked down $8.00 at the window.*
> *She tried to give him $4.00, but he refused*
> *to take it. So when they got inside, she*
> *bought him a large bag of popcorn.*

What did you infer is going on in the passage? Where were the people? What was their relationship? When I have read this passage with learners in the United States, the inferences are that the people are at a movie and that the woman does not want it to be considered a date, so she wants to make sure to pay. The cultural knowledge used to make those inferences is that movie theaters have ticket windows and popcorn. The social knowledge used to make those inferences is that men are expected to pay on dates. Some learners might infer that the woman is fine with it being a date, but is trying to break down traditional gender stereotypes.

On the other hand, when I read this passage with learners in Belize, there was a completely different set of inferences made. Those learners made the inference that it was a mother and son at a festival. Their conclusions still fit the evidence provided in the text and were based on their cultural experiences and social norms.

Critical Perspectives on Adolescent Literacy

According to a National Council of Teachers of English (NCTE, 2018) report, a critical perspective on adolescent literacy means "seeing, thinking, reading, writing, listening, and discussing in ways that critically confront and bridge social, cultural, and personal differences" (para. 6). Adolescents need to think critically about texts including analysis and evaluation. Critical analysis and evaluation of text enable learners to:

- Recognize writer's craft and how the writer uses craft to create effect,
- Infer beyond literal interpretations,
- Understand multiple meanings and layers of complexity, and
- Question the social, political, and historical context of text.

As social and mass media become increasingly prevalent in adolescents' lives, so too does the need for **critical media literacy**. Critical media literacy is the application of critical literacy to print and digital media. Critical analysis and evaluation of media enable learners to:

- Detect bias,
- Identify whose voices are reported and whose are missing,
- Analyze the purpose behind media messages, and
- Evaluate the credibility of a source.

As adolescents are developing their identity as individuals independent of yet connected to their family and community, they are also developing their beliefs and their voice. A critical aspect of adolescent literacy is providing opportunities for students to express themselves. These practices and more examples are displayed in Figure 1.5.

Critical Literacy Practices

Evaluate the reliability of information and credibility of sources

Reflect on one's thinking and ways of knowing

Reflect on one's cultural beliefs and values

Analyze the purpose behind media and text structures

Listen to diverse perspectives

Investigate who benefits and who is disadvantaged by access or policies

Question social, political, and historical context

Engage in conversations about social and political issues

Create counternarratives and remix texts to create versions that promotes equity

Revise claims as new evidence is presented

Figure 1.5 Critical Literacy Practices.

Conclusion

We must attend to the body of evidence-based scientific research and offer explicit and systematic instruction in reading and writing skills that are integrated and contextualized. But we can't stop there, as literacy is so much more than traditional academic skills. We need to provide ways to value diverse social and cultural literacy practices and bridge outside-of-school literacies with in-school literacies. And, we have to be open to the evolving nature of literacy and be willing to continuously evolve our instruction.

Reflect

Use a Thinking Routine to help you reflect on your learning: *I Used to Think … Now I Think …*

Questions to consider:

- How did you define literacy before reading this chapter?
- How would you define literacy now? Look back at your annotations or notes for what squared with you and your takeaways.
- How does your new understanding empower your teaching of literacy?
- How does your new understanding complicate your teaching of literacy?

Discuss

Questions for discussion to learn from and with each other:

- What questions or ideas are circling in your head? Refer to your annotations and notes that you took when actively reading.
- How does your definition of literacy compare with your peers' definitions? Can you come to consensus to build a shared definition of literacy?
- Listen to Dr. Robert Petron's podcast episode on *Rethinking Adolescent Literacy* (https://podcasters.spotify.com/pod/show/showmeliteracies/episodes/Adolescent-Literacy-e1j63i0/a-a80seut). How does his definition of adolescence as a social construct compare to your prior knowledge about adolescence?

- How does your new understanding of literacy and adolescence empower your teaching of literacy?
- How does your new understanding of literacy and adolescence complicate your teaching of literacy?

More to Explore

Adichie, C. N. (2009, October 7). *Chimamanda Ngozi Adichie: The danger of a single story* [Video]. YouTube. https://www.youtube.com/watch?v=D9Ihs241zeg

Boroditsky, L. (2018, May 2). *How language shapes the way we think* [Video]. YouTube. https://youtu.be/RKK7wGAYP6k?si=iEWBTz9N-UgoYSPI

Peterson, A. (2020). Literacy is more than just reading and writing [Blog]. *Literacy & NCTE Blog.* https://ncte.org/blog/2020/03/literacy-just-reading-writing/

Petron, R. (2022). *Rethinking adolescent literacy* [Podcast episode]. Show Me Literacies Podcast. https://podcasters.spotify.com/pod/show/showmeliteracies/episodes/Adolescent-Literacy-e1j63i0/a-a80seut

References

Bishop, R. S. (2015). Multicultural literacy: Mirrors, windows, and sliding glass doors. *Perspectives: Choosing and Using Books for the Classroom, 6*(3), 1–2. https://www.readingrockets.org/sites/default/files/migrated/Mirrors-Windows-and-Sliding-Glass-Doors.pdf

Cartwright, K. B. (2021, November 6). Executive function: The glue that holds together reading's many processes. *Dystinct,* (6), 21–31. https://on.dystinct.org/issue-06-november-2021/

Center for Advanced Research on Language Acquisition. (n.d.). *What is culture?* https://carla.umn.edu/culture/definitions.html

Compton-Lilly, C., Ellison, T. L., & Rogers, R. (2019). The promise of family literacy: Possibilities and practices for educators. *Language Arts, 97*(1), 25–35. http://doi.org/10.58680/la201930235

Ehri, L. C. (2022). What teachers need to know and do to teach letter-sounds, phonemic awareness, word reading, and phonics. *The Reading Teacher, 76*(1), 53–61. https://doi.org/10.1002/trtr.2095

Frankel, K. K., Becker, B. L. C., Rowe, M. W., & Pearson, P. D. (2016). From "what is reading?" to what is literacy? *Journal of Education, 196*(3), 7–17. https://doi.org/10.1177/002205741619600303

Freire, P., & Macedo, D. (2005). *Literacy: Reading the word and the world.* Routledge. https://doi.org/10.4324/9780203986103

Guthrie, J. T. (2008). Engaging adolescents in reading. In J. T. Guthrie (Ed.), *Reading motivation and engagement in middle and high school: Appraisal and Intervention* (pp. 1–16). Corwin Press.

Hall, L. (2022, March 24). *How reading instruction fails students | TEDxLander* [Video]. YouTube. https://www.youtube.com/watch?v=Mww43LkV6o0

International Literacy Association. (2025). Literacy glossary. https://www.literacyworldwide.org/get-resources/literacy-glossary

Kress, G. (2015). Semiotic work: Applied linguistics and a social semiotic account of multimodality. *Aila Review, 28*(1), 49–71.

Leland, C. H., Lewison, M., & Harste, J. C. (2020). *Teaching K–8 reading: Disrupting 10 literacy myths.* Routledge. https://doi.org/10.4324/9780429320736

Lent, R. C. (2009). *Literacy for real: Reading, thinking, and learning in the content areas.* Teachers College Press.

National Council of Teachers of English. (2018, July 17). *A call to action: What we know about adolescent literacy instruction.* https://ncte.org/statement/adolescentliteracy/

Pearson, P. D., Palincsar, A. S., Biancarosa, G., & Berman, A. I. (Eds.). (2020). *Reaping the rewards of the reading for understanding initiative.* National Academy of Education. https://doi.org/10.31094/2020/2

Skerrett, A. (2016). Attending to pleasure and purpose in multiliteracies instructional practices: Insights from transnational youths. *Journal of Adolescent & Adult Literacy, 60*(2), 115–20. https://doi.org/10.1002/jaal.571

Spires, H. A., Kerkhoff, S. N., & Graham, A. C. (2016). Disciplinary literacy and inquiry: Teaching for deeper content learning. *Journal of Adolescent & Adult Literacy, 60*(2), 151–61. https://doi.org/10.1002/jaal.577

Spires, H. A., Kerkhoff, S. N., & Paul, C. M. (2020). *Read, write, inquire: Disciplinary literacy in grades 6–12.* Teachers College Press.

Street, B. V. (2017). New literacies, new times: Developments in literacy studies. In B. V. Street & S. May (Eds.), *Literacies and language education: Encyclopedia of language and education* (pp. 3–16). Springer.

UNESCO (2007). *Promoting literacy in multilingual contexts.* https://unesdoc.unesco.org/ark:/48223/pf0000150704.locale=en

Zapata, A., & Laman, T. T. (2016). "I write to show how beautiful my languages are": Translingual writing instruction in English-dominant classrooms. *Language Arts, 93*(5), 366–78. https://doi.org/10.58680/la20162859

Literature Cited

Connell, R. (1924). *The most dangerous game.* Collier's.

Munsch, R. N. (2010). *The paper bag princess* (M. Martchenko, Illus.). Annick Press.

Willems, M. (2015). *I really like slop!* Hyperion Books for Children.

Diving Into the Science of Reading

2

In Chapter 1, we looked at literacy broadly to include reading, writing, speaking, listening, viewing, and visually representing; to include literacy as the knowledge and skills of an individual and as social and cultural practices; and to include multiple theoretical perspectives. This chapter zooms in on learning to read. We dive inside the reader's mind to examine research-based models of the mental processes that take place when reading, or what is sometimes referred to as the Science of Reading.

In this book, literacy is viewed as a social practice and learning is viewed as something we do together—not just things that happen silently in our heads. As such, this chapter takes a sociocognitive approach to literacy, which blends social learning models with cognitive research. For example, when students read a complex text and then discuss it in small groups, they're not just practicing **comprehension**, they're co-constructing meaning, drawing on each other's ideas, **background knowledge**, and perspectives. This approach recognizes that reading happens within social, cultural, historical, and political contexts—and that effective instruction must take all of these into account.

The Science of Reading has been gaining attention in the media and in governments. In fact, forty states and the District of Columbia have recently passed laws related to the Science of Reading. Unfortunately, many of these policies rely on an oversimplified understanding of the Science of Reading. In this chapter, you will learn that there is nothing simple about the Science of Reading.

Literacy Strategy: SQ3R

SQ3R is a strategy for informational texts that stands for Survey, Question, Read, Recite, and Review. You are invited to use these steps to actively engage with this chapter. (1) Survey the chapter to preview headings and images. (2) Create questions about what you want to learn based on the headings. Use the questions to guide note-taking. (3) Read to answer the questions and take notes. (4) Recite what you can recall after reading without looking at your notes. (5) Review your notes to see how well you recalled the important parts, and review the reading or consult other resources for any parts that you do not understand.

Preview Key Vocabulary

grapheme: letters of written language

orthography: study of how graphemes (letters) and phonemes (sounds) relate to form words

phoneme: smallest unit of sound in words

phonics: understanding that sounds are connected to graphemes, the name for written letters

phonological awareness: understanding that words are made up of sounds and the ability to recognize spoken parts of words

A Timeline of Reading Models

In 1955, a book called *Why Johnny Can't Read* launched the nation into debates about reading instruction. These debates questioned the premise of the book, with some arguing that there was a literacy crisis and others asserting that the book was sensationalizing the issue. Other debates questioned the claim that teaching **phonics** was the answer, with some rallying around the systematic teaching of phonics and others arguing for a more holistic approach to reading education. These debates continued into the 1980s and became known as the Reading Wars. We pick up our examination of research-based models of the reading process here in the 1980s with the simple view of reading. Many credit the simple view of reading as the foundation of modern Science of Reading models. The purpose of this section is to give a brief overview to illustrate the progression of research. The next section will give explanations about the interactive processes involved in reading. We then discuss the active view of reading and whether the Reading Wars are settled.

Figure 2.1 The Simple View of Reading.

1986

In 1986, Gough and Tunmer published the Simple View of Reading (see Figure 2.1) in a research journal that stated that reading equals the product of **decoding** and word recognition (WR) and listening and language comprehension (LC). Together these two parts equal reading comprehension. Word recognition refers to being able to decode or recognize the word in written text. Language comprehension refers to being able to understand spoken language.

1 (WR) × 1 (LC) = 1 (successful reading comprehension)

0 (WR) × 1 (LC) = 0 (decoding difficulty, often seen with dyslexia)

1 (WR) × 0 (LC) = 0 (oral language comprehension difficulty, often seen with hyperlexia)

2000

Through a review of the research on reading instruction, the National Reading Panel (2000) identified five components as key areas of reading and offered recommendations for explicit and systematic instruction in these five. The components are now widely referred to as the five pillars of reading instruction.

2001

Scarborough's (2001) reading rope (Figure 2.2) is often used as a metaphor for the strands that weave together to create meaning through texts. The

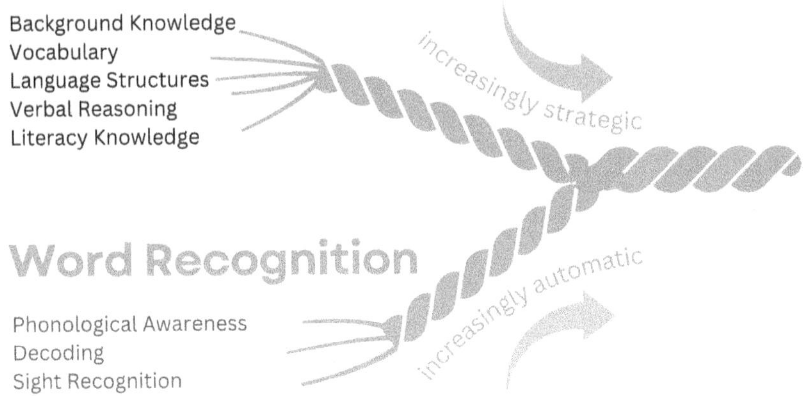

Figure 2.2 Scarborough's Reading Rope.

rope illustrates five strands in language comprehension: background knowledge, vocabulary, language structures (**syntax**, semantics, etc.), verbal reasoning (inference, metaphor, etc.), and literacy-specific knowledge. Word recognition includes three strands: phonological awareness, decoding, and sight recognition of familiar words.

2002

In 2002, Catherine Snow led a team at RAND to define reading comprehension. The three-way interaction between the reader, the text, and the activity occurs within a sociocultural context that impacts and is impacted by the reader throughout the reading process.

2015

To signify the importance of knowledge in the process of reading, Cervetti and Hiebert (2015) made a case for adding background knowledge to the five National Reading Panel components to make the 5+1 Model. A review of research by the National Academy of Education corroborated that "knowledge is cause, consequence, and covariate of reading comprehension" (Pearson et al., 2020, p. 2).

2020

Kim (2020) presents the direct and indirect effects model of reading contributing to the idea that both background knowledge and knowledge about language and reading are important and that **affect** (e.g., **motivation** and emotions) as well as executive function (e.g., working memory and attention) are integrated with reading comprehension. The model includes the following skills and knowledge: word reading, listening comprehension, fluency, background knowledge, affect, higher-order cognition (e.g., inference, perspective-taking, reasoning, and comprehension monitoring), vocabulary, syntax knowledge, phonology, morphology, orthography, and executive function.

2021

Building on the models that came before, the Active View of Reading by Duke and Cartwright (2021; see Figure 2.3) takes a deeper dive into the reader component to explain how word recognition and language comprehension have some overlapping components, and it adds active **self-regulation** through executive skills to the reader model. They note that this explains

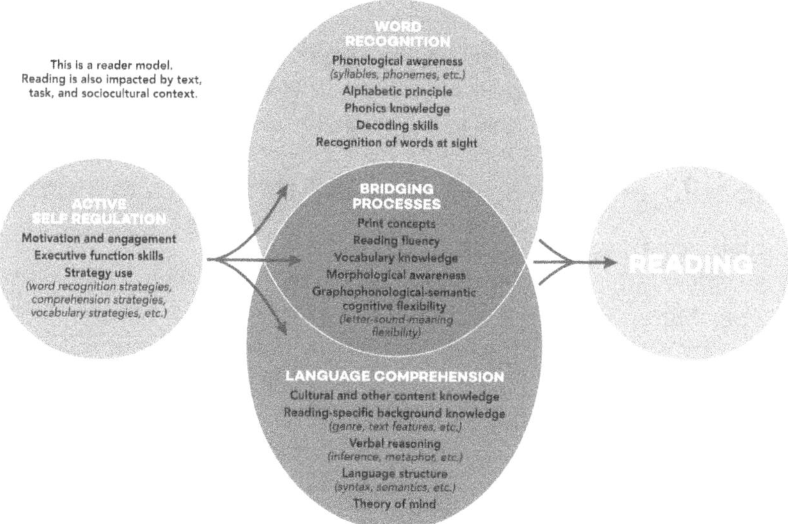

Figure 2.3 The Active View of Reading. From Duke and Cartwright (2021).

what the reader does, but that comprehension is also impacted by the text, task, and context of reading, as the RAND Model explains.

Diving Deeper into the Active View of Reading

Research continues to evolve and improve our understanding about what happens in the brain when we read. Today, we understand that word recognition and language comprehension are both important components of reading. However, the active view of reading, and our definition of literacy from the first chapter, suggest that there is nothing simple about the process of learning to read.

Duke and Cartwright (2021) built the Active View of Reading model, which consists of four components: word recognition, bridging processes, language comprehension, and active self-regulation. We will take a look at the four components more closely in this section. In later chapters, we will explore the research base for how to teach those components in developmentally appropriate ways.

Word Recognition

Word recognition is represented by the top circle in the model. Inside this component are **phonological awareness**, alphabetic principle, phonics knowledge, decoding skills, and recognition of words on sight.

Phonological Awareness and Alphabetic Principle

Phonological awareness is understanding that speech sounds connect together to create words. Teaching phonological awareness should progress from easier to more difficult skills, such as an awareness that sentences are made up of words, that words are made up of syllables, and then that words are made up of individual sounds called **phonemes**. Syllables in the English language are words or word parts organized around a vowel sound, for example, the word phonological has five: pho/ no/ log/ i /cal. Learning the individual sounds is called phonemic awareness and typically develops from simpler skills, like rhyme recognition, rhyme production, syllable segmentation, and onset-rime identification, to more advanced skills like phoneme blending, deleting, and segmentation.

Phonological awareness is built through explicit teaching and authentic application. When teaching children to read, they first need to learn the sounds in words before they learn to attach those sounds to written letters. The alphabetic principle is knowing that letters represent sounds.

A great way to help young children develop phonological awareness is through using songs and games. Children can repeat tongue twisters for building awareness of initial sounds, play rhyming games for end sounds, or clap the number of syllables in a word. When engaging older children in phonological awareness learning, it's important to not make it seem babyish. For example, rather than songs to enhance phonemic awareness, we can read and write poetry with alliteration and rhymes, such as Edgar Allen Poe's "The Raven." Take for instance these lines from the poem that repeat the sound /g/ and rhymes yore with nevermore.

What this grim, un**g**ainly, **gh**astly, **g**aunt, and ominous bird of y**ore**
Meant in croaking "Neverm**ore**."

Phonics Knowledge and Decoding Skills

Phonics is the relationship between the **graphemes** (written letters) of written language and the phonemes (individual sounds) of spoken language. This relationship is quite predictable in the English language with 84 percent predictable spelling patterns (Moats, 2005–2006). Most people need explicit phonics instruction in order to learn to read.

Effective literacy instruction in upper grades continues to advance children's knowledge of phonics strategies to read and write grade-level words. Specifically, educators can model and provide feedback on two phonics strategies for intermediate and adolescent learners: decoding and analogizing (Ehri, 2014). Decoding converts the graphemes (written letters) into a blend of phonemes (sounds) to say the word. The English language consists of fifty-two graphemes (capital and lowercase). There are forty-six phonemes in English produced by consonants, vowels, and digraphs. A digraph is a letter team that makes one sound, for example, ch says /ch/ as in the word *church*. What is tricky in English is that one letter can make different sounds and different letters sometimes make the same sound, for example the letter *C* says /k/ and /s/. And what is especially tricky are the many vowel combinations; for example, the word *read* can be pronounced two ways, and readers must determine whether the context is in the present or past to determine how to pronounce the word. Readers have to constantly check to see if their word reading makes sense in context.

Adolescents may need explicit help reading **multisyllabic** words. We can help adolescents remember to break down multisyllabic words into syllables in order to decode. First, we can teach students about syllables. Then, we can teach a flexible decoding routine that students can learn to use independently. The routine can look like this. First, underline the vowels or vowel groups. Then, draw a line to separate the syllables with one vowel or vowel group in each syllable. Next, say each syllable separately and then all together. Finally, check to see if the pronounced word makes sense in the context of the reading (e.g., se/man/tics). What is tricky about the last step when teaching adolescents is that often the word is unfamiliar even after pronouncing it. For example, a middle schooler might be able to pronounce semantics but still not know the word because they do not know the meaning. (Ironically, semantics means word meaning.)

Analogizing looks for patterns and is useful when readers know a lot of words. Readers identify patterns and use known words to decode unknown words. For example, if a reader knows how to decode the word "name," they can use the long-A pattern to decode the word "same." An engaging way to teach patterns is to play word ladder games where learners delete, add, or substitute phonemes. For example, write *fable*; now, instead of the beginning sound /f/ use the beginning sound /t/. To keep the teaching of advanced phonics from seeming babyish, we can use the linguistic terms for the patterns with our students, such as morpheme and syntax.

Recognition of Words on Sight

Orthography is knowing how letters and sounds relate to form words and create meaning. Reading and writing language call on multiple parts of the brain to connect the regions responsible for processing the visual symbols, the sounds in spoken language, the relationship of the letters and sounds, as well as the meaning being communicated.

Over repeated exposure to words in print, our brain creates an orthographic map (Figure 2.4) that connects the spelling, sounds, and meaning together and stores the map in long-term memory. When we have an orthographic map of a word, we can recognize it on sight. The more words we have an orthographic

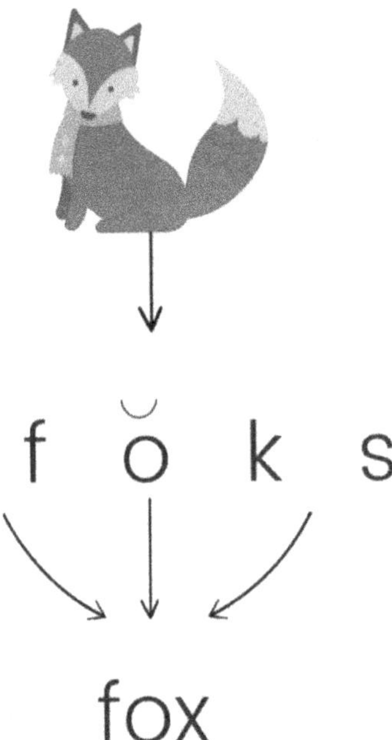

Figure 2.4 Orthographic Map.

map for, the less time and energy we have to spend to decode or spell (Ehri, 2014).

Bridging Components

Language processing for proficient reading includes the phonological and orthographic awareness described in the previous section as well as knowledge about words, language, and text.

Concepts about Print

Concepts about print refer to knowledge about books and how we read text. It is understanding that letters come together to form words, and that words, spaces, and punctuation create sentences, and so forth. It also includes knowing book parts. As young children, we learn that books have a front cover, back cover, and a spine. In upper grades, we learn more advanced information about texts, such as where to find the information needed for citations and how to use **text** features to increase reading comprehension. Teachers can use a document camera or projector to point out the front matter (e.g., title page and copyright page) and text features (e.g., headings and glossary).

Concepts about print include learning directionality, such as how to hold a book right-side-up and how to turn the pages. In English, we read from left to right and top to bottom. For most texts, this is straightforward, but when I started reading graphic novels, I needed help. One of my students was a fan, and she shared with me the formula. Comics and graphic novels are read from left to right, top to bottom in a Z pattern (as seen in the movement from panels 1 to 4 in Figure 2.5). They also use a nested system, so you read inside each panel from the top left corner to the right and down before moving to the next panel (as seen in panels 9 and 10).

Concepts about print also include learning how texts are structured. Narratives, like the novels we check out from the library and read for enjoyment, are typically meant to be read from beginning to end, following a clear structure with a beginning, middle, and end. In contrast, informational books and textbooks often use a variety of organizational patterns, such as cause and effect or problem and solution. They also include helpful features like a table of contents and an index, which allow readers to easily locate specific sections or topics without reading the entire book cover to cover.

Although this component is traditionally referred to as concepts about print, children and adolescents also need to understand concepts related to

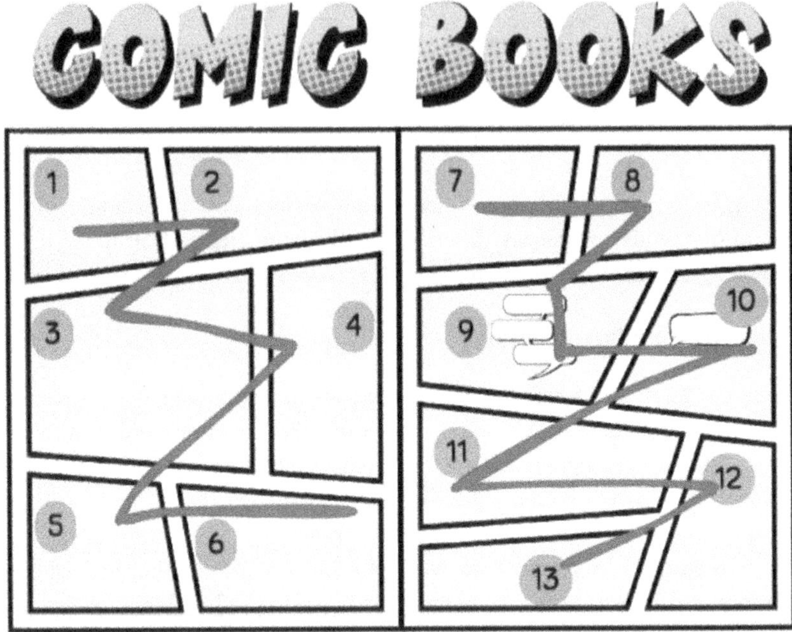

Figure 2.5 How to Read a Comic Book.

digital texts. Print texts have a cover and spine, and are read with the spine on the left. Pages are then read in the order from left to right. However, digital texts have hyperlinks and could be read in a variety of different orders depending on what links are clicked. Print texts that are informational often have a table of contents in the front and an index in the back. With digital texts, readers have to figure out how to navigate the text. Teachers can point out features available in a digital text that they will be using in class and model how to navigate back and forth in the text.

Fluency

Fluency is reading with accuracy, automaticity, and prosody. Accuracy is reading words correctly and automaticity is related to speed. Accuracy and automaticity are important because when readers can identify words automatically, they can devote effort that might have gone to decoding to understanding the text. The faster a student reads, the less effort their working memory has to contribute. Working memory is what links the pronunciation of words stored in our long-term memory in order to decode what we are reading. Working memory is responsible for holding sounds for spelling and ideas for composing when we are writing.

Of great importance in the intermediate grades is the connection of fluency and reading comprehension. According to the International Dyslexia Association (2020),

> When reading a long sentence, paragraph or passage, working memory is what allows us to hold on to and integrate information we read early on with information that comes later. Students with strong decoding skills but weak working memories often comment that they "can't remember anything!" from a page that they just read (para. 13).

By the end of sixth grade, students should be able to read 146 correct words per minute, whereas by the end of eighth grade, students should be able to read 151 words correct per minute (Hasbrouck & Tindal, 2017; ILA, 2018). Again, speed is not the goal, comprehension is the goal, but these benchmarks can help teachers identify where a problem lies if a reader is having difficulty comprehending grade-level texts.

Prosody is reading in a way that sounds like natural speech. It includes readers using appropriate phrasing and expression to make meaning. This sentence can mean two different things depending on whether or not you pause.

> Let's hunt, Grandpa.
> Let's hunt Grandpa.

We can teach phrasing and expression by helping students connect what they are learning about punctuation and formatting to their reading comprehension. For example, a comma means a small pause, a period means a longer pause, an exclamation point means strong emotion, and all caps with an exclamation point is REALLY STRONG EMOTION!

Students who need support with fluency can be encouraged to listen to audiobooks while reading along in the print version or to turn on the captions when streaming videos. This can help them with orthographic mapping while also hearing a model of fluent reading.

Vocabulary Knowledge and Morphological Awareness

Readers use their oral vocabulary to make sense of words in texts. Teachers can help children build their vocabulary indirectly, through reading aloud and conversations using technical vocabulary, and directly, through direct instruction of words before reading. Choosing which of the words from a text to preteach requires a Goldilocks approach, enough to aid comprehension but not so many that students are overwhelmed by the number or no longer required to build their independent word learning skills.

As students progress through school, texts become more technical and include more discipline-specific vocabulary. Adolescent students need explicit vocabulary instruction in content area classes, such as English, social studies, and science. Explicit instruction refers to two practices: (1) direct instruction on a word's meaning and (2) instruction on word learning strategies.

Research-based direct instruction includes previewing new words before reading and providing multiple opportunities for students to hear, read, speak, and write the words. Having students work in small groups gives them the opportunity to hear, read, speak, and write with words. Additionally, teaching vocabulary involves teaching the denotation and connotation of words so that students can use inference to make meaning from text and evaluate bias in text.

Research-based word-learning strategies include modeling how to use Context Clues and learning patterns in the English language. Regarding patterns, adolescents can study the relationship of morphology (roots, prefixes, and suffixes) and semantics (meaning). See Figure 2.6 to see the word parts in the word morphology. Morphological awareness is considered a bridging process because it aids readers in decoding words and making meaning. View these slides to see an example lesson on how students build advanced decoding skills by starting with breaking down multisyllabic words and then adding their knowledge of morphology to dissect words by scanning the QR code in Figure 2.7 or following this case sensitive link (https://bit.ly/3EQsol8).

GSF

Graphophonological semantic cognitive flexibility (GSF) is defined by Duke and colleagues (2021) as "the ability to simultaneously attend to, and flexibly switch between, the letters and sounds in words (graphophonological) and the meanings of words (semantic)" (p. 664). As such, GSF is interrelated to many of the previously described components of the model. What GSF adds to what we discussed previously is the idea of flexibility.

The English language does not have a one-to-one correspondence of graphemes to

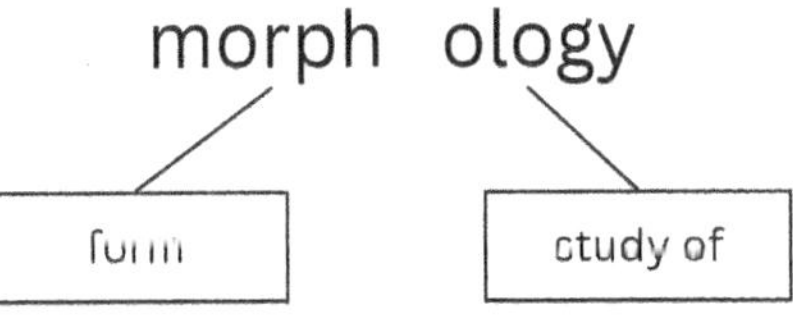

Figure 2.6 The Morphology of Morphology.

Figure 2.7

phonemes. In other words, one letter can make different sounds or no sound at all. For example, the letter e can make a short vowel sound like in *wreck*, a long vowel sound like in *week*, or be silent like in *woke*. When readers reach an unfamiliar word, they may have to try a few possible sounds before finding one that sounds right.

Context also matters. If you are on a hike and your partner says, "bear to the right," they are probably telling you to turn right, but you should still check to make sure there is not a grizzly. The same cognitive flexibility is needed in reading. Readers have to apply strategies flexibly and attend to context in order to figure out what the mystery word is.

Comprehension Components

Language comprehension is the ability to understand spoken and written words. As readers develop, they build listening comprehension that increases their capacity for reading comprehension. A predictor of reading comprehension is the knowledge a reader brings to the text. Children have both "in-the-head" and "in-the-world" knowledge (Compton-Lilly, 2013, p. 2). Their "in-the-head" knowledge includes reading-specific knowledge and understanding how language works. Their "in-the-world" knowledge includes cultural and content knowledge about how the world works.

Reading-Specific Background Knowledge

Knowledge about reading includes print concepts. Knowledge about reading also includes more advanced knowledge like understanding author presence and **genre**. We might take for granted that texts are written by authors and what that means. After all, authors are people, and people are not perfect. When an author makes a mistake unintentionally, that is called misinformation. When an author makes a mistake intentionally, that is called disinformation. In order to evaluate the reliability of the information we are reading, we need reading-specific background knowledge so that we can determine the author's purpose and genre. The author's purpose can be to entertain, which could mean that the text is a piece of fiction and not intended to accurately represent real people or events. The author's purpose can also be to persuade, which could mean that the author is sharing their opinion, not necessarily representing facts in a balanced manner. In journalism, for example, the genre of editorials is for the purpose of sharing the author's opinions and perspectives, whereas the genre of news is for the purpose of objectively informing the public. Just because something falls into the genre of news, this does not mean there will not be mistakes or even disinformation; but, knowing that something falls into the genre of an editorial means that we understand that the author is not trying to be objective necessarily, which signals that we should approach the reading more cautiously.

Language Structure Knowledge

Knowledge of language structure means understanding how language works. Structure includes word choice, semantics, as well as how words and phrases are arranged together to form sentences, which is technically called syntax. There is everyday language structure and **academic language** structure. Students learn everyday language structure through their social experiences, but they need intentional conversations with teachers to build knowledge of academic language structures. For example, academic informational texts include precise terminology and complex sentences.

Cultural and Other Content Knowledge

Readers must be able to activate knowledge that relates to the text and use this knowledge to understand main ideas and to make inferences. For example, one of my friends was in a spelling bee in elementary school. It came down to two spellers left on stage. The next word: buckwheat. The first speller did not know what the word meant and spelled the word *baquete*. My friend had cultural contextual knowledge of the words wheat and buckwheat and had seen the words in their environment on food packages. Because they had this cultural knowledge, they knew that they could break the word into two parts: buck and wheat. They won! If students do not have the necessary conceptual or cultural knowledge needed to recognize a word or understand a text, teachers can help by building the knowledge before reading or teaching strategies and resources to use independently.

Readers also need academic vocabulary and content knowledge. The more students read, the more words, facts, and concepts they learn. But, authors make assumptions about what knowledge their readers are bringing to a text. If there is a gap between what the author assumes the reader knows and what the reader actually knows, then teachers can step in and provide the knowledge. Sometimes building background knowledge can be a quick comment, such as "This text uses the word *spanner*, which is the British word for *wrench*." Or, if students might not know what a wrench is, then the teacher could also bring one in for students to see and touch. Check out the Tried and True lesson example to see building background knowledge in practice.

Tried and True Strategy by Dr. Katherine O'Daniels

Lesson Name: Building Background Knowledge Before Reading "The Mutants"

Context: Developmental Reading class in St. Louis, Missouri

Before reading the short story "The Mutants" by Joyce Carol Oates, I begin by filling the gap between what the author assumes the reader knows and what my students would have as background knowledge. However, one of the interesting storytelling features that the author uses is dramatic irony, where the reader knows something that the character does not. The author describes the setting and the action in a way that the reader figures out what is going on before the character does, like solving a mystery. Although I want students to be able to access the story, we don't want to take away the challenge of solving the mystery for them, because that is what makes the story so interesting to read! Instead, we want to only scaffold for what the author assumes the reader knows, such as some of the vocabulary words that are necessary to know in order to figure out the setting and some biological facts about what happens to the body when a threat is perceived: the fight or flight responses.

Before reading, I say:

"Today we are reading a short story called 'The Mutants' by Joyce Carol Oates. In this story we have one main character. She is really the only character in the book, but there are mentions of a fiancé and family. Also, she is never named. In the story, the character experiences a traumatic event. The plot unfolds over a single day as she is experiencing this traumatic event. Oates uses third person limited narration, so as readers we experience the events unfolding as she does.

Traumatic, dangerous, or threatening events trigger a fight or flight response in humans. Have you heard of this before? Essentially, it is a biological response that is evolutionary in nature. Stemming from the times when humans more regularly face life-threatening situations, we developed an instinctual physiological response that allowed our body to respond to a perceived threat by either fighting—or taking action to eliminate the danger, or by fleeing, which involves escaping the danger. This is where the term fight or flight comes from, and it is still an instinctual response we have today to help keep us safe from danger, even though we aren't as likely to encounter as many dangerous or threatening situations as early humans did. However, our character is in a traumatic situation, so before we start reading, we're going to watch this short video that talks about what happens to your body when you are scared. This can provide some perspective on our character's behaviors throughout the story."

We then watch a short informational video by UW Medicine called "Your Body on Fear." After the video, I instruct my students to look for evidence showing how the character is responding to the traumatic situation she faces as they read.

Verbal Reasoning and Theory of Mind

In addition to cultural and other content knowledge, readers also need the ability to relate their knowledge to what they are reading in order to read between the lines and draw reasonable inferences and logical conclusions. This is called verbal reasoning. When we read, especially narratives about people, we also need perspective taking. This is called Theory of Mind.

Theory of Mind is the ability to recognize and understand that other people have their own thoughts, feelings, desires, and beliefs, which may be different from your own. It is a key cognitive skill that allows individuals to interpret and predict others' behaviors by considering their mental states. For example, understanding that a friend might act distant because they're upset, even if they haven't said so, involves using Theory of Mind. This concept is fundamental in reading because it explains how we make inferences and interpret characters.

Theory of Mind also plays a role in developing empathy for characters while reading because it enables readers to imagine and understand the thoughts and emotions of characters. When engaging with a story, readers use their Theory of Mind to step into the perspectives of characters, interpreting their motivations, feelings, and decisions. This mental process not only makes the narrative more engaging but also fosters a deeper emotional connection with the characters. For instance, understanding why a character makes a difficult choice or empathizing with their struggles enhances the reader's ability to relate to diverse experiences and viewpoints, enriching both their understanding of the story and their capacity for empathy in real life (Kerkhoff & Falter, 2021).

Teachers can model verbal reasoning and Theory of Mind through Teacher Think Alouds, which involves reading a portion of text aloud and then explaining what they are thinking about when they read that part in order to make meaning.

Active Self-Regulation

Active self-regulation is separate from reading but impacts reading in direct and indirect ways. It consists of affective and cognitive components as described below.

Motivation and Engagement

Earlier, we talked about how we can't forget that authors are people. We can't forget that readers are people too, with their own feelings, thoughts, desires, and beliefs that they bring with them to school. Adolescents who believe that they can succeed at reading are more likely to be highly motivated. And, highly motivated readers are likely to engage with texts and to persevere through challenging texts.

Executive Function Skills

Our brain has to control many things when we read. According to Cartwright (2021), there are three core executive function skills (Figure 2.8) that our brain manages when reading:

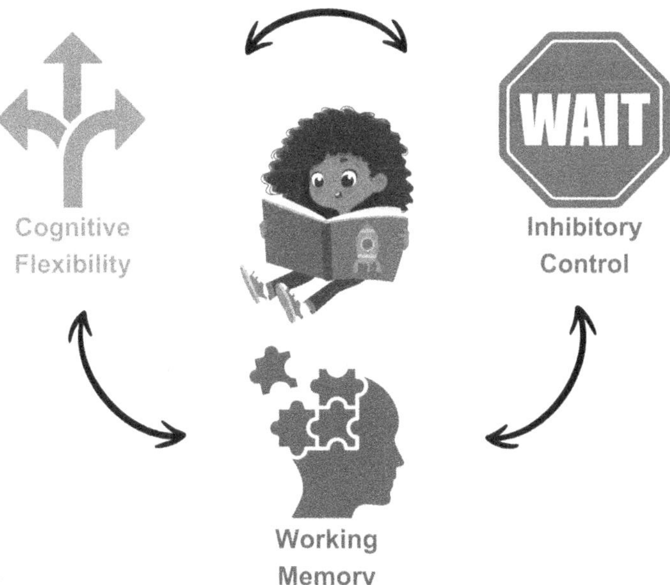

Figure 2.8 Core Executive Function Skills for Reading.

- Cognitive flexibility—Ability to switch among, and back and forth between, types of information or tasks (also called switching)
- Inhibitory control—Ability to refrain from responding, to wait, or to stop and think before responding (also called inhibition or self-control)
- Working memory—Ability to hold information in mind and work with, transform, or update part of that information as you work on a task. (p. 23)

Strategy Use

Reading strategies are purposeful ways readers try to make sense of text. Some people use word recognition and word-learning strategies when they come to a word they do not know, but others may simply skip the word and keep going. Likewise, some intuitively monitor comprehension as they read, but some do not. Reviews of research suggest that word recognition, word learning, comprehension, and metacognitive strategies improve reading performance for all students (National Reading Panel, 2000; Duke & Cartwright, 2021). Because these strategies are not easily seen, students are unlikely to learn them implicitly, which is why explicit strategy instruction benefits all learners.

What Research Says about Reading

Although some people may feel that the Reading Wars are still going strong, there is agreement in the field that children should learn phonics in a systematic and explicit way and that reading instruction should consider the whole child and attend to cultural, social, emotional, and motivational aspects too. Here is a summary of where the field stands today, but we need to remember that scientific research is always evolving.

Reading Is an Interactive Process

Reading is an interactive process involving many components and different parts of the brain. One part of the brain houses the phonological processor, which recognizes sounds. Phonological processing results in the awareness of the sounds in words, called phonemic awareness. Another part of the brain visually processes the graphical representation of letters. Another part is called the orthographic processor, which connects those sounds to the graphical representation of the letters and maps those sounds and letters together to make words. Phonics is understanding that written letters make sounds.

The meaning processor connects the word that is read to what the word means. Sometimes a word can have multiple meanings, such as the word "bark." The meaning processor also activates reasoning to choose the meaning that makes the most sense based on the context surrounding the word. The interactive process is not linear, but recursive as each processor helps the others and pulls from prior knowledge about the world to make meaning (Duke & Cartwright, 2021).

Reading and Knowledge Are Reciprocal

Background knowledge has a **reciprocal** relationship with reading comprehension. In other words, if you have background knowledge about the topic of the text, you will find the text easier to comprehend. At the same time, when you read about a topic, you build knowledge about the topic, which then in turn helps you comprehend other texts on similar topics (Hattan & Lupo, 2020). Reading authentic texts connected to real-world contexts can help students activate their background knowledge and build knowledge about the world around them. Research shows that foundational skills, comprehension skills, and knowledge develop simultaneously, not sequentially, and that literacy instruction that supports knowledge building is essential even before students have mastered foundational skills (e.g., Rapp et al., 2007).

Reading happens within a sociocultural context and that context impacts the reader. Readers and writers bring their social and cultural knowledge to the texts they read in order to make inferences. If the author and the reader have different experiences, that can impede comprehension. The context can also impact how a reader or writer approaches a text. Adolescents need a purpose for reading or writing, whether that purpose is to learn something useful or for enjoyment. Students' motivation to read or write in school is impacted by the purpose as well as their history of success or failure and by what their peers think. Students' ability to grow as readers is impacted by the opportunities to talk about texts with others, to get constructive feedback from their teachers, and to build upon their successes.

Reading should not be taught in a skills-only approach decontextualized from students' cultures and identities. As Gholdy Muhammad (2023) asserts, "As long as inequities and oppressions exist in the world and society, we need literacy instruction that nurtures students' identities and criticality in equal value to the teaching of skills" (p. 6). Students deserve to see their own identities and languages reflected in the literacy learning process. When applying the Science of Reading in our classrooms, we must consider the affective, social, and cultural dimensions of learning in addition to the cognitive skills we intend to teach. We can be intentional about using instructional materials that (a) represent the diversity of our students' identities and lived experiences, (b) nurture engagement and joy in learning, and (c) align to research-based reading instruction. After all, our goal is to nurture a love of reading and help every student experience the power of literacy.

Conclusion

Exploring the components of reading and investigating how to teach reading are two different areas of research. This chapter focuses on scientific models that describe the components of reading and how the components relate. Chapters in section two will provide insight into the complexity of teaching reading and instructional routines to use with learners as they develop advanced literacy skills and knowledge.

More to Explore

- In this video called *Explicit Instruction in Literacy,* I explain what the research says about explicit instruction: https://www.youtube.com/watch?v=hbN7D8pPxeE

- This video titled *The Reading Brain* explains the neuroscience connected to reading: https://youtu.be/A2HHrKpjlYM?si=HDi5ICg0OGo1uQ6n

- Listen to Jennifer Gonzalez with guests Kelly Cartwright and Jennifer Serravallo and in this podcast episode called "Untangling the Debate over Reading Instruction": https://www.cultofpedagogy.com/reading-instruction/

- Steve Graham discusses the reading and writing connection in this episode of *Science of Reading: The Podcast*: https://amplify.com/episode/science-of-reading-the-podcast/season-7/episode-8-writing-your-way-to-better-reading/

Reflect

For this reflection activity, you will use the Making Metaphors strategy. Making metaphors aids learning by helping to make connections, create mental images, and enhance memory retention. Metaphors bridge the known with the unknown, allowing learners to understand abstract concepts by relating them to familiar experiences or ideas. Create a metaphor representing your understanding of the reading process. For example, Scarborough (2001) used the metaphor of the reading rope. Cartwright and Duke (2019) talk about driving as a metaphor:

> A metaphor of driving, which likens reading to an everyday practice, demystifies complexities inherent in reading. Both reading and driving are active, strategic processes. Just as drivers deploy multifaceted driving processes to reach destinations on different types of roads in varied contexts and conditions, readers deploy multifaceted reading processes to reach reading goals with different types of texts in varied reading contexts and conditions. (p. 13)

You may express your metaphor via text and images. If it is helpful, you can choose one of the images in Figure 2.9 to prompt your thinking.

Figure 2.9 Inspiration for Reading Metaphor.

Discuss

Questions for discussion to learn from and with each other:

- What do you identify as the components of reading and how do the components relate to each other?
- How is reading a recursive process?
- What is a metaphor that helps you understand reading?
- How does the information in this chapter connect to your own experiences with teaching or learning to read?
- What would you consider to be the "look fors" when evaluating instructional materials to develop foundational reading skills?

References

Cartwright, K. B. (2021, November 6). Executive function: The glue that holds together reading's many processes. *Dystinct*, (6), 21–31. https://on.dystinct.org/issue-06-november-2021

Cartwright, K. B., & Duke, N. K. (2019). The DRIVE model of reading: Making the complexity of reading accessible. *The Reading Teacher*, *73*(1), 7–15. https://doi.org/10.1002/trtr.1818

Cervetti, G. N., & Hiebert, E. H. (2015). The sixth pillar of reading instruction: Knowledge development. *The Reading Teacher*, *68*(7), 548–51. https://doi.org/10.1002/trtr.1343

Compton-Lilly, C. (2013). Building on what children bring: Cognitive and sociocultural approaches to teaching literacy. *Journal of Balanced Literacy Research and Instruction*, *1*(1), Article 3. https://repository.lsu.edu/jblri/vol1/iss1/3/

Duke, N. K., & Cartwright, K. B. (2021). The science of reading progresses: Communicating advances beyond the simple view of reading. *Reading Research Quarterly*, *56*(S1), S25–S44. https://doi.org/10.1002/rrq.411

Duke, N. K., Ward, A. E., & Pearson, P. D. (2021). The science of reading comprehension instruction. *The Reading Teacher*, *74*(6), 663–72. https://doi.org/10.1002/trtr.1993

Ehri, L. C. (2014). Orthographic mapping in the acquisition of sight word reading, spelling memory, and vocabulary learning. *Scientific Studies of Reading*, *18*(1), 5–21. https://doi.org/10.1080/10888438.2013.819356

Gough, P. B., & Tunmer, W. E. (1986). Decoding, reading, and reading disability. *Remedial and Special Education, 7*(1), 6–10. https://doi.org/10.1177/074193258600700104

Hasbrouck, J. & Tindal, G. (2017). *An update to compiled ORF norms* (Technical Report No. 1702). Behavioral Research and Teaching, University of Oregon. https://www.readingrockets.org/sites/default/files/2023-08/2017_ORF_NORMS.pdf

Hattan, C., & Lupo, S. M. (2020). Rethinking the role of knowledge in the literacy classroom. *Reading Research Quarterly, 55*(S1), S283–S298. https://doi.org/10.1002/rrq.350

International Dyslexia Association. (2020). *Working memory: The engine for learning.* https://dyslexiaida.org/working-memory-the-engine-for-learning/

International Literacy Association. (2018). *Reading fluently does not mean reading fast.* Author.

Kerkhoff, S., & Falter, M. (2021). Going the distance: Using Flipgrid to mediate race discussions across two young adult literature courses. *Contemporary Issues in Technology and Teacher Education, 21*(4), 589–625. https://www.learntechlib.org/primary/p/217706/

Kim, Y. S. G. (2020). Toward integrative reading science: The direct and indirect effects model of reading. *Journal of Learning Disabilities, 53*(6), 469–91.

Moats, L. C. (2005–2006). *How spelling supports reading: And why it is more regular and predictable than you may think.* American Educator. https://www.aft.org/ae/winter2005-2006/moats

Muhammad, G. G. (2023). *Culturally and historically responsive education* [Policy research brief]. National Council of Teachers of English. https://ncte.org/wp-content/uploads/2023/05/2023-NCTE-Squire-Office_Culturally-and-Historically-Responsive-Education.pdf

National Reading Panel. (2000). *Teaching children to read: An evidence-based assessment of the scientific research literature on reading and its implications for reading instructions.* https://www.nichd.nih.gov/sites/default/files/publications/pubs/nrp/Documents/report.pdf

Pearson, P. D., Palincsar, A., Biancarosa, G., & Berman, A. (Eds.). (2020). *Reaping the rewards of the reading for understanding initiative.* National Academy of Education. https://doi.org/10.31094/2020/2

Rapp, D. N., Broek, P. V. D., McMaster, K. L., Kendeou, P., & Espin, C. A. (2007). Higher-order comprehension processes in struggling readers: A perspective for research and intervention. *Scientific Studies of Reading, 11*(4), 289–312. https://doi.org/10.1080/10888430701530417

Scarborough, H. S. (2001). Connecting early language and literacy to later reading (dis)abilities: Evidence, theory, and practice. In S. Neuman & D. Dickinson (Eds.), *Handbook for research in early literacy* (pp. 23–38). Guilford Press.

Snow, C. E. (2002). *Reading for understanding: Toward an R & D program in reading comprehension.* RAND Corporation. https://www.rand.org/pubs/monograph_reports/MR1465.html

Literature Cited

Flesch, R. (1955). *Why Johnny can't read: And what you can do about it.* HarperCollins.

Oates, J. C. (2004). The mutants. In J. Oates (Ed.), *I am no one you know* (pp. 281–7). Ecco.

Poe, E. A. (1845, January 29). The raven. *New York Evening Mirror*.

UW Medicine (2019, October 29). *Your body on fear* [Video]. YouTube. https://www.youtube.com/watch?v=zSwMn9g4OgQ

Shining a Light on the Science of Writing

3

Learning to write is both an art and a science, and like learning to read, it does not happen by accident. In this chapter, *learning the ropes* takes on a new meaning. Building on the familiar concepts in the science of reading, authors have also introduced the simple view of writing and the writing rope to illustrate the interconnected strands that contribute to skilled writing. Just as reading fluency depends on vocabulary, **decoding**, and **background knowledge**, writing proficiency requires a woven set of abilities, from transcription skills, like handwriting and spelling, to higher-order processes, like planning, revising, and crafting language for impact. Understanding the science of writing helps teachers break down the components in order to intentionally teach each. This chapter unpacks what writing development looks like, why explicit instruction matters, and how educators can support every student in becoming a confident, capable writer—strand by strand.

Literacy Strategy: Big 3 Questions

As you read, annotate the chapter with your thinking by highlighting important points and writing in the margins. Consider the Big 3 Questions from Beers and Probst (2015) to guide you in annotating.

1 What surprised me? (mark new insights with an !)

2 What does the author think I already knew? (mark with a ? and write any questions you have in the margins)

3 What challenged or confirmed what I already knew? (mark with an * and make connections in the margins)

You can also <u>underline</u> any new words.

These three questions normalize that reading is hard work. Sometimes when we read, we uncover ideas that we need to think more about.

And, sometimes when we read, the author does not provide all of the background information that we need to comprehend. That's not the reader's fault. In fact, in this case, that would be my fault!

Preview Vocabulary

genre: category defined by shared features that shape how a text is crafted and understood

meta-analysis: a type of research that analyzes a large body of research to determine the strength and consistency of the results of previous research by calculating effect size

rhetorical awareness: conception of audience, purpose, and context of writing

self-efficacy: believing that one is capable of succeeding

self-regulation: monitoring and managing a process, such as the writing process

syntactic awareness: understanding how sentences are structured

syntax: how sentences are structured

The Relationship of Reading and Writing

Reading and writing are deeply connected, but not in identical ways. If you think about it, you can read without writing but writing depends on reading. To write well, students draw on the vocabulary, structure, ideas, and models they've encountered through texts. On the other hand, reading does not always require writing. We can understand a **text** without ever picking up a pen. But when we do write about what we read, our **comprehension** often deepens. The relationship between reading and writing can be described as interrelated, **reciprocal**, and synergistic.

Two Buckets, One Well: Interrelated Relationship

Reading and writing are interrelated with common knowledge bases and cognitive processes. Picture two buckets at a well. The reading bucket and the writing bucket draw from the same well of knowledge (Fitzgerald & Shanahan, 2000). They draw on shared knowledge of vocabulary, text structure, **genre** conventions, and **rhetorical awareness**. Reading and writing are also closely connected in skills, strategies, and cognitive processes. For example, understanding how a scientific argument is structured can help adolescents both analyze similar texts and write their own.

Two for the Price of One: Reciprocal Relationship

Reading and writing have a reciprocal relationship in that when we teach one, they both improve (Slavin et al., 2019). When students read more, their writing improves. When students write more, their reading improves. For example, learning spelling patterns improves **encoding** *and* **decoding**. Writing about texts improves reading comprehension and writing fluency.

I'll never forget reading late one night during my first year of college—not because I was gripped by a page-turner, but because I had an 8 a.m. humanities class looming over me. The assignment? Dante's *Inferno*. The experience? Let's just say I was pretty sure I'd landed myself in the fourth circle of hell—my eyes felt like sandpaper, the smell of burnt coffee hung in the air, and my brain was wandering in circles trying to make sense of the text. My professor, Dr. Barb Stedman, had assigned a reading response journal. So I started scrawling a stream of consciousness questions, each one proving my complete and utter confusion. But somewhere between "What does this even mean?" and "Why would anyone put a pope in a hole?!" I realized—maybe confusion was the point. By the time I capped my pen, I realized maybe the point of reading Dante wasn't to "get it," but to wrestle with questions about humanity itself. Writing had nudged me from baffled to just a glimmer of clarity, like finding a candle in Dante's dark.

In fact, this night wasn't an isolated incident. And, in my own classroom, I witnessed how my students came to deep insights through writing about what we were reading, my experiences aligning with the science before I was even aware of the research.

Two Are Better than One: Synergistic Relationship

Reading and writing are synergistic, together producing more learning than either would alone. Think of a ballad—the melody can be beautiful, and the lyrics touching, but together they create a heartrending punch that neither could do alone.

When students use both reading and writing to learn new content, their content learning outcomes improve, but also their vocabulary, reading, and writing outcomes improve (Graham et al., 2020; Taǧa & Kalenderoǧlu, 2022). Activities like journaling about a book or summarizing an article are valuable not for the final piece of writing, but for the deep thinking that happens while creating it. For this reason, using **artificial intelligence (AI)** to create the reading response or summary paragraph would not have the same benefit.

Written Conversations about text is a tried and true strategy that integrates reading, writing, discussion, and content learning. See how Written Conversations work in the classroom in the section by Marsha Tyson below.

Together, reading and writing create a powerful synergy for learning. As you read the next section about the timeline of writing models, compare the models to the reading models presented in Chapter 2. As you read this section, try not to get bogged down in remembering all of the technical language. The purpose of the timeline section is to describe how the research evolved. The section that comes after the timeline is where we will put names to the important concepts in writing science.

Tried and True Strategy by Marsha Tyson

Strategy Name: Written Conversations

Context: Ms. Tyson's ninth-grade physics class in Columbia, Missouri

I first learned about Written Conversations from Harvey "Smokey" Daniels at a Write to Learn Conference, and it quickly became a favorite strategy in my high school physics classroom. Students sit in groups of three or four and write letters on a shared topic—whether it is a concept we're studying, a text we have read, or a recent field trip we have taken. Each student responds to a peer's letter and asks questions to keep the dialogue going, as shown in Figure 3.1. After a third round of responses, the original writer reads the full exchange and stars one or two ideas to discuss aloud.

This strategy promotes deep thinking, encourages students to cite evidence, and helps them make connections across texts and experiences. I have used it as a spin on jigsaw reading, a vocabulary-rich unit review, and even to reflect on museum exhibits not all students were able to see. It's a powerful and meaningful way to bring writing into science.

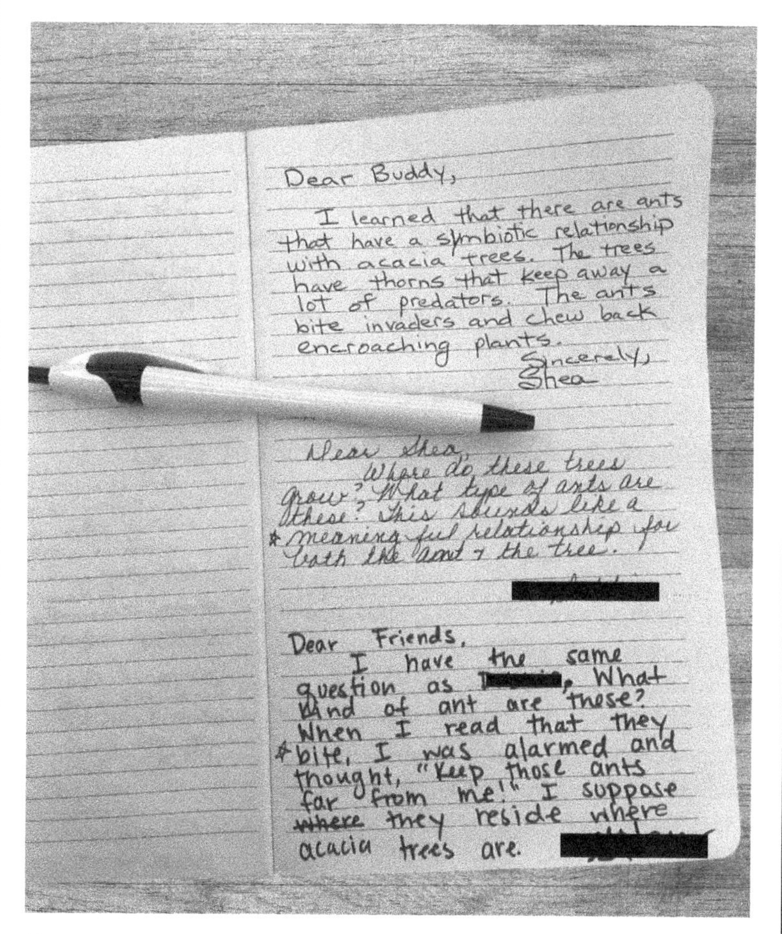

Figure 3.1 Written Conversations Example.

A Timeline of Writing Models

Traditionally, the teaching of writing included penmanship and spelling. Students used writing to demonstrate learning in school, but it was not an established subject of research until the 1980s. Around this time, composition became a research specialization in academia, and theories and models of writing began to spring from English departments and education departments on college campuses. The purpose of the theories and models was to identify and name the cognitive processes underlying writing. We pick up our timeline of writing models here in the 1980s.

1981

In 1981, Flower and Hayes published an article called "A cognitive process theory of writing." In it, they broke away from a product-focused view of writing to describe a process-focused model that continues to inform the teaching of writing today. They describe their theory here:

> A cognitive process theory of writing, such as the one presented here, represents a major departure from the traditional paradigm of stages in this way: in a stage model the major units of analysis are stages of completion which reflect the growth of a written product, and these stages are organized in a linear sequence or structure. In a process model, the major units of analysis are elementary mental processes, such as the process of generating ideas. And these processes have a hierarchical structure such that idea generation, for example, is a sub-process of Planning. Furthermore, each of these mental acts may occur at any time in the composing process. (p. 367)

Their writing process phases include planning (with sub-processes of idea generation, organizing, and goal-setting), translating (meaning putting the ideas into words), and reviewing (with the sub-processes of revising and editing). Throughout the process, the writer attends to both the audience and purpose as well as their own goals in writing. View the slideshow on the cognitive process approach linked here to learn more (https://bit.ly/cognitiveprocess).

1986

On the other end of the grade-level spectrum, researchers were thinking about how to teach the foundations of writing to young children and created the simple view of writing (Juel et al., 1986) to parallel the simple view of reading (Gough & Tunmer, 1986). The model consisted of two parts: ideation + spelling = writing.

2002–2006

The simple view of writing continued to evolve as Berninger and colleagues added handwriting and executive function to the model. In 2006, Berninger and Winn presented the "not-so-simple view of internal functional writing

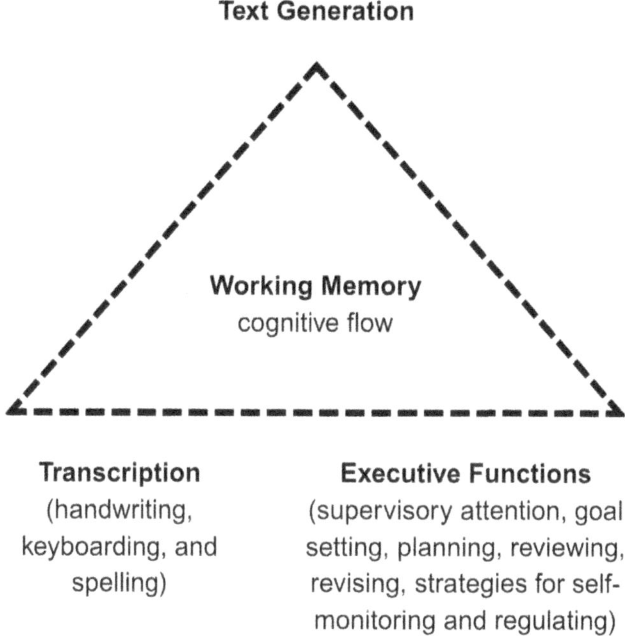

Figure 3.2 The Not-So-Simple View of Writing.

systems" (p. 97). This iteration named the lower-level skills transcription, which referred to handwriting, keyboarding, and spelling, and higher-order skills called text generation that included ideation from the original model. In addition, the not-so-simple view of writing expanded the model by adding executive functions (e.g., attention, goal setting, and reviewing) and emphasizing working memory, which taps into both short-term and long-term memory depending on the writing task. An implication of the model is that automaticity in transcription skills allows cognitive resources such as attention and working memory to be available for higher-order processes, as displayed in Figure 3.2 (Berninger & Winn, 2006).

1997

Activity theory offered a different triangle to serve as a model for writing with one point being the writer; the second point being the tools the writer uses; and the third the goals, motives, or objectives of the writing, which all lead to the product (Russell, 1997). From a sociocultural perspective, researchers built on activity theory as a helpful framework for understanding how people write by looking at the goals and tools as well as the social context around the writer(s). Instead of seeing writing as just a set of skills to acquire, activity theory shows that writing happens within a system of interactions: writers use tools (like oral language, digital platforms, or graphic organizers) to work toward a goal or objective (such as completing an essay or expressing an idea). This system is shaped by rules (e.g., classroom norms, language conventions, and genres), community (e.g., peers, teachers, and audience), and division of labor (e.g., who chooses the topic, who gives feedback, and who revises). For writing teachers, this means recognizing that students' writing development is deeply influenced by their environment, the tools they use, and the people they collaborate with—not just by individual ability or effort.

2016

The 2016 **meta-analysis** sponsored by the Institute for Education Sciences, What Works Clearinghouse, authored by Steve Graham and colleagues, in addition to putting forth implications for practice, codified the cognitive components that happen in writers' minds during the writing process. Their model included planning, goal-setting, drafting, evaluating, revising, and editing. The researchers stated that components of the writing process can be repeated, occur in different sequences, or even take place simultaneously. Purpose and audience are attended to throughout the process, as shown in Figure 3.3. (The report was revised in 2019.)

2018

Steve Graham's writer(s)-within-community (2018) model conceptualizes writing as a complex social activity affected by both the cognitive capabilities of the writer(s) and the context in which writing occurs. The cognitive capabilities include transcription, ideation, and translation as well as executive function and memory. This model relates the cognitive process approach to the component of executive function (i.e., planning, goal setting, monitoring, and evaluating) and describes the role of memory (i.e., long-term, short-term, and working) in relation to multiple components.

The model emphasizes that writing does not happen in isolation. Writers are also influenced by their community, including the expectations of the audience, the purpose of the writing task, cultural norms, and the type of writing being done. According to Graham et al. (2025), writing is shaped by the following contextual factors:

Figure 3.3 Components of the Writing Process.

its purposes, including writing goals, values, motives, audiences, established norms, social practices, writing supports, writing stance/ identity, available writing tools, typified writing practices, types of writing products produced, experiences and resources of members (teachers and students in classrooms), physical and social environment, and collective history of the community ... [and] by institutional, social, cultural, political, and historical factors operating outside the writing community. (p. 977)

In classrooms, this means writing instruction should address both the internal development of writing processes and the external factors that shape writing—like authentic purposes; a supportive, collaborative environment; and opportunities to write for real audiences.

2019

In 2019, Joan Sedita created the writing rope to parallel the reading rope (Scarborough, 2001), although the two have different purposes. While the reading rope illustrates the mental processes involved in reading, the writing rope serves as a framework to help educators evaluate writing programs and curricula. The writing rope consists of five components that contribute to skilled writing at a foundational literacy level, see Figure 3.4. Building on earlier writing models, it keeps the strand of transcription (i.e., handwriting, keyboarding, and spelling). It embeds idea generation, executive function, and the writing process into a strand called critical thinking. Between these two strands are **syntax** (e.g., sentence writing, grammar, and punctuation), text structure (e.g., whole text structure, paragraph structure, **patterns of organization**, and transitions), and writing craft (e.g., word choice, rhetorical awareness, and literary devices).

2019

Kim and Park's (2019) direct and indirect effects model of writing highlights how multiple cognitive, linguistic, and affective factors work together to support writing development. The model shows that foundational skills—such as transcription, oral language, and **self-regulation**—have both direct effects on writing quality and indirect effects through higher-order cognitive processes—such as planning, revising, and text generation. Essentially, writing is influenced not just by what students know, but by how they

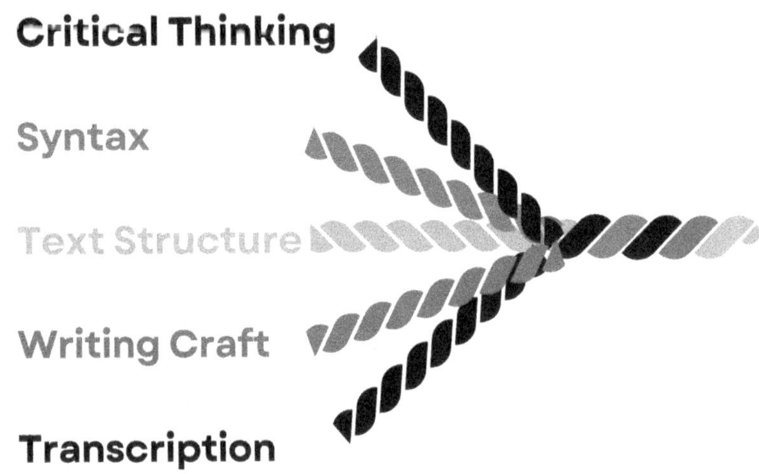

Figure 3.4 The Writing Rope. Adapted from Sedita (2019).

Table 3.1 Direct and Indirect Effects Model of Writing

Component	Characteristics
Background knowledge	Content knowledge (i.e., knowledge about the topic) and domain knowledge (i.e., knowledge about writing) needed for generating ideas and aligning structure and conventions to writing purpose
Affect	Motivation and self-efficacy developed alongside writing development
Transcription	Spelling and handwriting or keyboarding needed to produce writing
Emergent literacy skills and metalinguistic awareness	Phonological awareness, orthography, and morphology needed for word reading and spelling
Foundational oral language	Vocabulary and sentence comprehension and construction needed for syntax and word choice
Oral composition or discourse oral language	Generate and represent ideas in oral language at the discourse level, similar to ideation (Juel et al., 1986) or text generation (Berninger & Winn, 2006)
Higher-order cognition and self-regulation	Reasoning, inference, perspective-taking (e.g., audience awareness), goal-setting, and monitoring needed for coherence, evaluation, and strategy use
Executive functions (domain-general cognitions)	Working memory and control and shifting of attention necessary for all learning tasks and processes, including writing

manage and apply that knowledge during the writing process. This model emphasizes the complex, interconnected nature of writing and the need for comprehensive instruction that addresses both foundational and strategic components. Table 3.1 is an adapted version of Kim and Park's model.

Toward an Active View of Writing

The active view of writing brings activity theory and its iterations into conversation with research on the simple view of writing and its iterations. The active view of writing draws on Duke and Cartwright's (2021) organizational structure for the active view of reading to highlight the interrelationship of reading and writing and to emphasize the dynamic interaction of components of writing. As a sociocognitive model, this view contends that writing is a social activity shaped by the sociocultural context and happens in community, sometimes with other writers and always with a reader, even if that reader is the writer themself. The model zooms in on the writer and consists of four overarching categories: active self-regulation, transcription, bridging processes, and text generation.

Active Self-Regulation

Active self-regulation in writing is highlighted in many of the models described above as well as numerous meta-analyses on the teaching of writing cited throughout the chapter (e.g., Graham et al., 2016/2019, 2025). Following the organizational structure of the active view of reading, components under the umbrella of self-regulation include executive function, **motivation** and **self-efficacy**, and strategy use. Placing active self-regulation as related but separate from writing aligns with research by Ahmed and colleagues (2022).

Executive Function

Executive function refers to a set of cognitive processes that enable individuals to manage their thoughts, actions, and emotions in order to achieve goals. Harris et al. (n.d.) explain the role of executive function this way:

> While negotiating the rules and mechanics for writing, the writer must maintain focus on factors such as organization, form and features, purposes and goals, audience needs and perspectives, and evaluation of the communication between author and reader. Self-regulation of the writing process is critical; the writer must be goal-oriented, resourceful, and reflective … For skilled authors, writing is a flexible, goal-directed activity, scaffolded by a rich source of cognitive processes and strategies for planning, text production, and revision. (paras. 1 and 3)

Writing is, above all, a goal-oriented activity.

In writing, executive function supports students' attention, working memory, and self-regulation. "Working memory may reflect the ability to maintain attention and focus throughout an activity. It is possible that the same is true for writing" (Poch & Lembke, 2007, p. 37). Adolescents are still developing these self-regulatory abilities, so explicit instruction and scaffolding in goal setting and process monitoring can significantly improve their writing outcomes. Research has shown that when students are taught to use strategies, such as setting specific writing goals, checking their progress, and reflecting on their work, they become more effective writers (Graham et al., 2025; Graham & Harris, 2018). Supporting executive function in writing not only enhances composition skills but also transfers to other academic processes.

Motivation and Self-Efficacy

Especially important considerations in adolescent literacy are attention to motivation dispositions and writing self-efficacy. Motivation is key to sustaining **engagement** in planning, drafting, and revising. "Motivational dispositions affect what writers do as those possessing a positive attitude are more likely to plan, set challenging goals, and persist as writers" (Saddler et al., 2018, p. 193). Writing for authentic audiences, choice of topics or genres, and collaborative writing are all instructional approaches that foster motivation and increase engagement in writing.

Self-efficacy refers to the writer's confidence that they can achieve the writing goal. Much like motivation, this confidence plays a crucial role in how people approach writing—those with high self-efficacy are more likely to take on challenging writing assignments, persist through difficulties, and revise their work thoughtfully. Setting personal goals, receiving meaningful feedback, and celebrating growth are methods that enhance self-efficacy.

Strategy Use

Writing includes the use of self-regulation strategies (e.g., planning, goal setting, monitoring, and evaluating) and writing strategies (e.g., brainstorming, drawing, outlining, and using graphic organizers) (Graham et al., 2016/2019, 2025). Writers make decisions about what strategies to deploy when. Some strategies require the use of tools in writing. Likewise, writers choose the right tool for the job.

Transcription

Transcription is the ability to put words on the page, which involves skills like handwriting and spelling. This is also where conventions like capitalization, punctuation, spacing, and formatting play a role. For digital texts, keyboarding plays a role. In primary grades, transcription is best taught alongside **phonics** with lessons that integrate decoding and encoding. Through explicit and systematic instruction, students learn the sound–symbol correspondences for graphemes and how to form the letters. Handwriting instruction in early grades includes formation of lower- and upper-case letters, spacing between words, automaticity, and legibility. Starting in fourth grade, students should have the opportunity to practice transcription with word processing tools (Graham & Perin, 2007).

The more automatically students can spell and print or type, the more fluent they can become. Just as automaticity in word recognition enables fluency and allows readers to concentrate on comprehension, gaining automaticity in spelling, conventions, and handwriting/keyboarding helps students shift their cognitive resources to the more complex elements of text generation (Feng et al., 2019).

Evidence demonstrates that spelling instruction should focus on patterns, not random word lists, and be connected to the reading and writing that students are doing (Stone, 2021). In early grades, this includes having students see, hear, say, and write words. In older grades, this could look like teaching morphemes that change parts of speech (-tion/-sion, -ory/-ary/-ery) and practicing writing words using the morpheme under study.

Bridging Processes

Bridging processes are the cognitive mechanisms that connect transcription and text generation. There are three in writing: vocabulary, fluency, and sentence-level composition.

Vocabulary

Vocabulary refers to oral language proficiency and understanding of denotative and connotative word meanings. Vocabulary shares a reciprocal relationship with oral language proficiency, phonemic awareness, and orthographic mapping, where the ability to hear and manipulate sounds supports accurate spelling, spelling reinforces the mapping of sounds to written words, and growing oral language enhances understanding and use of words during writing. As students encounter longer, **multisyllabic** words—especially in content areas like science or social studies—the ability to recognize roots, prefixes, and suffixes becomes essential.

Semantic knowledge complements this process by giving meaning to those word parts. Knowing that "unbelievable" breaks down into un- (not), believe, and -able (able to be) helps students both spell it and use it in their writing with greater confidence. As Duke and Cartwright (2021) explain, "Morphological awareness has a particular value in written text. For example, morphological awareness allows a reader to recognize that the written words magic and magician are semantically related despite considerable differences in their oral pronunciation" (p. 530). Increasing both oral and written language proficiency affects writing fluency, the next bridging component.

Fluency

Fluency in writing is the ability to generate ideas, translate the ideas into words with ease, and transcribe the words automatically. According to Datchuk et al. (2022), "Arguably, the most well-researched and widely used writing fluency task is curriculum-based measurement of written expression" (CBM-WE; p. 155). Following standard CBM-WE procedures, students are provided with a writing prompt (e.g., story starter or picture) and then are given specific time limits for planning and writing. The writer gets one minute to plan, and a set time limit for writing (no longer than ten minutes is necessary). The writing can be scored for total words written (TWW). National norms for TWW in three minutes are displayed in Table 3.2 (AIMSweb, 2017).

However, research shows that transcription components like spelling are more important to fluency than the length of writing (Skar et al., 2024). In this case, a better measure of fluency would be words spelled correctly (WSC) or correct writing sequences (CWS) that takes spelling, capitalization, punctuation, grammar, and syntax into account. Regardless of the measure, the goal is that transcription becomes fluent to the point of automaticity, and that sentence composition becomes fluent, though composition will never be completely automatic because it is a thinking activity.

Syntactic Awareness

Sentences are the building blocks of writing. Sentence-level composition is considered a bridging process in adolescence literacy because Poch and Lembke (2007) found that sentence-level composition was more closely related to transcription than text generation for adolescents: "For high school

Table 3.2 Total Words Written (TWW) Norms by Grade Level

Percentile	TWW 6th grade	TWW 8th grade
75	73	79
50	59	69
25	47	58

students, the ability to generate and combine sentences is a basic or lower-level writing skill that is essential for generating connected text" (p. 37).

Sentence-level composition is supported by oral language, vocabulary, grammatical knowledge, and active self-regulation. The science of writing emphasizes the importance of building **syntactic awareness** (i.e., knowledge of grammar and how sentences are arranged) through sentence-level work because it helps students develop the foundational skills necessary for clear, coherent, and sophisticated writing. Research indicates that teaching sentence types improves students' ability to write more complex and varied sentences, which supports overall writing fluency and quality. See Table 3.3 for examples of sentence types.

When students practice manipulating sentence structures—such as combining, expanding, or rearranging clauses—they gain a deeper understanding of how language works to convey meaning and emphasis. Additionally, working at the sentence level strengthens students' grasp of grammar and mechanics in context, making it more likely they will apply

Table 3.3 Four Sentence Types

Sentence Type	Example Structures	Example Sentences
Simple	Subject predicate. Subject and/or subject predicate. Subject predicate and/or predicate.	The dog howls. The pup and the kitten play. The dog howls and howls.
Compound	Subject predicate, coordinating conjunction subject predicate. Subject predicate; subject predicate.	The dog howls, and I wince. The fire truck siren roars; the dog howls.
Complex	Subject predicate relative pronoun subject predicate. Subject predicate subordinating conjunction subject predicate. Subordinating conjunction, subject predicate, subject predicate.	I need a dog who is not yappy. I love when it rains. When it thunders, my dog howls.
Compound–Complex	Subordinating conjunction subject predicate, subject predicate, conjunction subject predicate.	When it rains, we make hot chocolate, and I read books all day.

these skills independently in their own writing. Teachers can provide explicit instruction on effective sentence writing, including elements of structure and grammar. However, research indicates that teaching grammar should not be decontextualized from students' writing (Graham & Harris, 2018).

Text Generation

Text generation is the composition of connected text with three levels: sentence-, paragraph-, and discourse-level writing. Discourse level refers to the text as a whole. Text generation includes higher-order cognition, cultural and content knowledge, writing-specific background knowledge, text structure, and writing craft.

Higher-Order Cognition

To generate ideas, writers need creative thinking and critical thinking, both of which are higher-order cognitive domains. Higher-order cognition is essential for producing coherent and high-quality written compositions, because they help writers originate and connect ideas effectively. Writers engage in higher-order cognition for conceptualizing, reasoning, perspective-taking, and evaluating information (Kim & Park, 2019).

Cultural and Other Content Knowledge

Idea generation relies on what writers know about the world—both the cultural knowledge they've gained from their own lived experiences and the content knowledge they've learned from school, books, media, and other sources. As Graham (2018) states, "Studies have shown that one's knowledge about a topic predicts the quality of the text produced, but this can depend upon what one is writing about" (p. 291). For example, I had a student who followed the National Football League closely and could easily explain game rules, defensive strategies, and league history. With their deep topic knowledge, they were able to write a detailed argument about the pros and cons of league rule changes to protect defenseless players. Their writing was better than what I could have produced—even as the teacher—because of my limited knowledge about the topic.

Background knowledge fuels the content of writing, and memory is the system that stores and delivers it when needed. Everything a writer knows—from cultural experiences to academic facts—gets stored in long-term memory. When we write, we pull relevant information from long-term memory into working memory so we can actively use it.

Writers with rich, well-organized background knowledge can focus more on crafting sentences and arguments because they don't have to stop and "fill in gaps" with research.

Without enough stored knowledge, working memory has less material to work with, making it harder to generate ideas or maintain coherence. In short, the more background knowledge a writer has, the less mental strain it takes to write.

Writing-Specific Background Knowledge

Knowledge specific to the domain of writing is the next component. Writing-specific background knowledge includes procedural knowledge from putting the pen to paper to cycling through the writing process. It also includes conceptual knowledge, such as rhetorical awareness of audience and purpose. Research shows that writers develop procedural fluency not in isolation but in tandem with conceptual insight; understanding why certain choices matter helps generate effective writing strategies, and practicing those strategies deepens that conceptual clarity.

Text Structure

Text structure is unique to written language (Sedita, 2023).Writers apply knowledge of text structure at paragraph and discourse levels. Writers use knowledge of modes, genres, and patterns of organization. Modes of structure are categorized based on the primary purpose and include narrative, descriptive, expository, argument, and persuasive. Genres are categorized by their form and content; examples include biography, artist statement, infographic, and op-ed article. Common patterns of organization in writing include chronological, sequence, cause and effect, compare and contrast, problem and solution, and spatial. Mode and patterns of organization cut across genres. For example, social media storytime videos and children's picture books are different genres but both are narratives and commonly told in chronological order. Similarly, tutorial videos on social media and instructions in technical writing are both expository and use sequential order.

At both the paragraph and discourse levels, writers use transitions to connect text in order to communicate coherently. For example, in a paragraph, writers use transition words and phrases to connect ideas, and in an essay, writers use transition sentences to connect paragraphs. Knowledge of patterns of organization and transitions contributes to coherent and organized writing.

Writing Craft

Writing craft is the "art" side of writing—the choices that make a piece not just correct, but compelling. It starts with rhetorical awareness, which is simply knowing the audience, purpose, and context. Skilled writers constantly ask themselves questions like, *"Who will read this?"* and *"What do I want them to think, feel, or do?"* From there, they choose the right genre, style, and tone for the situation—like a teacher picking the perfect journal prompt for the day's mood. Word choice also matters. Knowing both the denotative (dictionary) meaning and the connotative (emotional) meaning of a word helps writers select just the right term for precision or impact. And then there's the flair: literary devices such as imagery, metaphor, and symbolism, which can turn abstract ideas into vivid experiences and leave a lasting impression on the reader.

An example of a writer's craft technique is to show the reader what is happening through imagery and figurative language, rather than telling them explicitly. This makes the reading more interesting and detailed. The Show, Don't Tell strategy has been used by authors across disciplines, including creative nonfiction, personal narrative, and biography. For example, in *How the Word is Passed*, author Clint Smith uses imagery, personification, and symbolism when describing the living quarters of people who were enslaved at Monticello. "A blade of light cut through the open doorframe" (p. 31) and "whisper of sunlight squeezing through" (p. 34). Read the Tried and True lesson below to see what this looks like in a high school classroom.

Tried and True by Shea Kerkhoff

Lesson Name: Show, Don't Tell

Context: Ninth-grade English class in Knightdale, North Carolina

In my class, I would use the gradual release of responsibility method to teach the sentence expansion strategy of Show, Don't Tell. I would start by explaining to students that in creative and descriptive writing, authors use imagery to paint a picture with words for the reader and bring the writing to life.

First is the I Do. I would think aloud as I modeled writing a sentence that shows the reader rather than directly states for the reader what is happening. Next is We Do, we would collaboratively create a couple of sentences together. Here's what students came up with for expanding the sentence *I was sad.*

> **Show, Don't Tell Sentence:** *I was overcome with emotion as tears rained down my face like a waterfall off a cliff.*
>
> Then, I have them practice independently for the You Do part of the lesson using a prompt like the following.
>
> **Prompt:** *Write about a time that you felt a very strong emotion (anger, sadness, joy, disgust, nostalgia, fear, envy, ennui, embarrassment, anxiety, etc.), but do not use that specific word (or synonyms for that word). Instead, you must show the reader this emotion through description, dialogue, or action.*
>
> I let students know in advance that they'll be sharing their writing with their peers, so they can choose a topic that they feel comfortable sharing with others. The expectation is to write an elaborate sentence using imagery. They can write more than one sentence if they would like to. After five minutes, students read their writing to each other and try to guess the emotion that the writer was describing.

Writing Next

As teachers, it's important to have knowledge about writing. But if you are like me, what you really want to know is, *how do I apply this research to my teaching?* One of the most influential publications on research-based writing instruction for adolescent literacy is Graham and Perin's (2007) meta-analysis titled *"Writing Next."* The researchers identified eleven evidence-based strategies for improving writing in grades 4–12. Research since this publication has continued to corroborate these practices and suggest a Model–Practice–Reflect instructional routine (Graham et al., 2016/2019). Here are the headlines, and we will go into more depth in Chapter 10.

- Writing Strategies—Teach students planning, organizing, revising, and editing strategies to improve the quality and structure of their writing.
- Summarization—Instruct students on how to summarize texts, which helps improve reading comprehension and writing focus.
- Collaborative Writing—Have students work together to plan, draft, revise, and edit their writing to enhance idea development and feedback skills.
- Specific Product Goals—Set clear, specific goals for writing tasks (e.g., include a claim and three supporting pieces of evidence).

- Word Processing—Use computers for writing assignments to support greater output and easier revision, especially utilizing assistive technology.

- Sentence Combining—Teach students how to merge short, choppy sentences into more complex, coherent ones to improve fluency and style.

- Prewriting—Provide strategies and time for students to plan their writing before drafting (e.g., brainstorming, outlining).

- Inquiry Activities—Engage students in content-related exploration and data analysis to develop ideas for their writing (e.g., compare/contrast, cause/effect).

- Process Writing Approach—Teach writing as a process involving a cycle of multiple steps (e.g., planning, drafting, revising, editing, and publishing) with opportunities for extended writing and writing for authentic audiences.

- Study of Models—Show students examples of good writing and guide them in analyzing these models for structure, style, and technique.

- Writing for Content Learning (Writing Across the Curriculum)—Integrate writing into content areas (e.g., science and social studies) to deepen subject-matter understanding through written expression.

Conclusion

In Chapters 2 and 3, we have been learning the ropes about the Sciences of Reading and Writing. We can use this knowledge to evaluate curricular and instructional materials to determine if they are interpreting the science accurately. The rest of the chapters of the book will focus on evidence-based strategies for reading and writing that we can apply in our teaching and learning.

More to Explore

Barth, K. (2024). The science of writing: Integrating reading and writing for enhanced literacy. *SRSD Online.* https://srsdonline.org/the-science-of-writing-integrating-reading-and-writing-for-enhanced-literacy/

Graham, S., & Lyskawa, L. (2017, February 2). *Strategies to improve secondary students' writing skills: Lessons from a WWC practice guide* [Video]. Institute for Educational Sciences. https://youtu.be/yiPvvKMp-mQ?si=rYvsehFyGqf_EQdb

Knezel, S. (2028). Sketch noting: Using listening and drawing to change the world. [Video]. TEDx. https://www.ted.com/talks/sherrill_knezel_sketch_noting_using_listening_and_drawing_to_change_the_world

Lambert, S. (Host). (2025, February 26). S9 E11: Writing the way to better reading, with Judith Hochman, Ed.D. [Audio podcast episode]. *The Science of Reading Podcast.* https://amplify.com/episode/science-of-reading-the-podcast/season-9/episode-11-writing-the-way-to-better-reading-with-judith-hochman-ed-d/

Shanahan, T. (2025, May 5). How to teach writing fluency [Reading Rockets]. *Shanahan on Literacy.* https://www.readingrockets.org/blogs/shanahan-on-literacy/how-teach-writing-fluency (original work published January 8, 2022).

Reflect

Continue to use the Big 3 Questions to guide self-reflection about the ideas in this chapter.

1 What surprised me?

2 What did I learn?

3 What challenged or confirmed what I already knew?

Discuss

Questions for discussion to learn from and with each other:

1 Which model of writing resonates with you the most?

2 How can you use the science of writing research as a framework to evaluate instructional materials to develop writing processes and orthographic knowledge of learners?

3 What are the implications of the science of writing on the teaching of writing?

References

Ahmed, Y., Kent, S., Cirino, P. T., & Keller-Margulis, M. (2022). The not-so-simple view of writing in struggling readers/writers. *Reading & Writing Quarterly, 38*(3), 272–96. https://doi.org/10.1080/10573569.202 1.1948374

AIMSweb®. (2017). AIMSweb national norms table: Written expression—Total words written. Pearson.

Beers, G. K., & Probst, R. E. (2015). *Reading nonfiction: Notice & note stances, signposts, and strategies* (p. 312). Heinemann.

Berninger, V. W., & Winn, W. D. (2006). Implications of advancements in brain research and technology for writing development, writing instruction, and educational evolution. In C. A. MacArthur, S. Graham, & J. Fitzgerald (Eds.), *Handbook of writing research* (pp. 96–114). The Guilford Press.

Datchuk, S. M., Rodgers, D. B., Wagner, K., Hier, B. O., & Moore, C. T. (2022). Effects of writing interventions on the level and trend of total words written: A meta-analysis. *Exceptional Children, 88*(2), 145–62. https://doi.org/10.1177/00144029211027537

Duke, N. K., & Cartwright, K. B. (2021). The science of reading progresses: Communicating advances beyond the simple view of reading. *Reading Research Quarterly, 56*(S1), S25–S44. https://doi.org/10.1002/rrq.411

Feng, L., Lindner, A., Ji, X. R., & Joshi, R. M. (2019). The roles of handwriting and keyboarding in writing: A meta-analytic review. *Reading & Writing, 32*, 33–63. https://doi.org/10.1007/s11145-017-9749-x

Fitzgerald, J., & Shanahan, T. (2000). Reading and writing relations and their development. *Educational Psychologist, 35*(1), 39–50. https://doi.org/https://doi.org/10.1207/S15326985EP3501_5

Flower, L., & Hayes, J. R. (1981). A cognitive process theory of writing. *College Composition and Communication, 32*(4), 365. https://doi.org/10.2307/356600

Gough, P. B., & Tunmer, W. E. (1986). Decoding, reading, and reading disability. *Remedial and Special Education, 7*(1), 6–10. https://doi.org/10.1177/074193258600700104

Graham, S. (2018). A revised writer(s)-within-community model of writing. *Educational Psychologist, 53*(4), 258–79. https://doi.org/10.1080/004615 20.2018.1481406

Graham, S., & Harris, K. R. (2018). Evidence-based writing practices: A meta-analysis of existing meta-analyses. In R. Fidalgo, K. R. Harris, &

M. Braaksma (Eds.), *Design principles for teaching effective writing: Theoretical and empirical grounded principles* (pp. 13–37). Brill.

Graham, S., & Perin, D. (2007). *Writing next: Effective strategies to improve writing of adolescents in middle and high schools* [Report]. Alliance for Excellent Education.

Graham, S., Kiuhara, S. A., & MacKay, M. (2020). The effects of writing on learning in science, social studies, and mathematics: A meta-analysis. *Review of Educational Research, 90*(2), 179–226. https://doi.org/10.3102/0034654320914744

Graham, S., Bruch, J., Fitzgerald, J., Friedrich, L., Furgeson, J., Greene, K., Kim, J., Lyskawa, J., Olson, C. B., & Smither Wulsin, C. (2019). *Teaching secondary students to write effectively* (NCEE Report 2017-4002). National Center for Education Evaluation and Regional Assistance (NCEE), Institute of Education Sciences, US Department of Education. https://ies.ed.gov/ncee/WWC/PracticeGuide/22 (original work published 2016).

Graham, S., Cao, Y., Kim, Y.-S. G., Lee, J., Tate, T., Collins, P., Cho, M., Moon, Y., Chung, H. Q., & Olson, C. B. (2025). Effective writing instruction for students in grades 6 to 12: A best evidence meta-analysis. *Reading and Writing, 38*(4), 1–46. https://doi.org/10.1007/s11145-024-10539-2

Harris, K. R., Schmidt, T., & Graham, S. (n.d.). *Strategies for composition and self-regulation in the writing process.* LD Online. https://www.ldonline.org/ld-topics/writing-spelling/strategies-composition-and-self-regulation-writing-process

Juel, C., Griffith, P. L., & Gough, P. B. (1986). Acquisition of literacy: A longitudinal study of children in first and second grade. *Journal of Educational Psychology, 78*(4), 243–55. https://doi.org/10.1037/0022-0663.78.4.243

Kim, Y.-S. G., & Park, S. (2019). Unpacking pathways using the Direct and Indirect Effects Model of Writing (DIEW) and the contributions of higher order cognitive skills to writing. *Reading and Writing: An Interdisciplinary Journal, 32*(5), 1319–43. https://doi.org/10.1007/s11145-018-9913-y

Poch, A. L., & Lembke, E. S. (2007). A not-so-simple view of adolescent writing. *International Journal for Research in Learning Disabilities, 3*(2), 27–44. http://doi.org/10.28987/ijrld.3.2.27

Russell, D. R. (1997). Rethinking genre in school and society: An activity theory analysis. *Written Communication, 14*(4), 504–54. https://doi.org/10.1177/0741088397014004004

Saddler, B., Ellis-Robinson, T., & Asaro-Saddler, K. (2018). Using sentence combining instruction to enhance the writing skills of children with learning disabilities. *Learning Disabilities: A Contemporary Journal, 16*(2), 191–202. https://files.eric.ed.gov/fulltext/EJ1194557.pdf

Scarborough, H. S. (2001). Connecting early language and literacy to later reading (dis)abilities: Evidence, theory, and practice. In S. Neuman & D. Dickinson (Eds.), *Handbook for research in early literacy* (pp. 23-38). Guilford Press.

Sedita, J. (2019). The writing rope: The strands that are woven into skilled writing. *Reading Rockets.* https://www.readingrockets.org/topics/writing/articles/writing-rope-strands-are-woven-skilled-writing

Sedita, J. (2023). *The writing rope.* Brookes Publishing.

Skar, G. B., Graham, S., Huebner, A., Kvistad, A. H., Johansen, M. B., & Aasen, A. J. (2024). A longitudinal intervention study of the effects of increasing amount of meaningful writing across grades 1 and 2. *Reading and Writing, 37*(6), 1345–73. https://doi.org/10.1007/s11145-023-10460-0

Slavin, R. E., Lake, C., Inns, A., Baye, A., Dachet, D., & Haslam, J. (2019). A quantitative synthesis of research on writing approaches in grades 2 to 12. *Best Evidence Encyclopedia.* https://orbi.uliege.be/bitstream/2268/236036/1/writing_grades2to12_April_2019_full.p

Stone, L. (2021). *Spelling for life: Uncovering the simplicity and science of spelling.* Routledge.

Tağa, T., & Kalenderoğlu, İ. (2022). Effect of vocabulary instruction integrated with writing exercises on word learning, retention, and awareness. *International Journal of Education & Literacy Studies, 10*(4), 81–90. https://doi.org/10.7575/AIAC.IJELS.V.10N.4P.81

Literature Cited

Alighieri, D. (2013). *Dante's Inferno* (H. F. Cary, Trans.). Burk Classics.

Smith, C. (2021). *How the word is passed: A reckoning with the history of slavery across America.* Dialogue Books.

Comparing Content Area and Disciplinary Literacy

4

Myth or fact: in early grades students "learn to read" and then in upper and secondary grades they "read to learn." It's actually a myth! We typically think of learning to read as "reading foundations" and reading to learn as "content area reading." However, this is a false dichotomy. In fact, even before they can read, children can listen to books about science and social studies topics that build knowledge. For example, kindergarteners can learn about science as teachers read aloud books like *From Seed to Pumpkin* and *My Five Senses*. In addition, the content knowledge they learn from books helps them become better readers as they recognize words and concepts in any new texts that they encounter. Reading informational texts also helps children learn about **text** features and structure. Throughout our lives, we are always learning from what we read and learning to be better readers.

In grades 4 through 12, students need to continue to advance as readers in order to access the types of texts that are prevalent in their content area classes. When we teach students *how* to read complex texts in our content areas, we're not just assigning reading—we're empowering them to inquire about the knowledge within. In this chapter, we will discuss advancing students' reading and writing across the curriculum.

Literacy Strategy: 3 Whys

As you read this chapter, think about literacy in the content area(s) that you teach using the 3 Whys.

1 Why does literacy matter to me?
2 Why does literacy matter to my community (in this case your students)?
3 Why does literacy matter to the world?

Figure 4.1

Preview Key Vocabulary

academic language: the formal language and vocabulary used in schools
content area literacy: reading, writing, and language strategies that can be used to support literacy in any content classroom
disciplinary literacy: the unique ways that disciplinary experts read, write, and use language in the disciplines

Literacy in Our Lives

Literacy plays a vital role across career and community roles, and students' literacy outcomes when they graduate high school support their future life outcomes. A marine biologist uses reading and writing to access scientific research, write reports, and communicate findings about ocean life. A business owner writes marketing materials to promote their services and interprets data to make smart decisions. A pediatrician reads medical charts, writes prescriptions, and explains health information clearly to families, skills rooted in strong reading **comprehension** and communication. A legal advocate must interpret laws, craft persuasive arguments, and write speeches, drawing from language arts, civics, and critical thinking. These examples show how literacy, combined with knowledge from science, mathematics, social studies, English, and other subject areas, empowers students to thrive in diverse careers and to participate meaningfully in their communities. Teachers can support students through the development of content area and disciplinary literacy.

Although content area and disciplinary literacy are sometimes used interchangeably, they are not the same thing. **Content area literacy** is broader and includes strategies that can be used for reading and writing in any content classroom. **Disciplinary literacy** refers to the specific ways that experts (e.g., scientists, historians, and mathematicians) use reading and writing within their discipline. Research demonstrates that we should teach both content area and disciplinary literacy in grades 4–12 (Spires et al., 2018). Content area literacy skills and strategies are high leverage because they can be applied to many contexts, but also they are high leverage because they enhance students' understanding. Disciplinary literacy helps students join in on important civic discussions and gets them ready for the kinds of literacy they'll face in college and future careers.

What Is Content Area Literacy?

Content area literacy is an overarching term that refers to a group of instructional strategies and classroom routines for content area reading, writing across the curriculum, and learning **academic language**. Content area is the term for common departments in secondary schools, such as social studies, science, mathematics, health and physical education, music, arts, family and consumer sciences, business, and so on.

Content Area Reading

Content area reading refers to teaching students skills and strategies in order to learn through reading in the content areas. From a content area view, reading is a tool to build knowledge. In fact, as mentioned in Chapter 2, Cervetti and Hiebert (2015) argue that knowledge is such an important element of reading that it should be considered the sixth pillar of reading (i.e., phonemic awareness, **phonics**, fluency, vocabulary, comprehension, and knowledge development). All too often, however, students keep their knowledge and strategies siloed and do not automatically bring something they learned in English to the text they are reading in science, for example. Teachers can make explicit these connections and scaffold students' comprehension of grade-level texts to help them build new knowledge. In order to do this, they must purposefully plan for the language, literacy, and knowledge needs of their students.

Writing Across the Curriculum

Writing across the curriculum consists of writing to learn content knowledge and to demonstrate learning. When we are learning something new, writing can help us think because we have to transfer the complex phenomenon or issue into words, which forces us to organize our thoughts, clarify our understanding, and make connections between ideas. As far as using writing to demonstrate learning, the essay exam is probably as old as school itself. However, there are many possibilities for writing to learn and writing to demonstrate learning that we will explore in this chapter and others.

Academic Language

Academic language is the formal language used in schools, textbooks, and tests. It includes vocabulary not found in everyday language; complex sentence structures; and the ability to summarize, analyze, and communicate ideas clearly. Students need academic language to understand what they read and hear in subjects like biology, history, and geometry. Textbooks, standardized tests, and classroom assignments often use academic language (like *summarize* and *analyze*), so students must be familiar with the language to perform well. This book does not support the idea that students should give up their home languages or ways of speaking. Instead, it encourages an **asset-based** view of language—one where schools help students build on the languages and literacy skills they have, adding not subtracting language knowledge and not viewing some languages or ways of speaking as better than others (see Valenzuela, 2010).

When we combine academic language, content area reading, and writing across the curriculum, we use the term content area literacy to talk about students using reading, writing, and language to learn in school throughout the day and across the curriculum. As teachers, we can support students' literacy development across the curriculum in the following ways:

- Before Reading—We can help students access academic texts through explicitly teaching academic vocabulary and employing the other before reading strategies described in Chapter 7, in order to prepare readers with the knowledge and skills that they will need to successfully navigate the texts in our class.

- During Reading—We can model how to approach reading textbooks and standardized tests, as well as other grade-level texts, through thinking aloud during reading. In a Teacher Think Aloud, the teacher actively reads the text aloud as students follow along in their own text. When the teacher has a question, connection, or other thought, they pause the reading and explain what they are thinking about. Also, we can scaffold students' independent reading of grade-level texts through the during reading strategies presented in Chapter 9.

- After Reading—We can ask students to reflect on their learning and extend or revise their thinking after reading through talking and writing. We can guide students to further their learning through online research projects, which are discussed in Chapter 11.

- Writing to Learn—Writing to learn is where students use writing to explore, understand, and reflect on what they are learning—not just to show what they already know. It focuses on using short, informal writing tasks (like journals, quick-writes, or reflections) to help students process ideas, clarify thinking, and make connections between concepts. Strategies for writing to learn appear in Chapter 10.

- Writing to Demonstrate Learning—This is where students show what they know through writing and can be either an **informal or formal assessment**. We can write in front of students to model various aspects of assessment writing and explain the moves we are making and why. More writing to demonstrate learning ideas is presented in Chapter 5.

Research across different subject areas shows that teaching literacy within content areas can boost students' understanding and achievement—not just in reading and writing, but in the subjects themselves (Baye et al., 2019; Graham et al., 2020). That's great news! But there's a catch: when instruction focuses only on general reading strategies without also diving into the unique ways each discipline thinks and works (such as how historians analyze sources or how scientists build explanations), students don't get the full benefit. To really support their learning, we need to blend literacy instruction with the rich, specific practices of each discipline, which is called disciplinary literacy.

What Is Disciplinary Literacy?

Although secondary schools are organized by content areas, each includes multiple disciplines. For example, science includes the disciplines of biology and chemistry. Social studies includes history, economics, and political science. English includes linguistics and literature. There are reading, writing, and sense-making practices that happen across disciplines, and each discipline has unique literacy practices. Although content area literacy strategies can help students access text and understand concepts, doing the work of the discipline requires the unique literacy practices also (Gabriel, 2023). Moreover, as teachers, we must help students to understand what strategies they can transfer from class to class and when there are differences (e.g., skills needed to read a mathematics textbook will differ from reading a play).

Disciplinary literacy includes the knowledge of discipline-specific vocabulary (like "photosynthesis" in biology), how knowledge is constructed, the criteria used to evaluate evidence, and how to make arguments in the discipline. After all, the work of disciplinary experts is knowledge construction and communication (Osborne et al., 2019). When adolescents learn how each subject uses language differently, it helps them understand that knowledge is created by people and that they can create knowledge, too. When we engage students in asking questions and then analyzing sources in order to answer those questions, we teach students both the procedural and the content knowledge of the disciplines. Zygouris-Coe (2012) proposes that in addition to knowledge and skills, disciplinary literacy also includes the "habits of mind associated with each discipline" (p. 42). This makes disciplinary literacy a stance as much as it is a set of literacy practices.

Examples from Secondary Classrooms

Let's walk through a few examples together of how content area and disciplinary literacy play out in secondary classrooms.

In a middle school family and consumer sciences class, students engage in inquiry-based learning. The teacher has created a Hyperdoc, a document with hyperlinks embedded, to walk students through the inquiry one step at a time with the resources they need for each step curated and linked. At the top are the parameters: You have an annual budget of $600 for your cell phone. Which cell phone plan is the best choice for you? Under the inquiry question, a cell phone company website is linked that takes students to a comparison table of the company's four plans available with three-month, six-month, and twelve-month payment options. Students work in partners to make meaning of the data. At the bottom of the Hyperdoc is where the students are instructed to write a paragraph that answers the inquiry question and justifies their choice. There are Sentence Stems that students could use if they would like to: *The best option is ... We think this because ... We figured this out by ... In the end ...* Student pairs then switch their papers with another pair and give them feedback on their paragraph before turning in their answer.

In a high school physical education class, students are learning about weightlifting. After an introduction to the weight room and general safety, they are each given a journal and instructed to write the date and time at the top of the page. They then copy the list of exercises from the board with this as the goal beside each: one set of ten reps. The goal for the first day is to see what weight they can do ten reps at and to record the information in their journal. Groups of three are assigned to a machine in the circuit to get started. At each machine, the teacher has printed the name of the exercise and pictorial instructions of how to do the exercise. Students add to their journal the weight used as they make their way around the circuit. At the beginning of the next class, students write a goal for the end of the two weeks: three sets of ten reps at X lbs. They record their progress each day. At the end of the unit, they reflect on whether they met their goal and make a plan on how to continue strength training in their lives.

In a middle school mathematics class, students engage in project-based learning that integrates math, literacy, and fun! Let's zoom in to Sharon Wright's mathematics class and see literacy in action.

Tried and True Strategy by Sharon Wright

Lesson: Plan my Road Trip

Context: Eighth-grade math class in Chalmers, Indiana

For this project, I used the RAFT acronym to design a disciplinary literacy project for my junior high math students.

R stands for the role of the writer: You are a travel agent.
A stands for audience: I am your client.
F stands for format: You will create and present a slide deck.
T stands for topic: Plan the ultimate vacation.

Students work with partners and present their trip to the class with a slide deck. Here's their task:

You are a travel agent that I have hired to plan a road trip for my family of five people. Your goal is to create the most enjoyable trip while keeping costs as low as possible. Change up variables to stretch the trip as long as possible—without sacrificing the fun!

- Destination: Where will we go?
- Lodging: Will we stay in a hotel, house rental, or camp?
- Entertainment: What will we do for entertainment each day? Plan one activity for each day.
- Length: How long will we stay? Plan between 3 and 5 days.

Use math to help you make the smartest choices. Write an equation to represent the total cost of the trip (c) based on the number of nights we stay (n) and cost of fuel based on my car's MPG of 35 (MPG is the average miles per gallon of fuel). Also, create a table that breaks down the total cost of the road trip.

After all the presentations, the class votes on which road trip they think my family should actually take!

Table 4.1 illustrates even more examples of the content area and disciplinary literacy practices students engage in throughout the day.

Inquiry and Argument

History educator Walter Parker said, "History is not only about what happened in the past (its substance) but also about how we know it (its method). Understanding history means grasping both. Like the wings of an airplane, neither works alone" (2004, p. 66). At the heart of the disciplines—whether it's history, literature, biology, or mathematics—is constructing knowledge through an inquiry method and sharing knowledge through writing. Making explicit the inquiry and writing processes shifts the focus from knowledge acquisition to knowledge construction. As opposed to a banking model of education, where teachers deposit factual knowledge into students' brains and students are expected to acquire the factual knowledge of a discipline without question, in a disciplinary literacy approach, teachers invite students into the process of knowledge construction (Freire, 1970; Spires et al., 2020).

In a disciplinary literacy approach, the primary mode of writing is argument. But not the pick-a-side kind or the fight-to-win kind students often associate with the word. We're talking about *argumentation*—the process of making a claim, backing it with evidence, and explaining the reasoning behind it.

Table 4.1 Examples of Content Area and Disciplinary Literacy Practices

Content Area	Assignment	Text Types	Content Area Literacy	Disciplinary Literacy
Physics	Egg drop challenge	Trade book *Aerospace Engineering and the Principles of Flight* by Anne Rooney	Summarize during reading	Draw models and record changes in engineer's journal Write up the results of experiment
Family and Consumer Sciences	Make an informed decision on a cell phone plan	Cell phone plans comparison table	Read with a partner Write a paragraph to justify a choice	Make a consumer decision based on information
Personal Finance	Create a monthly budget for your future self	Housing websites Examples of budgets	Take notes while reading Format a table	Create a personal budget
Child Development	Write a lesson plan for social and emotional learning	Book chapter on theories and strategies	Use sources in writing	Write learning objectives
Biology	Argue for which clean energy source the USA should invest in	Research articles Science journalism articles Graphs	Annotate while reading See, Think, Wonder routine	Write a paragraph with a claim, evidence, and reasoning
History	Connect articles of the UN Declaration of Human Rights to events during the Holocaust	Documentary about the Holocaust UN Declaration of Human Rights	Paraphrase complex sentences Analyze cause and effect	Analyze a primary source Explain historical significance

Content Area	Assignment	Text Types	Content Area Literacy	Disciplinary Literacy
Civics	Analyze a political cartoon	Political cartoon	See, Think, Wonder routine	Use historical context to interpret text
Geography	Create a museum exhibit about a country in Africa	Websites with words, photos, and maps	Gather sources Evaluate sources for credibility	Curate visuals, artifacts, and text to inform an audience
Mathematics	Plan a vacation by adjusting variables to get the most fun for the longest time	Websites with words and tables	Read with a partner Create a slide deck Write a paragraph to justify a choice	Highlight pertinent variables Calculate difference
Drama	Write an original play	Excerpts of scripts from multiple playwrights	Analyze mentor texts to understand how a genre is structured	Write a script with stage directions and dialogue
Production Agriculture	Judge soil quality	Informational texts Topography maps	Annotate while reading Write a paragraph to justify a choice	Use discipline-specific vocabulary (e.g., silt, granular, bedrock, ribbon)
Animal Science	Demonstrate understanding of medicine labels for beef, sheep, swine, and goats	Medicine labels and inserts	Read informational texts	Identify the parts of a medicine label Read a chart to calculate dosage

Content Area	Assignment	Text Types	Content Area Literacy	Disciplinary Literacy
Literature	Write a literary analysis of a "great American novel"	Literary fiction novel	Use sticky notes to mark important passages	Keep a reader response journal to record impact of authors' craft on you as a reader
Health and PE	Set and monitor progress of a fitness goal	Fitness plans	Write SMART goals Routinely write in a journal	Log physical activity using reps, sets, weights, duration, time, distance, or appropriate measure
Visual Art	Write an artist statement for your artwork that will be part of the school art show	Artist statements	Analyze mentor texts to understand how a genre is structured	Use discipline-specific vocabulary (e.g., acrylic, graphite, Surrealism, Minimalism)
Choir	Analyze a song's text and music	Lyrics Music score	Look up words that are unfamiliar Paraphrase in own words Underline important words	Identify poetic elements, such as rhyme, alliteration, assonance, and consonance
Computer Science	Understand how direction words impact program design	Programming directions	Use sequence text structure for sense-making Annotate while reading	Identify direction words

If we accept that knowledge is constructed by fallible humans (which it is), then anytime we share that knowledge, we're essentially saying: "Based on the evidence I have, this is the best understanding I have *right now*." That's an argument. Teaching students to read, write, and think through a disciplinary literacy approach equips them to participate in the conversations of each discipline—evaluating evidence, questioning conclusions, and building knowledge, not just memorizing it.

Bringing students into the knowledge construction and communication processes shifts authority in the classroom from solely residing with textbook authors and teachers, to shared authority among students, teachers, and authors. In this way, classrooms are places where students share control and construct meaning, two important factors of motivating and engaging learning experiences and factors consistent with culturally sustaining teaching practices. Students use literacy in the disciplines as tools to learn about the world and synthesize their ideas with the ideas of authors to create new ideas. Through Inquiry-Based Reading, students analyze and synthesize the ideas of others and through Source-Based Writing, they build upon the ideas of others to construct their claims backed by solid evidence.

As Sir Isaac Newton wrote in 1675, it is through standing on the shoulders of giants that we can reach higher and achieve further. From a disciplinary literacy approach, students use literacy to build on the work that came before them in order to achieve new heights of understanding. Let's examine what this looks like in fourth- to twelfth-grade classrooms.

Inquiry-Based Reading

Inquiry-Based Reading is an instructional approach that encourages students to actively engage with texts through questioning, exploration, and critical thinking. Instead of passively receiving information, students are guided to investigate big ideas, generate their own questions, and seek answers through reading and discussion. It aligns with inquiry-based learning practices used in science and social studies, and it applies to literacy development in each discipline by supporting how to locate credible and reliable disciplinary texts and scaffolding how to actively read these texts. Below are three ways to support Inquiry-Based Reading.

M&M Text Set

Creating a Multimodal and Multivoiced Text Set, or M&M Text Set for short, is an effective instructional strategy applicable to any topic. The purpose of the first text in an M&M Text Set is to build students' knowledge on the topic and spark curiosity. The first text introduces the topic in a way that all students can access, such as a provocative photograph, an interesting infographic, or a valuable video. From there, the next objective is to deepen students' knowledge of the issue and widen their perspective by presenting different points of view. Sometimes one carefully selected text can do both; other times, it may take two to accomplish this. The final reading in the set is a complex, content-rich text that pushes students to think critically and make connections across sources. As a whole, the set provides multiple modes to access the content and diverse perspectives to think critically about the issue.

Text sets can be created when designing curriculum, to supplement curriculum, or when needing to reteach a topic. But, it can be overwhelming to find appropriate texts. Although there are many online sources, most are written for adult audiences or the kid version is too babyish. Here are some of my go-to sources for that just-right reading. The *Science Journal for Kids and Teens* is unique in that it rewrites scientific journal articles for younger audiences and has the original authors check the rewrite for accuracy (sciencejournalforkids.org). Topics include agriculture, health, climate, technology, and social science articles too. *Newsela* has high-interest articles curated for fourth- to twelfth-grade levels and accompanying lesson plans for teachers (newsela.com). Public radio and television stations produce various types of **multimodal texts** including online videos and podcasts that are credible and interesting. I like to play the episode and give students a printed copy of the transcript that they can annotate as they listen. Check out your local stations for ways to connect your curriculum to your students' lives. The Library of Congress also has an education page with curation of texts for history, science, and poetry (loc.gov/education).

Text Roundup

A Text Roundup is an activity where students gather multiple texts related to a question. The activity is based on the article type used in journalism and marketing to summarize research or curate a group of texts on a common theme. See *The Scientist*'s Roundup for examples (https://www.the-scientist.com/tag/roundup). After a lesson on locating reliable information, a Text Roundup can be an assignment for students to practice gathering relevant, credible sources. Teachers can assign this activity for 3–10 texts around a common theme or inquiry question.

Table 4.2 displays an effective Text Roundup Graphic Organizer that works well for fourth- to twelfth-grade students. Having students note the year and the connection to the question helps them focus on timeliness and relevance. They can add a column for **genre** (e.g., peer-reviewed scientific journal article, magazine article, and government website) or author's purpose

Table 4.2 Text Roundup Organizer

Inquiry Question:					
Text Title	Author	Year	Main Idea/ Message	Key Quote or Evidence	Connection to Question

(e.g., persuade, inform, and entertain) to focus on credibility. Teachers can modify the number of columns to align with the learning goals or simplify the organizer by providing drop-down menu choices.

The students can turn in the organizer as a way for teachers to check students' ability to locate relevant and reliable sources. Teachers can facilitate discussion about what the texts had in common and how the texts offered different perspectives. As an extension, students can write a roundup article, such as *The Most Important Stories from the Year about Tariffs*, *Three Women from the U.S. Revolution You Should Know*, or *Pros and Cons of Nuclear Energy*.

Questions Into Paragraphs (Q→P)

This strategy takes an overarching topic and breaks it into two to four questions. The overarching topic can come from the curricular unit, and then students can work in small groups to identify lines of inquiry that they would like to follow. Students complete an organizer to answer the questions that help them track information across sources, compare perspectives, and deepen understanding. Then, students are guided to weave sources together in their writing, showing how different sources answer the same question. It's like hosting a panel discussion—except no one's talking over each other and citations are built in. You can find the free download with an example and student-friendly instructions by following the case-sensitive link or QR code in Figure 4.2 (https://bit.ly/QPorganizer)

Figure 4.2

Source-Based Writing

Imagine source-based writing as the art of weaving trusted materials—quotes, data, ideas—into your students' own voice to explain a concept or build an argument. It's more than summarizing; it's a strategic process of interpreting, selecting, synthesizing, and remixing information so students construct knowledge from sources. Teaching these skills supports richer classroom discussions, deeper content understanding, and more empowered writers.

Thinking Routines

Thinking Routines are game-changers when it comes to helping students engage with complex texts and visuals—especially in data-rich subjects. An example is Say, Mean, Matter for layering close reading of texts. This routine starts with the literal layer *Say* (On page #, the text says ...), moves to an interpretative layer *Mean* (I think this means that ...), and then an analysis layer *Matter* (This matters because ...). The routine can guide annotating, discussion, and writing about texts. It provides a clear structure that supports students as they annotate, discuss, and write. When annotating, students might highlight what the text says, such as key words, important details, or powerful quotes. During discussion, they share interpretations or inferences about what the author means. By breaking down the process of textual analysis into manageable, repeatable steps, this routine helps students think more deeply—whether they're explicating a poem, contextualizing a historical speech, or dissecting a scientific article.

Another example is See, Think, Wonder for close reading of visual texts, including photographs, data tables, and infographics. A great resource is the What's Going On in This Graph? collection, a collaboration between the American Statistical Association and the New York Times Learning Network, where students are invited to analyze real-world graphs. Students analyze the graph by first simply observing what is there (what do you *see*?), then thinking (what do you *think* is going on?), and finally questioning (what do you *wonder*?). This routine encourages critical thinking and inquiry, sparking thoughtful questions that can lead to rich class conversations or even drive research and writing.

Thinking Routines (Figure 4.3) work because they are structured yet open-ended—giving all students a way into the task, regardless of **background knowledge**. Plus, it mirrors the kind of analytical thinking that professionals use in the real world, making learning feel authentic and purposeful.

Visual Text

What do you **notice**? What do you **wonder**?
How does this **connect** to you and your community?

What do you **see**?
What do you **think** is going on?
What do you see that makes you think that?
What do you **wonder**?

What do you **see**?
What do you **think** about the work/image?
What connections can I make between the work and **me**?
How might **we** connect to the work? How might the work be connected to the world and our place in it?

Linguistic Text

What does the text **say**?
What does the text **mean**?
Why does it **matter**?

Speaker **O**ccasion **A**udience **P**urpose **S**ubject **Tone (SOAPStone)**

How do the ideas and information **connect** to what you already know?
What new ideas did you get that broaden your thinking or **extend** it in different directions?
What **challenge**, puzzle, or questions emerge?

It says... I say...

Figure 4.3 Thinking Routines for Textual Analysis.

Reading

I choose the quote from MLK Jr. "Freedom is never voluntarily given by the oppressor; it must be demanded by the oppressed." I chose this quote because I noticed the word demanded, and I think the author was very deliberate in choosing this strong word.

Writing

It makes me think of current social justice movements and how people are protesting around the country. It makes me wonder: Who decides when change happens, and what does it take to create real pressure? Do protests work to demand freedom? I think protests can be a powerful way to demand freedom because they bring attention to injustice and show that people are willing to stand up for their rights. While protests don't always lead to immediate change, they can inspire others, pressure leaders, and help build movements that eventually make a difference.

Figure 4.4 Dialectical Notebook Example.

Dialectical Notebook

Dialectical Notebooks are a simple yet powerful tool that can boost student thinking across all content areas. At their core, Dialectical Notebooks integrate reading and writing. On the left side, students jot down a quote or idea from a text, and respond with their thoughts on the right, as shown in Figure 4.4.

It's like having a conversation with the content, encouraging students to slow down, think critically, and actively engage with texts as they read. Check out how Julie Sheerman infused the Tried and True strategy in her high school class.

> ## Tried and True Strategy by Julie Sheerman
>
> **Strategy:** Dialectical Notebooks
>
> **Context:** Senior composition class in Marceline, Missouri
>
> During the year-long senior composition course, my students used Dialectical Notebook entries regularly. With a short excerpt on the left pulled directly from the text, their right-side responses varied according to the text and its purpose in any given unit plan. Sometimes posing questions, sometimes noting surprise or concern, students deepened their critical thinking skills. Early in the school year, I often offered several excerpts from which they could choose. As the semester progressed, the work became more generative and thoughtful. When a text proved especially dense, I layered academic sentence frames to allow their responsive thinking to flow more easily. Not only did the use of dialectical entries prove useful as a reading response strategy, this work often helped students prepare for small-group discussion. Dialectical entries also helped during the early stages of formal writing assignments, as students could review and track their thinking over the span of a unit.

Dialectical Notebooks, as described above, can be used as part of the writing process to layer reading sources with initial writing to begin generating students' own ideas. Layered reading and writing, rather than reading sources first and writing second, integrates the two in a way that better prepares students for the creation of a source-based writing product. Students use the left side to gather important ideas, record powerful quotes, and note interesting evidence. Students then use the right side to process their thinking and generate their own ideas about the topic under investigation.

Document-Based Questions

Document-Based Questions (DBQs) are a powerful strategy that integrates reading, writing, and critical thinking by asking students to analyze a set of sources and use them to construct an evidence-based written response. Instead of simply recalling facts, students investigate sources to answer a compelling question. For example, a science teacher could use a DBQ to explore the question: *"Should humans colonize Mars?"* Students would examine a curated set of sources, such as excerpts from NASA reports, climate data from Mars, expert opinions, and even sci-fi portrayals. They'd analyze each source for reliability and scientific reasoning, then write an argument using evidence to support their position. See how Mrs. Walsh uses DBQs in her middle school social studies classroom in the Tried and True example.

> ## Tried and True Strategy by Veronica Walsh
>
> **Strategy Name:** Document-Based Question
>
> **Context:** Middle school social studies class in New Jersey
>
> In my social studies class, students examine historical primary and secondary source documents to create a claim about the historical figure Alexander the Great. The compelling question is: *Should Alexander the Great be remembered as a hero or a villain?* Documents include a map of Alexander the Great's empire, a short excerpt from Lucius Flavius Arrianus's history from 130 CE, "The Legend of the Helmet" by two different biographers, and a chart with statistics related to the size of the empire at Alexander's death. For each document, I provide questions to guide analysis. Class discussion follows. Then, students write an essay about their claim using evidence from the texts. To scaffold the writing process, I provide an outline that they are invited to use in planning.

This method mirrors the work of real scientists and historians. DBQs are effective because they deepen content understanding while building disciplinary literacy skills, and they invite students into the role of meaning-makers, not just fact-memorizing test-takers. Plus, when the question connects to a big idea or present-day issue, it can stimulate authentic **engagement** and lively classroom debate.

Critiquing Arguments

In disciplinary literacy, reading and writing arguments go hand in hand with critiquing them—students must learn not only to evaluate their own claims but also to evaluate the strength, credibility, and logic of others' arguments within the norms of each subject area.

Co-Create Criteria

Each discipline has its own standards: what counts as strong evidence in a science lab isn't the same as what builds a compelling argument in a literary analysis. When students co-create criteria to evaluate evidence, they're not just learning how to think—they're learning to think like scientists, historians, or literary critics. Inviting students to collectively define these criteria gives them a clearer sense of what matters in the discipline and why.

What criteria do you use to evaluate evidence? List, Group, Label

Class A Categorized into 6 Groups | Class B Categorized into 7 groups

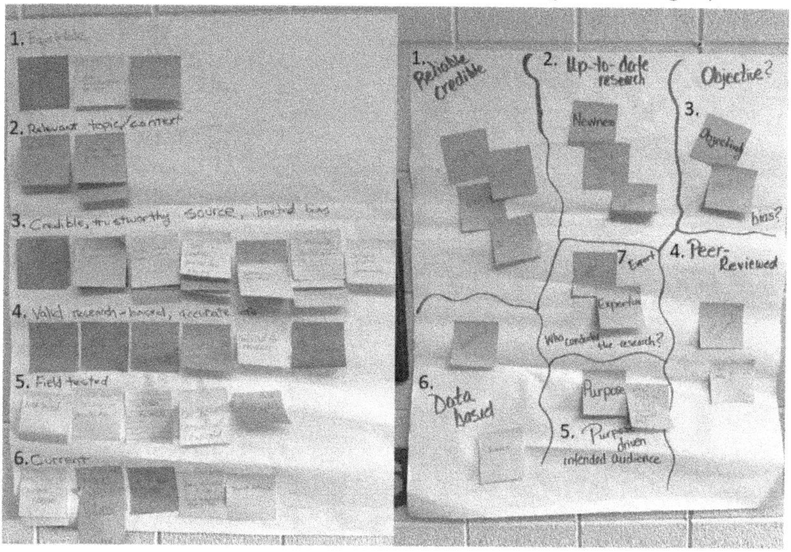

Figure 4.5 Criteria to Evaluate Evidence Example.

Plus, co-creating the criteria fosters ownership and **autonomy**. They're more likely to apply standards they had a hand in shaping. It transforms critiquing arguments from a guessing game into a thoughtful, discipline-specific process where students feel invested and empowered. In Figure 4.5, my class used the List, Group, Label routine to enact the Co-Create Criteria strategy. In the context of our learning, our guiding question was *What criteria do you use to evaluate evidence?* First, each person brainstormed a list of answers, putting one idea per sticky note. Then, in small groups, they placed like answers together and labeled each grouping using either the most common language from the sticky notes or an overarching label. We then did a Gallery Walk to view each group's answers and then discussed as a whole class to come to a consensus. I recorded the consensus on an Anchor Chart so that we could revisit the criteria throughout the year.

Atwoodian Table

An Atwoodian Table is an instructional strategy that invites students to visualize academic argument as a conversation—one where each author has a seat at the table. This approach helps students understand that when they join an argument, they're stepping into an ongoing dialogue, not starting from scratch. Students draw a table on their paper and assign each "seat"

1. Draw a round table.
2. On the table, write the issue.
3. Draw 6 chairs, one for each person at the table.
4. Beside each chair, draw a word balloon.
5. As you read the texts, write the name of the source by the chair. Paraphrase their main claim and some supporting evidence in the word balloon.
6. For the 6th chair, add your own voice!

Figure 4.6 Atwoodian Table.
Adapted from the National Writing Project.

to a different voice in the conversation (see Figure 4.6). For example, in a discussion about nuclear energy, one seat might belong to a scientist advocating for it as a clean, efficient alternative to fossil fuels, supported by data on low-carbon emissions. Another seat might be taken by an environmental activist concerned about radioactive waste and the risk of accidents, citing incidents like Fukushima. A policymaker might take a third seat, weighing economic and regulatory factors, including the high upfront costs, long construction timelines, and challenges related to scaling nuclear energy in a cost-effective way. As students map out these voices and ideas, they begin to see how arguments interact—agreeing, critiquing, or complicating—and where their own voice might fit in. This routine supports considering multiple perspectives and evaluating evidence before constructing claims.

Social Annotation

Social Annotations use computer-mediated communication to combine the active reading strategy of annotation with the power of hearing others' perspectives. When students notice a move an author is making, they can highlight the quote and add a comment to name the rhetorical technique and explicate the impact of the move on the reader. After reading, students can discuss which quote they thought was most powerful or convincing. This practice goes beyond surface-level engagement—it trains students to read like insiders in the discipline. In English, they may analyze persuasive appeals; in history, they might evaluate primary source bias; in science, they could question the strength of reasoning in a research claim. Critiquing arguments is a cornerstone of disciplinary literacy—it helps students recognize how knowledge is built and debated within each subject area. Social Annotations give adolescents a low-stakes way to practice this skill collaboratively, developing both their analytical thinking and their confidence to challenge ideas with evidence.

Conclusion

Reading, writing, speaking, and listening are at the heart of the disciplines. Teaching both content area and disciplinary literacy in middle and high school across the day is important. Academic language helps students access and understand academic texts, encourages them to express their thinking clearly and accurately, and prepares them for the demands of college, career, and community. Learning the unique structures of the disciplines enhances students' ability to enter civic conversations and prepares them for a future of knowledge creation.

More to Explore

- In this episode of the Classroom Caffeine podcast, Dr. Elizabeth Moje discusses disciplinary literacy and the power of literacy in life: https://www.classroomcaffeine.com/guests/elizabeth-moje

- In this video, two teachers from different disciplines think aloud during a close reading: https://youtu.be/xoPtpdMcNcc?si=NZmFJgiTaGykGVo5

- In this episode of the *Journal of Adolescent & Adult Literacy* podcast, Dr. John Strong and Dr. Laura Tortorelli discuss the Read STOP Write program, a multicomponent informational reading and writing intervention: https://podcasts.apple.com/us/podcast/read-stop-write-with-drs-john-strong-and-laura-tortorelli/id1678225245?i=1000706686927

Reflect

Grab your notebook, it's time for a Quick Write. The goal of a Quick Write is to get your thoughts down on paper quickly and freely, without worrying about making mistakes. Set a timer for five minutes, and write as much as you can about the following questions.

1 How is literacy a part of your discipline?

2 What literacy skills and strategies are unique to your discipline?

3 How would you support students in acquiring these skills and strategies?

Discuss

Questions for discussion to learn from and with each other:

- Do you think teachers across content areas should be responsible for teaching literacy?
- If you had to choose three literacy strategies that students would learn to use across content areas, which would you choose?
- What do you want teachers from other disciplines to know about literacy in your discipline?

References

Baye, A., Lake, C., Inns, A. & Slavin, R. E. (2019). A synthesis of quantitative research on reading programs for secondary students. *Reading Research Quarterly, 54* (2), 133–66. https://doi.org/10.1002/rrq.229

Cervetti, G. N., & Hiebert, E. H. (2015). The sixth pillar of reading instruction: Knowledge development. *The Reading Teacher, 68*(7), 548–51. https://doi.org/10.1002/trtr.1343

Freire, P. (1970). *Pedagogy of the oppressed.* Continuum.

Gabriel, R. E. (2023). *Doing disciplinary literacy: Teaching reading and writing across the content areas.* Teachers College Press.

Graham, S., Kiuhara, S. A., & MacKay, M. (2020). The effects of writing on learning in science, social studies, and mathematics: A meta-analysis. *Review of Educational Research, 90*(2), 179–226. https://doi.org/10.3102/0034654320914744

Osborne, J. F., Borko, H., Fishman, E., Gomez Zaccarelli, F., Berson, E., Busch, K. C., Reigh, E., & Tseng, A. (2019). Impacts of a practice-based professional development program on elementary teachers' facilitation of and student engagement with scientific argumentation. *American Educational Research Journal, 56*(4), 1067–112. https://doi.org/10.3102/0002831218812059

Parker, W. C. (2024). Backtalk: Teaching historical reasoning helps democracy thrive. *Phi Delta Kappan, 105*(5), 66–7.

Spires, H. A., Kerkhoff, S. N., & Paul, C. M. (2020). *Read, write, inquire: Disciplinary literacy in grades 6–12.* Teachers College Press.

Spires, H. A., Kerkhoff, S. N., Graham, A. C., Thompson, I., & Lee, J. K. (2018). Operationalizing and validating disciplinary literacy in secondary education. *Reading and Writing, 31*(6), 1401–34. https://doi.org/10.1007/s11145-018-9839-4

Valenzuela, A. (2010). *Subtractive schooling: US–Mexican youth and the politics of caring.* Suny Press.

Zygouris-Coe, V. I. (2012). Disciplinary literacy and the common core state standards. *Topics in Language Disorders, 32*(1), 35–50. http://doi.org/10.1097/TLD.0b013e31824561a2

Literature Cited

Aliki. (1989). *My five senses.* Scholastic.

American Statistical Association and the New York Times Learning Network (2025). What's Going on in the Graph? https://www.amstat.org/whats-going-on-in-this-graph.

Pfeffer, W., & Hale, J. G. (2015). *From seed to pumpkin.* Harper.

Informing Instruction Through Literacy Assessment

5

There is more than one way to get to the top of any mountain. If we think about the academic standard as being the summit, we want all students to reach it, but we can offer different paths to get to the top. Some paths might be more steep and rugged and other paths might take a more gradual climb. Also, we can offer different amounts of support for students.

When I first went rock climbing, I needed a guide to set up the top-roping system for me. A safe system requires the rope to be properly threaded through multiple anchor points at the top and secured to the harness correctly, none of which I knew how to do. Then, I could concentrate on learning the climbing part itself. Having to learn how to build a safe system and how to scale the rock face would have been too much at once. I would have felt overwhelmed before I even began!

With the system in place, I was able to concentrate my energy on learning how to position my body. As I would scramble for each new hold, the guide would observe and give feedback on my body position, which meant I heard "use your legs" about twenty times on my way up the rock face. My sister—who was right beside me, at least for the first two minutes—hardly needed any reminders as she ascended the wall like a spider. When we reached the top, it didn't matter that I climbed awkwardly while she did so gracefully, we both made it. And after, I stayed at the top for a while to rest and take in the view of the lush Chestnut Oak forest while she couldn't wait for the thrill of rappelling down. The point is that, although it looked different for both of us, we both reached the goal. And, one of us fell in love with rock climbing! I know, you probably guessed that was my sister, but though it might have been easier for my sister, it's actually me who fell in love!

This chapter will describe effective strategies for creating literacy assessments that support all learners in inclusive and equitable ways. We will explore key principles and strategies for designing assessments that cater to diverse student needs while ensuring alignment with **learning objectives** and **academic standards**.

Literacy Strategy: It Says / I Say

Make a T-Chart as shown in Table 5.1 below to take notes as you read this chapter. Label the left side "It Says" and note claims from the text. Label the right column "I Say" and respond to the text with your ideas. As you are reading and thinking, consider how assessments position students in ways that impact their reading and writing identities.

Table 5.1

It Says	I Say

Preview Vocabulary

academic standards: agreed-upon goals for what students should know and be able to do by the end of each grade level

asset-based: an approach that focuses on the strengths, skills, and resources that individuals or communities possess, rather than concentrating on weaknesses or deficits

deep learning: shift from rote memorization to the ability to understand, apply, and connect concepts across different contexts

formal assessment: structured assessments, like tests or portfolios, used to measure learning in an official way

formative assessment: assessment during learning to check how well students are understanding

informal assessment: less-structured assessments, like class discussions or observations, to gauge learning in a low-risk way

learning objective: specific statement of what students should know or be able to do by the end of the lesson

proficiency scale: assessment tool that delineates levels of a skill or understanding

rubric: assessment tool that clearly outlines the criteria for evaluating a student's work

summative assessment: final assessments, like tests or projects, of what students have learned at the end of a unit or course to measure student outcomes

Purpose of Assessment

Literacy assessments serve multiple purposes in schools, from guiding classroom instruction to determining eligibility for special education services. They typically fall into five main categories: screening, diagnostic, progress monitoring, formative, and summative. This includes both **formal assessment** and **informal assessment**, and a single test may fulfill more than one purpose. Figure 5.1 gives an overview of different types of assessment.

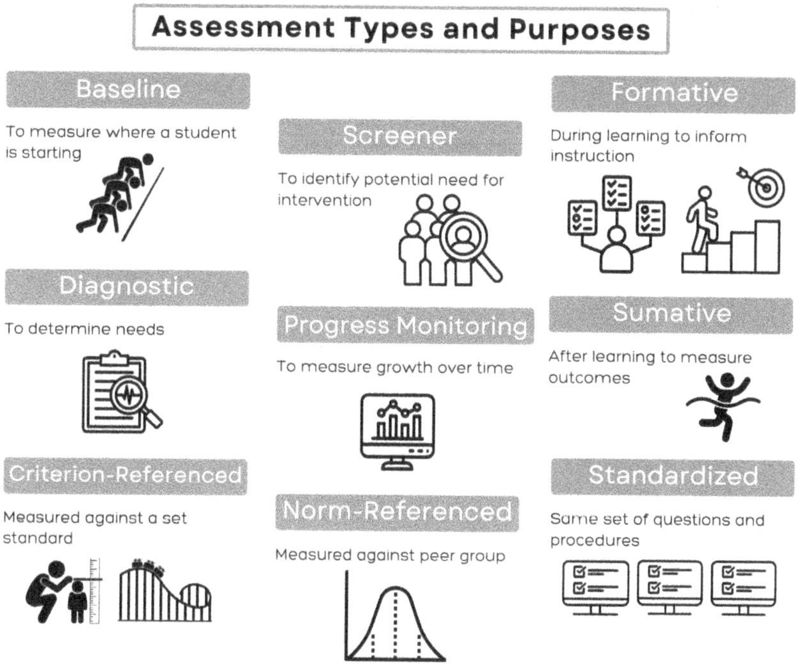

Figure 5.1 Assessment Types and Purposes.

Universal Screeners

A screener is a quick check to see if any students need extra help or have special learning needs. Students identified by the screener are then given a diagnostic test, a deeper assessment to identify the points of difficulty. For example, the eye chart at a doctor's office quickly checks if a person might have a vision problem—it tells you *that* something might be wrong. A diagnostic test goes further, identifying *what* the specific vision issue is, such as astigmatism or nearsightedness, so a treatment plan can be made.

School districts often administer a universal screener at the beginning and/ or middle of the year. *Universal* refers to being given to all children. School districts make the choice of which screener will be administered between the many available, reliable, and valid standardized tests. That might sound like a lot of jargon, so let's break it down—here's what those terms actually mean.

Standardized refers to tests that have predetermined sets of questions and are administered and scored the same for all students. *Reliable* means the assessment consistently produces the same results under the same conditions, like a thermometer that consistently shows that your body temperature is ninety-five degrees Fahrenheit. If that thermometer read that your body temperature was ninety-eight degrees, then you would know that you have a fever because the temperature is raised, even though it is not an accurate reading. *Valid* means that the test is measuring what it is intended to measure—think of darts hitting the dart board where a person is aiming. When an assessment is valid and reliable, it means the developer used a scientific process to show that the assessment accurately measures what it is intended to consistently over time. Think of darts hitting *exactly* where a person is aiming *every time*, as illustrated in Figure 5.2. The value of an assessment is in how well it consistently and accurately measures evidence of the learning outcomes.

Standardized assessments compare scores to criteria or national norms. Criterion-referenced tests measure specific skills or content based on a set standard—not how students compare to others. The Phonological Awareness Screening Test (PAST; Kilpatrick, 2024) is an example of a criterion-referenced assessment designed to determine whether a student has mastered specific skills based on developmental milestones. This screener is conducted one on one, grouped by skill, and increases in difficulty in the sequence of the items. Let's look at an item to give you a sense of how the screener is structured. Item: "Say craft. Now say craft but instead of /f/ say /k/." Answer: "If you say craft, and change the /f/ to /k/, you get cracked." The level of difficulty that the student is able to do correctly can be compared

Figure 5.2 Meaning of Reliable and Valid.

to a set standard, such as a table with ages of typical development, in order to determine if there is a difference.

In comparison, norm referenced tests compare a student's performance to a national sample of peers to see where they stand. An example is the Comprehensive Test of Phonological Processing (CTOPP-2; Wagner et al., 2013) that compares a student's performance to a national norm group. Either criterion- or norm-referenced screeners can be used to identify potential risk of a developmental delay, learning difference, or disability. If a risk is identified, the next step is a diagnostic test.

Diagnostic Tests

Diagnostic assessments are used to pinpoint individual strengths and needs in reading and writing. Typically administered after a student shows risk on a screener, a formal diagnostic test can help point to language, spelling, **decoding**, or reading **comprehension** issues and lead to targeted instruction (Reading Rockets, 2025). In some cases, it also leads to an intervention plan and may result in a learning disability diagnosis. A commonly used diagnostic test is the Basic Reading Inventory (Johns, 2016), which provides information on word recognition, fluency, and comprehension. For an option that can work in a classroom setting, teachers of adolescents can give the Words Their Way Upper Level Spelling Inventory (2020, pp. 326–9). A teacher can deliver the Upper Level Spelling Inventory to their whole class to gather information on students' knowledge of **phonics**, orthographic patterns, and morphological structures. It's designed to be administered quickly—often in under twenty minutes—and provides information that is useful for grouping and tailoring instruction.

Informal diagnostic tests, more commonly referred to as pretests, are given at the start of a school year or unit to find out what students already know and are able to do. The results help teachers plan instruction based on students' current skills and knowledge. For example, a high school writing teacher might use a pretest essay to see how well students can organize their ideas, use evidence, and write clearly. This information helps the teacher decide which writing skills to focus on first. Formal and informal diagnostic assessments can be used as often as needed to gather information.

Progress Monitoring Tools

Progress monitoring tools track a student's development in reading and writing throughout instruction and/or intervention. Progress monitoring can start with a benchmark to mark where a student is beginning. Then, depending on the level of support a student needs, progress monitoring might happen every two or four weeks. The results help educators chart growth over time and make informed decisions about the next instructional steps to meet the students' needs.

Progress monitoring and **formative assessments** have similar purposes, to see what students know and can do in order to inform instruction. But, progress monitoring is scheduled at regular intervals and formative assessment is responsive to students' immediate learning needs, sometimes in real time.

Formative Assessment

Formative assessments are conducted as part of the learning process, enabling educators to gauge student understanding, adjust instruction accordingly, and inform next steps in teaching. To be effective, the assessment must be closely aligned with the learning objectives established for the lesson. This alignment helps to monitor skills, knowledge, and abilities that students are expected to acquire. Based on results of formative assessments, teachers can differentiate instruction for groups or individual students.

Formative assessments can include informal checks for understanding that give teachers instantaneous information and are not for a grade, like observations of student performance, discussions with students, classroom polls, exit slips, and the following two strategies.

Fist to Five

Fist to Five is a nonverbal check-for-understanding strategy that gives teachers information in real time. The teacher poses a question (e.g., "Do you understand photosynthesis?"). Students respond by holding up a number of fingers:

- 0 fingers (fist)—"I'm so confused."
- 1 finger—"I kind of get it."
- 2 fingers—"I am getting it but still have a lot of questions."
- 3 fingers—"I understand but want to understand more."
- 4 fingers—"I understand well."
- 5 fingers—"I'm so confident, I could explain this to a classmate."

If most of the students are at a four or above, the teacher can ask a student who held up five fingers to explain the concept to the class. By hearing a peer explain the concept in their own words, other students may gain clarity from a relatable explanation, build confidence in their own ability to grasp the material, and deepen their understanding. If most of the students are at a three or below, the Anonymous Questions strategy, described next, comes in handy.

Anonymous Questions

Anonymous Questions are a low-risk way for students to clarify their learning and for the teacher to see where students need more support. This can be done physically or digitally. Students write their question, leaving their name off, on a piece of paper; crumple the paper into a snowball; and throw it to the front of the room. The teacher reads the questions for the class to answer. Digitally, this can be done with an anonymous digital survey or whiteboard tool. The reverse can also work, where the teacher asks a question and students anonymously answer on paper or a digital tool.

Exit Ticket

An Exit Ticket is a quick, low-stakes way to check what students have learned before they head out the door—think of it as their "ticket to leave" the classroom. It's a classic example of formative assessment because it provides timely insight into student understanding *during* the learning process, not after it's too late to course-correct. Thinking Routines make great exit ticket prompts, such as Connect, Extend, Challenge: What connections do you notice? What ideas extend your thinking further or in a new direction? What challenges or questions emerge?

The popular 3-2-1 Prompt is an easy, customizable exit ticket format that teachers can tailor to any lesson. You just create your own version to match your goals—like asking students to list three facts they learned, two ideas they found interesting, and one question they still have. It's simple to write, quick for students to complete, and gives teachers a clear snapshot of what stuck, what sparked curiosity, and what is still muddy.

Teachers can also create their own short, focused prompts to match the learning goals. For example, a high school social studies teacher might ask: "In one sentence, explain the main cause of the American Revolution" or "Which Enlightenment thinker do you most agree with and why?" The responses are like mini-windows into their brains—and unlike concert tickets, these are priceless. Bonus? It keeps students engaged till the final bell.

Summative Assessment

Whereas formative assessments are *for* learning, **summative assessments** are *of* learning. Summative assessments evaluate student learning at the end of the unit or course, measuring the extent to which learning objectives have been met. In summative assessments, the focus should be on measuring the proficiency of these skills and knowledge against the intended standards, ensuring that the assessment serves as a true reflection of what students have learned and not just their test-taking skills. Summative assessments in adolescent literacy are often evaluated through the use of rubrics, checklists, scoring guides, or **proficiency scales**.

When the use of the results of a single summative assessment is used to make important decisions about student promotion or teacher effectiveness, they are referred to as high-stakes assessments. High-stakes assessments carry a significant risk of serious consequences, which means that they are often anxiety-producing. Offering low-risk opportunities to monitor progress along the way can help reduce the anxiety for teachers, students, and their families.

While a single assessment provides a snapshot of student performance, a portfolio presents a photo album of their learning. A portfolio is a curated collection of a student's work that demonstrates their growth over time. Using portfolios to assess adolescent reading and writing offers a more authentic, student-centered, and asset-based approach to assessment. Rather than relying solely on one-time tests, portfolios allow students to showcase learning through a collection of work that includes drafts, reflections, self-assessments, and final pieces. This summative tool supports equity-focused, competency-based assessment, giving teachers a fuller picture of students' progress. Portfolios also promote metacognition and **self-regulation** as students reflect on their strengths, set goals, and take ownership of their literacy development.

Design Principles

When designing literacy instruction and assessment, the Universal Design for Learning (UDL) framework outlines evidence-based principles that respect learner differences and emphasize fairness without sacrificing rigor (CAST, 2024).

Asset-Based Assessment

Asset-based assessments notice and name what students can do rather than concentrating on what they may lack. From an asset-based lens, literacy assessments should tap into students' cultural knowledge and community practices as resources (Hammond, 2014). For example, when designing prompts or questions, teachers can draw from topics familiar to students, making the assessment about literacy and not **background knowledge**. One effective strategy is to incorporate culturally relevant texts that reflect students' backgrounds and lived experiences. For example, teachers can provide choices among culturally relevant passages for a reading comprehension assessment or as examples for a writing assessment.

Another asset-based practice is celebrating bilingualism and linguistic diversity as strengths. Inviting students to use their home languages—especially when annotating reading and in stages of the writing process—can support both comprehension and expression, providing a richer and more authentic demonstration of their literacy skills (Garcia & Kleifgen, 2020). Students can write in their home language first and then translate to English or translanguage by using both languages simultaneously. By integrating these **culturally sustaining** approaches, teachers can create assessments that center students, build their confidence, and enhance their literacy development.

An asset-based approach is grounded in evidence-based practices that prioritize culturally relevant and sustaining teaching, which affirms students' cultural and linguistic identities while promoting academic success (Dunham et al., 2022). Instead of viewing students' diverse experiences or languages as barriers to learning, educators see them as rich resources that can enhance academic success and contribute to the classroom environment. This approach helps create a more positive, inclusive, and supportive learning space, where all students' strengths are acknowledged and leveraged for growth.

Multiple Means of Representation and Expression

When designing assessments, it is crucial to proactively identify barriers that could impede student success. The UDL framework highlights how representation (i.e., language and symbols) can hinder access to the task. When students do not fully understand the language or symbols used in an assessment, it can create barriers to comprehension and prevent students from accurately demonstrating what they know. To proactively remove barriers, teachers can facilitate multiple representations for accessibility, clarity, and comprehensibility for all learners. Teachers can provide written instructions, read them aloud, and offer a visual example.

Some learners have a specific need. For example, to increase accessibility for multilingual learners, teachers can help learners translate the assessment in their first language before beginning. To increase accessibility for a student with an information processing disability, a teacher can break long assessments into smaller tasks, such as presenting one question at a time for an essay exam.

In addition to challenges with language reception, difficulties with language expression can also hinder a student's ability to effectively demonstrate their understanding and skills. The UDL principle of multiple means of action and expression refers to providing students with flexible, inclusive, and accessible options to show what they know. Teachers can offer choices for different modes of expression (e.g., text, visual, or audio) or alternative forms of assessment (e.g., oral exam or multimedia presentation), enabling students to showcase their understanding in ways that resonate with their individual learning needs and preferences.

By considering the potential barriers, educators can develop strategies that accommodate all learners tailored to their diverse needs. UDL categorizes scaffolds into three types:

- linguistic (e.g., providing audio instructions, word banks, speech-to-text)
- conceptual (e.g., offering templates or graphic organizers)
- social–cultural (e.g., encouraging revisions and retakes)

Assistive technology can facilitate support. Many free tools are available to add audio instructions, deliver read-aloud support for tests, and enable students to record their spoken responses (see Class Kick, 2025, in More to Explore). Google has browser extensions, like Translate and Dictionary, that readers can utilize to determine the meaning of new vocabulary they encounter when reading. Microsoft also has accessibility tools, like Translator and Immersive Reader, with voice settings, picture dictionary, and line focus. Online reading tools can highlight a few lines at a time or change text color to support eye tracking and focus (see BeeLine Reader, 2025). When creating assessments, teachers can use fonts like Dyslexie and Lexend that are designed to improve reading performance. Additional accessibility strategies include increasing the font size and ensuring good contrast between the text and the background.

So far, we have learned about multiple options for language representation and expression in assessment design. To support diverse learners, assessments also need to be student-centered and flexible. Flexibility is not about removing rigor. It's about removing the irrelevant variables from the equation. It's about embracing student voice and choice in communicating what they have learned. And, it's about equity and inclusion. As illustrated in Figure 5.3,

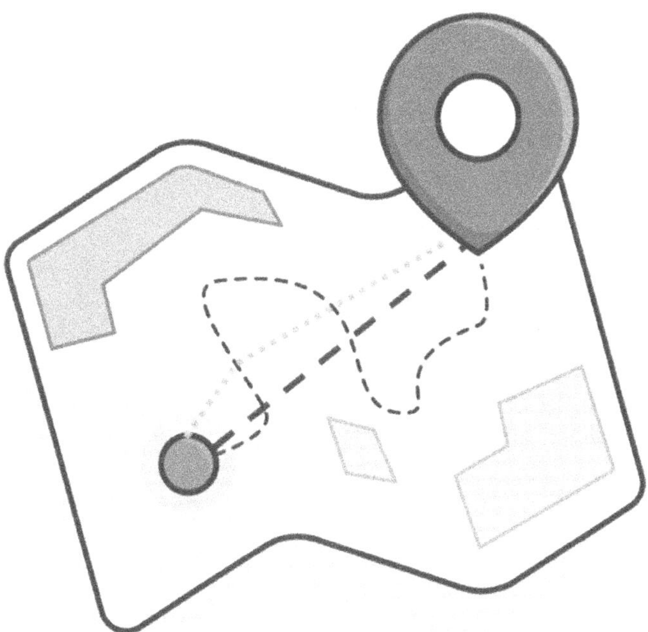

Figure 5.3 Flexibility in Assessment.

the goal is for all students to meet the standard, but they don't all have to do so in the same way and in the same amount of time. The following are examples of assessments that embrace flexibility in both the process and product.

Figure 5.4

Choice Board

A standards-aligned Choice Board grounded in UDL gives students multiple options to demonstrate their understanding of specific learning objectives, while honoring their individual strengths, interests, and needs. Each task on the board is intentionally designed to meet the same academic standards but offers varied modes of expression, such as writing, drawing, speaking, or using technology. This approach heightens **engagement** and deepens learning through student **autonomy**. And, the multiple means of action and expression support accessibility. Scan Figure 5.4 for an example.

Tic-Tac-Toe

The Tic-Tac-Toe strategy for summative assessment is similar to a choice board in that it presents choices aligned to specific learning objectives. What's different is that there are nine choices presented on a 3×3 grid. Students choose three in a row horizontally, vertically, or diagonally to complete a Tic-Tac-Toe. This strategy invites students to demonstrate their understanding in multiple ways to leverage their strengths while also encouraging them to stretch beyond their comfort zone.

Learning Menus

Learning Menus are also similar to choice boards, but they add a bit more structure in that students make a choice within categories, like starters, main course, and dessert! See the Tried and True Strategy for what it looked like when Diana Hammond introduced a Learning Menu for writing in her classroom.

One-Pager

A One-Pager is a creative, student-generated response to a **text** that combines visual and written elements—such as drawing, writing, key words, important ideas, quotations, connections, and elements of design—on a single sheet of paper. This strategy encourages students to engage deeply with content by synthesizing ideas, making interdisciplinary and personal connections, and demonstrating comprehension through both textual analysis and visual representation (see Potash, 2019, for examples). Check out the link for even more Choice Board (Figure 5.5), Tic-Tac-Toe, Learning Menu, and One-Pager examples (https://bit.ly/4nVyjYw)!

Tried and True Strategy by Diana Hammond

Assessment Strategy: Learning Menu

Context: Eleventh-grade English Language Arts class in St. Louis, Missouri

I wanted to provide my students with more choice and flexibility in their writing to promote ownership and engagement, while still meeting the same semester objectives as my colleagues. So, I created a menu of topic, mode, and genre options for students to select from, and I provided accompanying mini-lessons in class to teach the different options. Some students were resistant at first, finding it frustrating that I would not just tell them what to do. Conferring one-on-one during class helped students who were not used to making so many decisions during their writing process. At the end of the semester, I remember reading student reflections and coming across the same takeaway over and over: my writing is better when I care about the topic.

AFTER READING

CHOICE BOARD

Choose one task to demonstrate your learning

With a small group, write and perform a skit demonstrating your learning	Design an infographic based on the text	Present a TED Talk that inspires the audience to take action on the issue
Create a comic based on the text	With a partner, record a podcast that teaches the audience about the concepts in the text	Write a story from your experience that illustrates the issue

Figure 5.5 Choice Board Example.

Designing Rubrics and Proficiency Scales

The most important aspect of any evaluation is that it focuses on the intended objective or standard, not the method of expression. For instance, if an assessment is designed to measure students' understanding of science concepts, spelling errors should not impact their score. **Rubrics** are a valuable tool to support this focus by clearly outlining the criteria for success, which John Hattie's (2023) research found is paramount to student learning. Sometimes in a rubric, a standard or objective is tied to one criterion and sometimes a standard or objective is broken down so students can understand exactly what's expected, as shown in the Single-Point Rubric in Table 5.2.

When shared in advance, rubrics make the success criteria clear and help students plan and monitor their performance. Rubrics can guide self-assessment, peer feedback, and teacher evaluation of formative and summative assessments. Rubrics assist with consistency and transparency in grading and can reduce the time in grading. Even better, co-creating rubrics with students can deepen their understanding of effective reading and writing and increase ownership of their learning.

The three main types of rubrics include holistic, analytic, and single-point (Brookhart, 2013). A holistic rubric evaluates a product, like a student essay, as a whole and presents one score. An analytic rubric breaks down the components of the assignment into separate criteria and shows what is expected at different levels of performance. A single-point rubric outlines expectations for proficiency in the middle column, with space on either side for noting areas that exceed or fall short of the standard. A single-point rubric is the best of both worlds, in my opinion, because it combines the speed of the holistic and the detailed feedback from the analytic.

Table 5.2 shows a sample rubric used to assess an informational writing assignment following a lesson on hooks (i.e., attention-grabbing sentences that spark the reader's interest). In this assignment, students wrote letters to family members to share important information about preventing a disease covered in the unit that might be relevant to their loved ones.

A **proficiency scale** is a tool used in education to clearly define levels of student knowledge or skill in relation to a specific objective or standard. It outlines a progression of learning from limited to advanced performance and helps both teachers and students understand what competency looks like (Marzano, 2006). The most common

Table 5.2 Single-Point Rubric Example

Grows How to strengthen your work	Standards 6.2 a, b, d	Glows Strong aspects of your work
	Criteria 1 (6.2a) Introduce the topic in an interesting way.	
	Criteria 2 (6.2a) Include a topic sentence (for each paragraph if writing more than one).	
	Criteria 3 (6.2b) Develop the topic with relevant facts, definitions, details, or examples.	
	Criteria 4 (6.2d) Use at least three vocabulary words to inform the reader about the topic.	
	Criteria 5 Provide information that is factually correct.	

proficiency scale has four levels with the highest level referring to inferences, connections, or applications that go above and beyond what was explicitly taught. Level 3 describes what meeting the standard at a proficient level looks like. Level 2 refers to foundational knowledge or simple skills needed first in order to develop proficiency. Level 1 means that the student can get to Level 2 with teacher support, and Level 0 is that the standard is not met even when support is provided.

I made a proficiency scale based on the Common Core State Standards (National Governors Association, 2010) for Reading: Informational Text. The scale is to evaluate the Grades 9–10 standard for evaluating arguments in a text (RI.9–10.8). I started with Level 3 and unpacked the standard using language that I thought would make sense to students—to be honest, that first required me to make sense of the standard myself. I then used the evaluating argument standard for Grade 8 (RI.8.8) to help me construct Level 2. For writing Level 4, I looked at the standard for the Grades 11–12 band, but it was specific to US seminal texts, and my curriculum was World Literature, so that wasn't helpful. So then, I asked myself, *what do I really want my students to be able to do related to reading arguments?* And I realized, I really want them to be able to recognize authors' biases and hidden agendas, which requires inference because neither is explicitly stated. Here's what I came up with:

- **Level 4** (exceeds the standard): The student insightfully evaluates the validity of the author's argument; uses textual evidence when identifying logical fallacies or sound reasoning; points out bias, assumptions, or unstated motivations; and determines the credibility, relevance, and sufficiency of evidence.

- **Level 3** (proficient): The student accurately identifies the argument's claim; identifies examples of sound reasoning or logical fallacies; and correctly determines validity, relevance, and sufficiency of evidence.

- **Level 2** (developing): The student identifies the argument's claim, identifies at least one example of a logical fallacy or sound reasoning, and correctly determines the relevance and sufficiency of supporting evidence.

- **Level 1**: The student can reach level 2 with support of the teacher.

- **Level 0**: The student did not demonstrate level 2 even with support.

The proficiency scale supports students by making expectations transparent and helps teachers guide progress more strategically.

Although there are different tools for assessment, an effective design acknowledges that each student has unique strengths and needs and provides educators with space to tailor feedback accordingly. To sum up, educators should be able to answer the following questions when designing assessments:

- What do you want students to learn?

- How can you see that students learned what you wanted them to?

- What are some potential barriers that could affect students' being able to show you what they learned?

- Can you be flexible in the process and/or product?

- Where is support necessary in the assessment process?

Fueling Learning with Feedback

Feedback on students' reading and writing is essential because it helps them understand their strengths and identify specific areas for improvement. Effective feedback guides students toward deeper comprehension and clearer expression by highlighting not just *what* needs to change, but *why* it matters. In reading, feedback can support skills like inference, summarizing, and vocabulary use; whereas in writing, it can refine organization, clarity, and grammar. When feedback is timely, specific, supportive, understandable to the learner, and actional, it furthers learning in a significant way (Fisher et al., 2016). What's more, feedback reinforces a growth mindset, encourages meaningful revision, and fosters long-term development in literacy. Ultimately, quality feedback equips students to become more confident and independent readers and writers. According to writing gurus Graham, Karen, and Hebert (2011), "Writing improves when students are taught to evaluate the effectiveness of their own writing [and] when teachers and peers provide students with feedback about the effectiveness of their writing" (p. 6). Here are strategies for self, peer, and teacher feedback.

Self-Assessment and Peer Feedback

Students can and should reflect on their learning processes and products. Self-assessment is a powerful strategy that encourages students to take ownership of their learning by reflecting on their reading and writing progress. When students are taught how to self-assess using clear criteria, they can identify what they did well and what they need to improve. This process helps build metacognitive skills, thinking about one's own thinking, which strengthens both comprehension and communication. Likewise, peer feedback is powerful because it requires the student giving the feedback to internalize the success criteria and use higher-order thinking—analyzing the work to identify specific features and evaluating it to determine its strengths and areas for improvement.

Adolescents are often more motivated to use feedback from their peers because social connection and peer approval play a big role in how they think and behave at this age. However, in my experience, students need structure and coaching in order to give feedback that is helpful and not hurtful. Over time, giving each other feedback nurtures confidence, **motivation**, and a deeper understanding of effective reading and writing practices. Following self or peer feedback, students set a goal for the next stage of their learning, which might be revising their essay or applying a literacy strategy during the next assignment. Consider using the following strategies as part of the assessment.

Exam-Wrappers

Exam-Wrappers are a post exam or assignment activity where students self-reflect on their performance and study habits. It's short, often ungraded, and encourages students to analyze what they did well, what they struggled with, and how they can improve their learning strategies for future assessments (see Bergman, 2025, for an example).

Rose, Bud, Thorn

Rose, Bud, Thorn is a simple yet surprisingly insightful reflection routine that helps students pause and think about their reading and writing. The "rose" is something that went well—maybe they nailed a metaphor or actually enjoyed the article (gasp!). The "thorn" is a challenge or frustration, like getting lost in a dense text or wrestling with a thesis statement that just won't cooperate. The "bud" is something they're still curious about or looking forward to, like trying out a new writing style or diving into a topic that sparked their interest. It's like giving students a chance to say, "Here's what bloomed, here's what poked me, and here's what might still grow."

Playing Card Method

Before peers give each other feedback, the teacher uses the suits in a deck of playing cards as a metaphor to explain different types of feedback. Heart feedback is positive but vague. The equivalent of clicking the heart icon, it feels nice but isn't helpful. Diamond feedback is positive and pointed—in other words, valuable and specific. Club's feedback is not actionable, either because it is unclear or based on personal preference. It feels like being hit by a club—ouch! Spades feedback is negative but, as explained by TedEd (Kolaya, 2017), "Just like the little shovels they're named after, spades can help people dig themselves out of a hole. This feedback may be negative, but also specific, which makes it helpful" (para. 6). The goal is for each peer to provide diamonds and spades feedback.

Peer Conferences

For this activity, pairs of students receive an interview protocol with questions related to assessment goals. The questions ask about the student's process and product in order to foster self-reflection. I have used it in my own classroom and find it effective for several reasons. First of all, interviewing integrates the literacies of reading, writing, speaking, and listening. Second, it's collaborative in nature, and students learn from each other as they hear about others' processes. Third, an interview protocol introduces some structure, but students can control the direction and flow of the conversation. Examples of questions from the protocol I gave my students are: *What was your purpose for this writing? Who was your audience? What decisions did you make to connect with your audience and achieve your purpose?* and *What feedback would you like from me today?* This last question is especially powerful as it helps peers provide what experts call "just for me, just in time feedback" (Fisher et al., 2016, p. 66).

Asset-Based Teacher Feedback

When giving feedback on a writing assignment, adopting an asset-based approach can make a world of difference in how students perceive their growth and potential. Instead of concentrating solely on mistakes, teachers can highlight the strengths in students' work—whether it's their creativity, voice, or the way they've structured their argument. For instance, the teacher could say, "Your introduction begins in an engaging way and clearly presents your main idea," instead of just pointing out what's missing. If the student draws from their cultural or linguistic background, the teacher can notice and name that as an asset. Teachers also can celebrate how students' unique perspective enriches their writing: "I love the way you integrated your cultural experiences into this paragraph. It adds perspective and depth to your argument."

Giving feedback on student writing can feel overwhelming at times. Targeting feedback to the learning goals, and not trying to comment on everything or correct every error, keeps the task manageable for teachers and more constructive for students. Constructive feedback should always feel like an opportunity for growth. For example, if the learning target is to include textual evidence in writing, rather than saying, "The evidence is weak," try, "Your example is a great starting point—expand on your key idea by providing a quote from the text to illustrate your point for the reader." Framing challenges as chances for improvement helps students see their weaknesses as stepping stones. Sometimes, an educator's intended tone doesn't translate through written comments. Recording a video—or better yet, having a real conversation—adds in those powerful nonverbal cues like facial expressions and tone of voice that help students actually *feel* the encouragement (Fisher et al., 2016).

> A high school student writes a sentence like this:
>
> *"She don't know what to do about the problem."*
>
> Response telling the student:
>
> *"This should be 'She doesn't know ... ' because 'don't' is incorrect in this context."*
>
> Response asking a question:
>
> *"I noticed you used 'don't' instead of 'doesn't.' Is there a particular reason you chose to write it this way?"*

Asset-based feedback does not do the problem-solving for the learner. There are times when asking a question—instead of immediately making a correction or providing a suggestion—can be more effective in supporting the reader's thinking. When providing feedback on student writing, the question stance avoids the assumption that the writer made a mistake. Here's a scenario that illustrates using a question.

Asking rather than telling respects the writer's choices and keeps the agency with the student. Asking the question honors the possibility that the student deliberately chose to use "don't" for a specific reason—perhaps to reflect their authentic voice or a certain tone. The question doesn't assume that the word was an error, but instead shows curiosity about the student's thinking process. Sometimes, especially in creative or informal writing, what looks like an error might actually be a stylistic choice.

Questions center dialogue rather than directives. This helps build a relationship where the student feels that their voice and decisions are valued. The student is invited to reflect on their own writing choices, which encourages deeper engagement with literacy. Asking thoughtful questions encourages students to reflect on and explain their writing choices, while still allowing space for teachable moments about grammar and style.

When holding Reading and Writing Conferences with students, I like to start with an asset-based self-reflection question: "What part are you most proud of?" This enables students to recognize their strengths. Then I ask, "What part would you like feedback on?" From there we can work together to set goals for growth, which research shows is beneficial for adolescent reading (Hall, 2016) and writing (Graham et al., 2016). Setting literacy goals based on assessment personalizes the learning and reinforces the idea that literacy development is a process, not a one-time event.

By focusing on what students do well and offering constructive, strengths-based feedback, teachers can help students build confidence and motivation, making reading and writing empowering experiences for all learners. As Katherine O'Daniels, a literacy professor and teacher educator, says, "The language we use to respond to students' work and describe their literacy development has the power to shape literate identities" (personal communication, July 11, 2025).

Designing Next Instructional Steps

Diagnostic and formative assessments can help identify students' current levels of proficiency. However, the usefulness of these assessments depends on the quality of the data they report—invalid or poorly designed assessments can lead to misguided decisions. As they say, garbage in, garbage out. In addition, assessments are only useful if the conclusions drawn from them lead to meaningful instructional decisions. Teachers must be able to interpret assessment data—such as benchmarking results, progress monitoring trends, and observations of student performance—to make informed instructional decisions. With useful data, educators can tailor instruction to meet the needs of individuals, small groups, and the whole class, ensuring that literacy instruction is responsive and differentiated.

When it comes to literacy, there are constrained and unconstrained skills (Paris, 2005). Unconstrained skills have a clear endpoint and can be mastered. Foundational literacy consists of several constrained skills, such as phonics, spelling, and high-frequency word recognition. Either you know that the digraph *ph* makes the /f/ sound, or you do not. It's relatively straightforward to use the results from diagnostic or formative assessments of constrained skills to inform instruction. For students receiving small-group intervention, begin instruction with the next skill in the sequence following the one they've already mastered. Once students demonstrate proficiency, the intervention can be phased out or transitioned to another area of need.

For unconstrained skills, on the other hand, there is no ceiling. The skill can always be developed further, and development is never truly finished. Unconstrained literacy skills are harder to assess because they are complex and influenced by background knowledge, language exposure, and context. Unlike constrained skills, which can be measured with right-or-wrong answers, unconstrained skills require more nuanced assessment methods.

In my experience, the best way to assess reading comprehension is to listen to students read. In my high school class, students were not shy about reading aloud in small groups. I would circulate the room, conducting an informal assessment through listening. But, in order to ensure a safe space, teachers could consider listening one-on-one in a private space or having students audio record their reading. The reason that listening to students read is so powerful is because in order to use the appropriate prosody, that is, phrasing and expression, the reader needs an understanding of what the text is saying. This makes prosody a good proxy for comprehension while also being able to hear if there are other factors impeding comprehension. Along with one's professional judgment, resources to support the determination of where students are and what the next level would be include teacher-created proficiency scales as well as research-based analytic rubrics for reading fluency (see Rasinski, 2024, in More to Explore), comprehension (see Critical Reading Inventory, 2016), and writing (see National Writing Project, 2025).

Once the teacher has interpreted the results of assessment, they can use the results to plan the next learning experiences for the students. If the whole class met the learning goals, then the teacher can move on in the curriculum. If not, then comes the big question, *now what?* We can think about providing support to students in three tiers. Tier 1 is whole-class instruction. If the majority of the class did not meet the learning goals, then the teachers might want to reteach the whole class. Another option would be to pull a small group of students who meet the learning targets and provide the opportunity for enrichment, such as a virtual scavenger hunt or creative writing prompt, while reteaching the rest of the class. Free online programs for creating a scavenger hunt include Goosechase (https://goosechase.com) and TrackStar (trackstar.4teachers.org).

Tier 2 is small-group instruction, which allows for more individualized attention, immediate feedback, and targeted support based on their specific needs. It also creates a more comfortable environment for participation and asking questions, which maximizes the engagement needed for **deep learning**. Small group instruction can be managed by creating stations and grouping students by need. For example, in my tenth-grade class, while one group met with me for targeted support on writing thesis statements, another station guided students through peer review using structured checklists, a third engaged the small group of students at that station in collaboratively analyzing a **mentor text**, and the fourth station was for conducting Internet research to gather information for their essay. By rotating through stations, students get the support they need without one-size-fits-all instruction, and the teacher can zero in on skill gaps without leaving the rest of the class idle. It's not just efficient—it's empowering for both students and teachers.

Tier 3 provides the most individualized and intensive support for students who benefit from more focused instruction to fully engage with grade-level learning. This typically happens after ongoing progress monitoring shows that a student isn't making sufficient growth with Tier 2 support. However, in some cases such as a significant and immediate learning need, students may be placed directly into Tier 3 support. This level of support is typically delivered one-on-one or in very small groups, using assessment data to tailor instruction to each student's strengths and needs. Taking the time to reinforce key concepts before moving on helps create a strong foundation for future learning and supports long-term success.

Conclusion

Thoughtfully designed literacy assessments support students where they are and help them scale new heights in their learning. First, it's essential to recognize and build upon students' strengths and resources, otherwise known as an asset-based approach. Using an asset-based lens, teachers recognize students' personal, cultural, and linguistic backgrounds as valuable assets in the learning process. Second, assessment should focus on accurately capturing student learning while reducing barriers. By proactively identifying barriers, planning for variability, and implementing appropriate scaffolds, educators can design assessments that not only measure student learning effectively but also foster an inclusive learning environment where each learner's journey to the summit is supported and celebrated.

More to Explore

BeeLine Reader (2025). https://www.beelinereader.com/

Bergman, M. (2025). Exam-Wrapper. https://docs.google.com/document/d/1c8Fd_GMwp-pdF-biR2yk1Occe_raPnSJm4t6Y2EUqD8/edit?usp=sharing

Class Kick (2025). https://classkick.com/

Critical Reading Inventory (2016). https://thoughtfulliteracy.com/cri/video.htm#8

National Writing Project (2025). Civically-engaged writing analysis continuum. https://cewac.nwp.org/how-can-i-use-cewac/cewac-rubric/

Potash, B. (2019, May 26). *A simple trick for success with one-pagers*. Cult of Pedagogy. https://www.cultofpedagogy.com/one-pagers/

Rasinski, T. (2024). Multidimensional fluency rubric. http://www.timrasinski.com/presentations/multidimensional_fluency_rubric_4_factors.pdf

Reflect

Summarize your understanding of this chapter through one of the following choices:

- a movie or song title
- a haiku
- a Gist Statement

Here's mine using a movie title: Assessment does not have to be *Everything Everywhere All at Once*. Assessment should be aligned to the learning goals and inform next instructional steps.

Discuss

Questions for discussion to learn from and with each other:

1. What are the different types and purposes of literacy assessment?
2. How can assessment be used to promote intrinsic motivation for learning and growth rather than extrinsic motivation for a grade?
3. How does assessment position students in ways that impact their reading and writing identities?
4. Consider this quote from Katherine Bomer (2010): "I despise grading, testing, or instruction that forces young writers to produce texts similar to prefabricated homes with shrubs pruned into uniform balls, when what kids are writing comes from their precisely unconventional minds and hearts naming the world in new and unusual ways" (p. 3). How does the author's philosophy compare to your philosophy of assessing literacy?
5. Consider this quote from Gholdy Muhammad (2023): "Often schools and districts collect data related to students reading, writing, and math levels, yet schools fail to collect assessment data related to a child's identity, intellectual growth, criticality, and consciousness, or joy. These are just as important to nurture alongside skill development and so-called levels" (p. 7). How does the author's argument compare to your beliefs about assessing literacy?

References

Bergman, D. M. (2025, May 28). *Flexible paths to success: 7 UDL tips for action and expression*. Dr. Matt Bergman. https://drmattbergman.com/blog/f/flexible-paths-to-success-7-udl-tips-for-action-and-expression

Bomer, K. (2010). *Hidden gems: Naming and teaching from the brilliance in every student's writing*. Heinemann. https://www.heinemann.com/products/e02965.aspx

Brookhart, S. M. (2013). *How to create and use rubrics for formative assessment and grading*. ASCD.

CAST. (2024). The UDL guidelines. https://udlguidelines.cast.org/

Dunham, H., Murdter-Atkinson, J., Nash, B., & Wetzel, M. M. (2022). Building on linguistic strengths: Tenets of a culturally sustaining teacher. *The Reading Teacher*, *75*(6), 677–84. https://doi.org/10.1002/trtr.2094

Fisher, D., Hattie, J., & Frey, N. (2016). *Visible learning for literacy, grades K–12: Implementing the practices that work best to accelerate student learning*. SAGE Publications.

García, O., & Kleifgen, J. A. (2020). Translanguaging and literacies. *Reading Research Quarterly*, *55*(4), 553–71. https://doi.org/10.1002/rrq.286

Graham, S., Harris, K., & Hebert, M. (2011). *Informing writing: The benefits of formative assessment*. Alliance for Excellent Education.

Graham, S., Bruch, J., Fitzgerald, J., Friedrich, L., Furgeson, J., Greene, K., Kim, J., Lyskawa, J., Olson, C.B., & Smither Wulsin, C. (2016). *Teaching secondary students to write effectively* (NCEE Report 2017-4002). National Center for Education Evaluation and Regional Assistance (NCEE), Institute of Education Sciences, US Department of Education. https://ies.ed.gov/ncee/WWC/PracticeGuide/22

Hall, L. A. (2016). The role of identity in reading comprehension development. *Reading & Writing Quarterly*, *32*(1), 56–80. https://doi.org/10.1080/10573569.2013.861332

Hammond, Z. L. (2014). *Culturally responsive teaching and the brain*. Corwin Press.

Hattie, J. (2023). *Visible learning: The sequel*. New York: Routledge.

Johns, J. (2016). Basic Reading Inventory.

Kilpatrick, D. (2024). Instructions for the Phonological Awareness Screening Test. https://thepasttest.com/

Kolaya, A. (2017, November 9). How to give effective feedback on a talk. *TED-Ed Blog*. https://blog.ed.ted.com/2017/11/09/how-to-give-effective-feedback-on-a-talk/

Marzano, R. J. (2006). *Classroom assessment and grading that work.* ASCD.

Muhammad, G. G. (2023). *Culturally and historically responsive education: A policy research brief.* National Council of Teachers of English. https://ncte.org/wp-content/uploads/2023/05/2023-NCTE-Squire-Office_Culturally-and-Historically-Responsive-Education.pdf

National Governors Association. (2010). *Common core state standards.* Authors.

Paris, S. G. (2005). Reinterpreting the development of reading skills. *Reading Research Quarterly, 40*(2), 184–202.

Reading Rockets. (2025). *Screening and assessment.* https://www.readingrockets.org/helping-all-readers/screening-and-assessment

Wagner, R. K., Torgesen, J. K., Rashotte, C. A., & Pearson, N. A. (2013). *Comprehensive test of phonological processing—second edition (CTOPP-2).* Pro-Ed. https://doi.org/10.1037/t52630-000

Words Their Way. (2020). Upper Level Spelling Inventory. *Savvas.* https://mysavvastraining.com/assets/files/documents/WTW6e_Inventories_04202021_1619457927.pdf

Literature Cited

Scheinert, D., & Kwan, D. (Directors). (2022). *Everything everywhere all at once* [Film]. A24.

Motivating and Engaging Learners in Literacy

6

Think about a time you were really motivated to learn something. What did it look like? What did it feel like? Something sparked your **motivation** and kept you engaged. Psychologists have studied the factors that create and sustain motivation. Many of the same principles about motivation from psychology relate to literacy engagement. And there are some principles that are specific to literacy engagement that we will also learn about in this chapter.

Literacy Strategy: Thinking Hats

Choose a hat to wear as you read this chapter. Take notes based on the focus described in the list for that hat.

Thinking Hats

- Red Hat: Focuses on emotions, feelings, intuition, and connections.
- Black Hat: Identifies potential challenges, problems, risks, and critiques.
- Green Hat: Explores creative ideas, alternatives, new possibilities, and innovations.
- Blue Hat: Deals with facts, data, organization, and summarization.

The thinking hats strategy was adapted from de Bono's (2023) thinking hats book.

Preview Key Vocabulary

affective: relating to feelings and emotions
autonomy: able to decide for oneself what and how to learn
engagement: emotional connection to or active participation in learning
motivation: will or drive to do something

Setting Students Up for Success

Before students even pick up a text, there are things teachers can do to prepare them for success. There are instructional moves related to the cognitive (or thinking) dimensions of reading. Teachers can preview essential vocabulary, activate prior knowledge, set a purpose for reading, and model a strategy that students can use when reading, which will be discussed in later chapters. There are also instructional moves related to the affective (or feeling) aspects of reading (Afflerbach, 2022), which is the topic of this chapter.

Helping students develop their literacy *skills*—the cognitive—can help increase their *will*—the affective—to read and write more. In other words, when students have the skills needed to accomplish the task, they are more motivated to try. On the other hand, if students do not believe that they can be successful, they may not want to try and risk failing.

Also, literacy development is iterative. Meaning that the more students read and write, the more their skills and language grow. Helping students grow is, therefore, about both literacy skills and will iteratively. Consider this summary of previous research according to Brandt and colleagues (2021):

> Past research has shown that when motivation declines, reading scores typically do too. When students have little motivation to read, they read less, spend less time with texts, and are slower to develop early skills such as decoding and fluency. Conversely, students who read often become more proficient readers and thereby read more. This cycle is referred to in research as the Matthew Effect: a biblical reference from Matthew 25, indicating that "the rich get richer and the poor get poorer." (p. 723)

The good news is that teachers can help encourage student motivation for reading and writing with exponential payoffs. In fact, research shows that it is the teacher, not the curriculum or program, that makes the biggest school-based impact on literacy outcomes (Fisher et al., 2016).

Eight Cs of Motivation

Research shows that teachers have the potential to impact students' motivation for reading and writing. Specifically, we're going to talk about eight factors that are backed by scientific research from psychology and education: community, collaboration, control, consequence, confidence, challenge, constructing meaning, and **culturally sustaining**. Although each

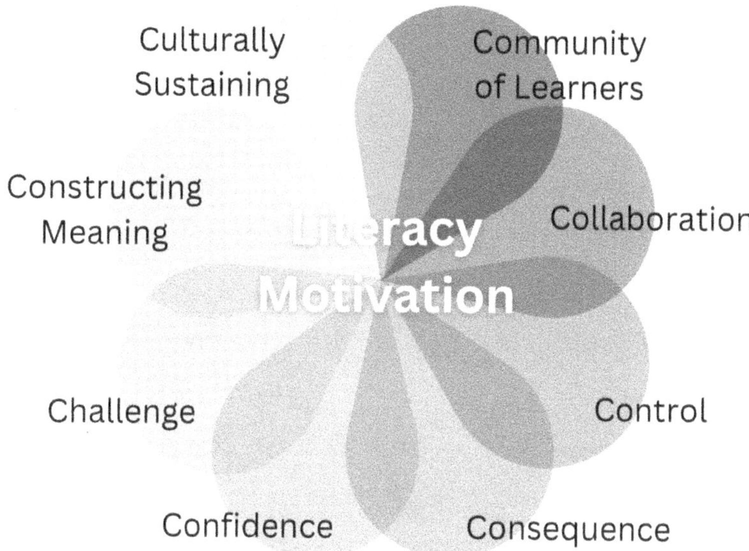

Figure 6.1 Eight C's of Motivation Blossom.

of these Cs is important in its own right, many aspects of motivation overlap, as illustrated by the blossom in Figure 6.1.

Community

The first C is about cultivating a community of learners. Community is created when students feel a sense of safety and belonging. Teachers enable community through building a relationship with each student and nurturing students' relationships with each other. This C follows the "Maslow before Bloom" principle, meaning that we have to attend to students' hierarchy of needs that Maslow (1943) identified before we can attend to students' higher-order cognitive development represented by Bloom's taxonomy (Bloom et al., 1956).

According to Maslow, people's physiological needs, such as food and water, as well as a sense of safety and belonging are foundational, and these needs must be met before people can concentrate on higher-order needs such as having a healthy self-esteem and making decisions that lead to the kind of life a person desires (Figure 6.2). The Maslow before Bloom principle in education means that all of these physical and psychological human needs are foundational to being able to learn. Although we should start by making sure our students' physiological needs are met and that students feel safe and

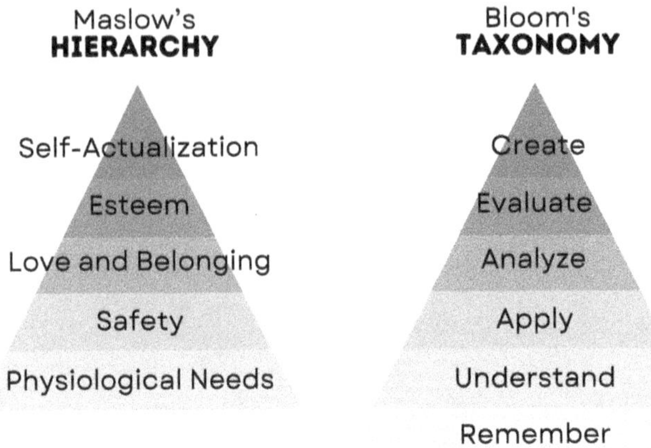

Figure 6.2 Maslow's Hierarchy of Needs and Bloom's Taxonomy of Cognitive Domains.

secure in our classroom, the point is not that everything else should then come in a step-by-step order. In fact, students should regularly have opportunities to work at the top of both pyramids. The point is that we should think about the whole child when we are teaching. When we remember that we all have physical, psychological, affective, and cognitive needs and desires, then we can attend to all of these dimensions proactively.

Another reason that building relationships with students is important is to be able to differentiate literacy learning based on students' needs and interests (Milner, 2021). In order to meet students where they are, we have to know where they are. In order to bring in or suggest interesting books, we have to know what students like. What one student thinks is fascinating might repel another child. When students' needs are met and they feel like their teacher cares about them, they are more likely to engage in learning. A strategy to get to know your students is the creation of Identity Webs.

Identity Webs

Middle school educator Sara Ahmed (2018) describes Identity Webs as "personalized graphic tools that help us consider the many factors that shape who we are." She goes on to say, "Identity webs help us find commonalities which springboard us to notice, wonder, and see the humanity in one another. What matters is not the web itself, but the dialogue that it makes possible and how that dialogue is a catalyst for rapport building" (p. 5). As students are creating their webs, the teacher can walk around the room, chatting with each student quietly with questions like *What do you want to share about your identity?* and *Is it okay to ask you about _____?* Figure 6.3 illustrates an example of an identity web.

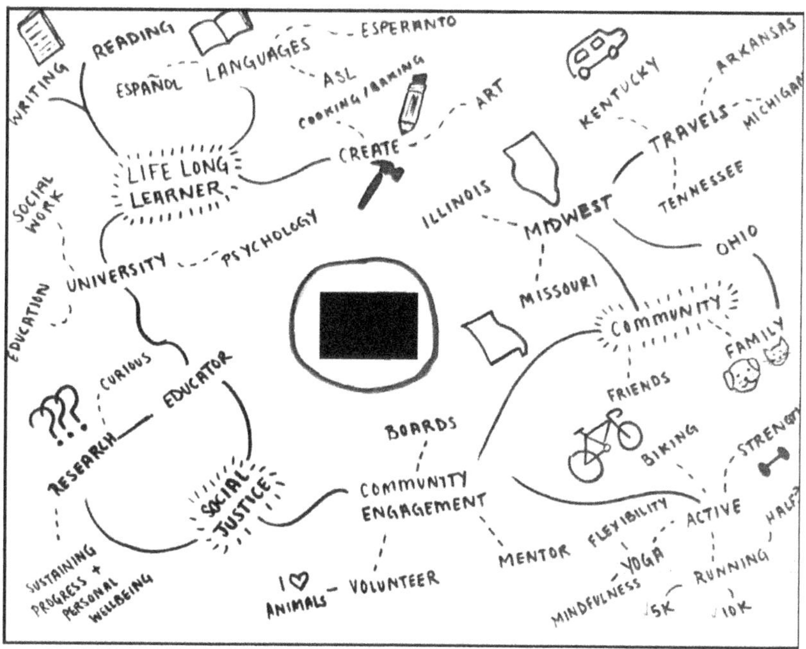

Figure 6.3 Identity Web Example.

In order to help students bond as a community of learners, teachers can be intentional about building students' relationships in the first week of school and continue to incorporate community building throughout the year. Students can share their identity webs with each other using the same two questions from the previous paragraph with the goal of making connections. But why stop there! Here are some more community building activities for the first week of school.

Alliteration Name Game

On the first day, I like to play the Alliteration Name Game. Everyone thinks of an adjective to describe themself that starts with the same sound as their name, like Curious Cory or Motivated Micah. We start in one corner of the room and the first person says their adjective and name: "Curious Cory." The next person has to remember and say the first person's alliterative name and then their own. "That is Curious Cory, and I am Motivated Micah." By the time we finish, I am well on my way to knowing everyone's name in the class and so are they! Knowing their names is very helpful for classroom management, but, most importantly, it is important for building relationships.

Acrostic Name Poem

The next day, I ask everyone to write an acrostic poem using their name. For each letter, they add an adjective that describes them. (Bonus: Talking about adjectives becomes a teachable moment to explain the function of words in the context of students' own writing, and research shows that teaching grammar in context is more motivating and engaging for adolescents.) Students already have the first adjective from the previous class, now they add the rest. We use markers and colored paper and hang the poems around the room. This is another way to help us continue to remember each other's names and to feel a sense of belonging in the physical space.

Create a Community Code

One of the first days of school, I have each class create its own code where they collectively create the shared norms for what is expected in our classroom. I prompt the discussion by asking students what they need in order to learn, what do they expect from me as their teacher, and what do they need from each other. I then ask what do we seem to agree about that should be in our code, and a volunteer records the Community Code on chart paper to display on the wall.

Collaboration

The second C is collaboration. A collaborative environment fosters a community of learners. Humans, and especially adolescents, are social beings, so whenever there is social interaction around literacy, that leverages our strength (Guthrie & McRae, 2017). Research supports students collaborating on reading or writing in small groups, with educators actively supporting their **engagement**. Students contribute their lived experiences and academic knowledge to discussions about their reading, working together to interpret text, and writing to explore content topics. This allows them to explore issues from multiple perspectives and collective resources. Teachers encourage students not only to collaborate but to enhance their understanding through learning from and challenging each other. Teachers provide support for collaborative learning by:

- establishing group norms in alignment with the class's community code and specific to the task at hand;
- offering sentence stems to support Accountable Talk, productive and civil discourse;

- moving from group to group to monitor understanding and intervening when necessary;

- asking questions that probe students to think more deeply and encouraging students to ask questions of each other;

- modeling productive strategies for handling friction and redirecting behavior if needed; and

- holding groups accountable for how they work together in addition to the product of their work.

The following are some collaborative group work strategies, where each person is accountable for their part and all parts are needed for the product of learning. The first takes the idea of each person holding a piece of the puzzle.

Jig-Saw

For a simple version of a Jig-Saw activity, each person in the group is assigned a different section of a **text** to read. In the end, they will teach their section to the rest of the group. It's important that the text used is able to be comprehended without reading the full thing. Not all texts lend themselves well to Jig-Saw for this reason. Another option is to have each person in the group read a different text, such as articles written from different perspectives on the same topic, and then share the perspective from the text with the group.

Once everyone has read their section, they summarize what they learned for the others. I like to give students a Jig-Saw notecatcher with a designated space for each section so that students can take notes on what their peers share. I collect the notecatchers at the end of the activity, so that I can assess if there are any gaps or misinformation that need to be cleared up in the next lesson. Then, I pass back the notecatchers so that students can keep them to study from. Being responsible for teaching their peers enhances motivation and filling out the notecatcher keeps each student accountable for learning all of the information.

Social Layered Annotation

This routine combines Social Annotation and Layered Annotation to create collaborative engagement with text (Castellano, 2024; Honore, 2025). Students work in small groups of two to three to annotate a text, as shown in Figure 6.4. Here are the steps for the routine:

1 Grab supplies for your group (tape, text passage, chart paper, three markers of different colors, and sticky notes). Tape the text passage to the middle of the chart paper.

  2 Assign roles and marker colors. Write your name in the corner with your marker.

    a Connector—connect to prior knowledge, connect to other class readings, connect to life, note how the author links words and ideas to create flow

    b Identifier—identify and define key words, note emphasis of words/ideas, summarize what the text is saying

    c Challenger—question or challenge the argument that is being made in the text, note whose perspectives are represented and whose perspectives are not, note what information is presented and what is left out, evaluate the author's purpose

  3 Read and annotate the passage on the chart paper according to your role (fifteen minutes).

  4 Grab some sticky notes, and go add your thoughts to other groups' annotations (fifteen minutes).

  5 Go back and read what others said on your paper. Add a layer of annotation to your original annotations and what others wrote. You do not have to annotate according to your role this time.

  6 Discuss in your group using Connect, Extend, Challenge. Choose a spokesperson who can share one connection, extension, and challenge to the class.

    a What connections do you notice now?

    b What extends your thinking further or in a new direction?

    c What challenges, puzzles, or questions emerge?

  7 Whole-class debrief. Spokesperson from each group shares out.

When I have used this routine, I find people usually use a mixture of talking, writing, and drawing while annotating in their small groups, which is perfectly fine. I also find that people enjoy viewing other groups' annotations and especially returning to their own group to see what others added to their annotations.

This activity, as with most collaborative group work, works better when people have designated roles. In the steps above, I included the roles that I used with my students, but these are adaptable (same as the thinking routine for the debrief). For example, the Thinking Hats presented at the beginning of this chapter could be adapted to engage with the text for Layered Social Annotation.

For even more motivation in collaborative group work, if possible, let students have a choice of whom to work with or compromise and let students

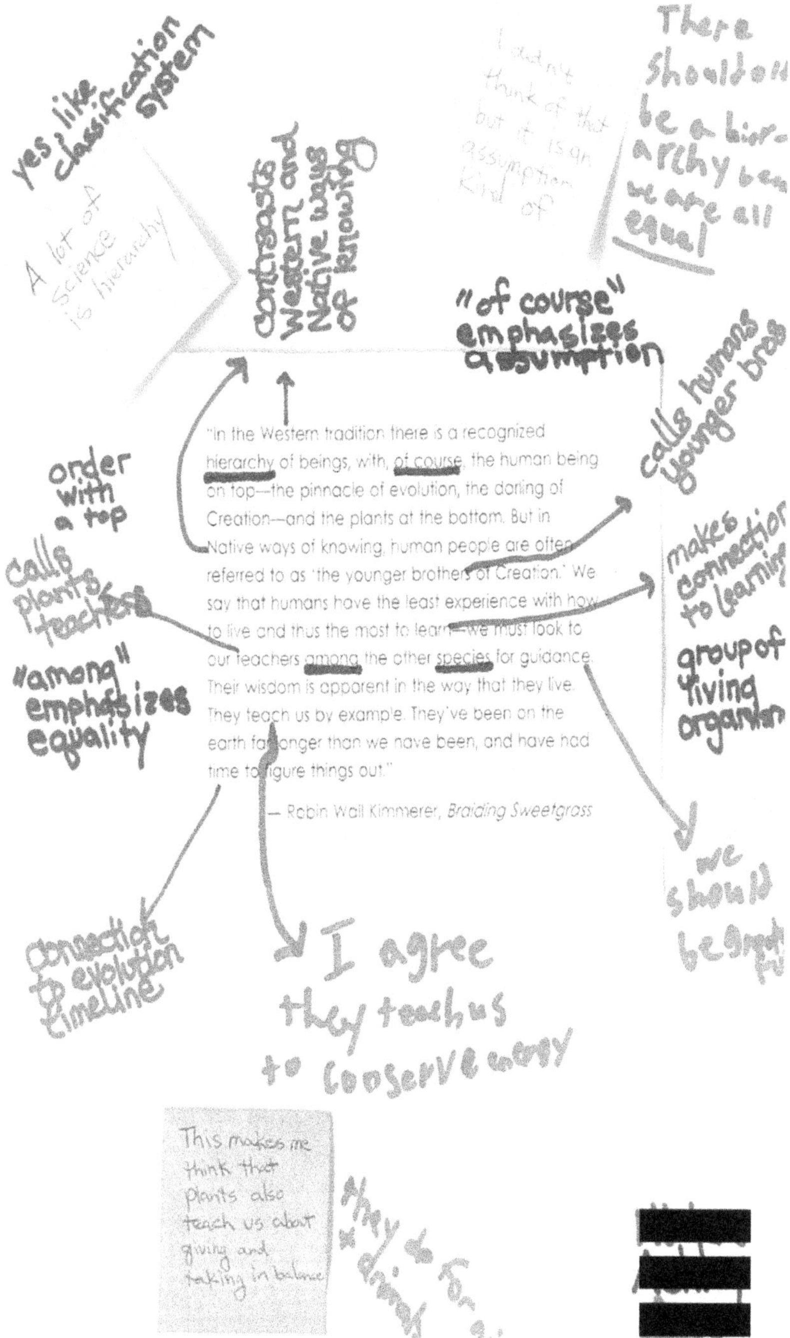

Figure 6.4 Social Layered Annotation Example.

choose a partner, but then you place partners together to form a group of four. Having some control over whom they get to work with is related to the principle behind the next C.

Control

Control relates to **autonomy** and self-determination. Teachers who support students' autonomy help them align personal motivations (such as the need to feel competent or to feel connected with others) with their daily classroom activities (such as building from students' strengths or working in small groups). These supportive teachers identify and nurture students' needs and interests, creating opportunities for students to let their intrinsic motivations guide their behavior. On the flip side, educators who hold all of the control disrupt students' self-determination by imposing a rigid instructional agenda that disconnects students from their internal motivations, telling them what they must do instead. I also recognize that control is often influenced by factors outside of the classroom, such as state mandates and parent expectations. Even with this layer of complexity, I encourage teachers to consider the control they do have in their classrooms and give themselves permission to let go.

Control does not have to be solely in the hands of the teacher or solely in the hands of the students. Instead, we can think of control along a continuum, with teachers and students negotiating the what, when, and how of learning together. Teachers can let go of some control by letting students choose from a set of approved choices or creating space for students to pursue their own interests. Instead of worrying that chaos might ensue, teachers can be encouraged that letting go actually has been shown to increase academic performance, intrinsic motivation, and persistence to graduation (Turner & Paris, 1995).

When we share control with students, we respect their humanity and agency. One way this plays out in literacy instruction is that instead of saying you are a 740 Lexile reader so you will read books from this shelf, we give students the strategies to make the best choice for themselves and provide the scaffolding to help them succeed in reading the texts they choose. In other words, teachers can empower their students by demonstrating how to choose a text, how to determine a purpose for reading, and how to choose the appropriate strategy to meet that purpose.

Choice is a way to provide students autonomy along the continuum. For example, the teacher could provide the options for what to read. When I taught ninth grade, I allowed students to choose to read either *Fahrenheit 451* or *The Last Book in the Universe*. Both were great dystopian books with similar themes, but *Fahrenheit 451* has an 890 Lexile level with 272 pages and *The Last Book in the Universe* has 740 with 240 pages. Students would respond in their Reading Journals and discuss literary elements in small groups with people who read the same book. We would also have whole-group discussions about the prominent themes across the books. Teachers can give students choices about how they will read or write (silently, in partners, or with technology) and where they will engage (on a beanbag, under the window, with a blanket).

Another possibility, teachers can give students choices of how to express their ideas, through poetry, pictures, and words, or recording a video. In fact, according to Brandt et al. (2021), "Technology motivates students with options for reading practice or response projects" (p. 723). Incorporating technology can relate in-school literacy with out-of-school literacy. However, recent research has pointed to technology fatigue among students (Klein, 2022). As this research continues to unfold, I suggest using a variety of modes. If you use technology a lot but are seeing a dip in motivation, try switching to paper and markers for an activity and see what happens! Here are some strategies that put the control of what to study or how to learn in students' hands.

KWHLAQ

You may have heard of the KWL chart, where students either individually or as a whole class answer the questions: *What do I already* know *about this topic? What do I* want *to know?* And then after the lesson return to fill out *What did I* learn? The expanded chart also includes How *do I find out?, What* action *will I take?*, and *What* questions *do I have now?*

Wonder Wall

Dedicate a space on the wall or a bulletin board for students to add questions that arise from what they are reading and studying. Students can use sticky notes to add what they are curious about and what they want to know more about. Use the wall to inform planning of future lessons.

Genius Hour

Dedicate time each week for students to pursue their own passions through inquiry-based learning (Krebs & Zvi, 2020). This strategy originated from Google's 20 percent time, where employees were allowed to work on personal projects the equivalent of one workday a week. Students design their project based on their personal values, their needs, and their curiosity and are able to make a plan in a self-directed and creative way. They can use the Wonder Wall for inspiration!

Consequence

The fourth C is consequence. If you've studied motivation before, you probably heard about intrinsic and extrinsic motivation. The aim is to get students to have intrinsic motivation because that comes from within themselves. Similar to how we want to teach students strategies and then empower them to choose the right strategies at the right time leading to them becoming independent readers and writers, we also want their motivation to become independent—to come from themselves. When we're helping students follow their curiosity to learn something new, giving them feedback to help them grow, and connecting the learning in class to the real world, these are all intrinsic reasons for learning.

Extrinsic motivation could be a grade, reward, or award. Although we might see that students are motivated by grades, reinforcing that external motivation can do more harm than good in the long run. Sometimes we can use extrinsic motivation as a bridge to intrinsic, meaning that the reward may originate as extrinsic but build to intrinsic motivation, such as receiving candy for participating in class or earning a pizza party for completing a read-a-thon. But, we don't want the focus of our class to be on extrinsic rewards for reading, writing, and participating as that is self-defeating in the long run for our students. And we definitely don't want to insert extrinsic rewards when students are already intrinsically motivated.

In school settings, when the learning is about growth rather than about performance, adolescents are more motivated. In other words, a growth view sees reading as a way to learn something new or writing as a way to figure something out, rather than to perform well for a teacher or in comparison to peers. As Alfie Kohn (2022) states,

> Those [performance] goals, unfortunately, are elicited by grades, tests, competition, and other features of traditional schooling that lead kids to focus more on their level of achievement—how well they're doing— than on what they're learning. They may be working hard, but often without the genuine enthusiasm and curiosity that promote cognitive engagement. (para. 12)

Reading and writing in class should be meaningful, authentic, and relevant. A focus on growing rather than grades leads not only to motivation to read and write but to engagement in learning. One strategy to help students focus on learning and growth is to have students set their own goals and reflect on their learning. For example, in family and consumer science, students can identify something that they want to learn how to cook, make a plan for how to learn it, and reflect on their experience in the end. In physical education, students can keep a journal to record and track their weight-lifting progress. In addition to fostering motivation, goal-setting and monitoring foster metacognition and **self-regulation**, two executive function skills that are key to literacy growth.

Confidence

The fifth C is Confidence. Teachers can help students build confidence as readers and writers. We rarely attempt something that we think we are going to fail at. We try when we think we at least *might* be able to do it. Teachers can help build students' confidence by explicitly teaching literacy skills and strategies and including time to practice. Practice is most effective when students have a chance to practice collaboratively and to get feedback before being graded on the skill. When students have the appropriate skills and strategies, then they're more confident that they are going to be successful.

So instead of thinking about reading or writing as something we either can do or can't do, we think about literacy as something that grows over time. We talk as a community of learners about how we can continue to build our skills and increase our repertoire of strategies to continuously become better readers and writers. As discussed in Chapter 1, our literacy ability is not fixed, it grows over our entire lifetime.

Another thing that teachers can do is help adolescents foster an identity as a reader and as a writer. Reading identity is thinking of oneself as a reader, valuing reading, and being a lifelong reader. Likewise, a writing identity is thinking of oneself as a writer.

Literacy Partnership Approach

An evidence-based instructional approach to support students in building robust literacy identities is the Literacy Partnership Approach (Hall, 2014, 2022). The Literacy Partnership Approach has three parts. First, teachers make identity explicit by asking students to share with them about their reading and writing identities. At this point, the teacher's job is to listen. The students might share an identity that surprises the teacher. A high achiever might share that they do not feel like they are a good reader. The teacher does not correct the child or try to convince the child that they should have a different identity. The teacher simply listens to understand the students' perspectives. See an example of a Tried and True strategy I use to collect information about students' perspectives on their literacy identities.

The second step is to help students strengthen their reading and writing identities. Teachers can do this through approaching literacy from a growth mindset stance. Rather than seeing literacy as fixed, either I am a good reader or a struggling reader, reading is actually something that we all can work on to improve. And, in actuality, we all struggle to read some texts sometimes. In fact, I remember one early October morning walking into class at Purdue University when it seemed the breeze just overnight had turned from refreshing to refrigeration. As I hugged the sweater over my shoulders a little tighter, I complained about how difficult the reading assignment had been. An audible exhale filled the room as the circle of students breathed a sigh of relief. I literally saw a circle of shoulders drop, and I realized that everyone had found the reading difficult, but everyone thought it was just them.

Tried and True Strategy by Shea Kerkhoff

Lesson Name: Using a Literacy Identity Questionnaire to Learn about Ourselves as Readers and Writers

Context: Literacy for Adolescent Learners class in St. Louis, Missouri

First, I asked my students to choose an image from a stack of photos on the front table (or displayed digitally like in Figure 6.5) that represents them as a reader and answer the following questions in their journal:

- What image did you choose?
- How does it describe you as a reader?
- Why do you think that description fits you?

I then ask for volunteers to share what they wrote, if they would like to. The next day, I ask students to complete this Google Form (adapted from Hall, 2022):

1   How would you describe yourself as a reader?
2   How would other people describe you as a reader?
3   How would you like to improve your reading abilities this year?
4   How might you achieve your reading goals?
5   What is something I could do to help you achieve your reading goals?

The next week, we repeat the process replacing reading with writing. I like to do them separately because I find that my students have distinct reading and writing identities.

Figure 6.5 Inspiration for Literacy Identity Metaphor.

We began to talk about how the reading was really dense, and the author expected us to have so much **background knowledge** that we were consistently going outside of the book in order to figure out what the author was talking about. So many starts and stops made it hard to comprehend.

Teachers can talk to students about how all readers, including teachers themselves, struggle with some texts and how all readers can get better at reading if they work on it. It's important that teachers do not reinforce the false dichotomy of good readers and poor readers through their language. Rather than referring to "what good readers do," teachers should drop any adjectives and only talk about "readers" in their class. Teachers can also reinforce how we are all writers by having students keep a Writers' Notebook and encouraging students to share their writing with each other. In addition to being intentional about how they talk, teachers can explain the power of self-talk. Students can write in their notebooks positive mantras and words of encouragement, like "progress not perfection," "I can do hard things!" "My ideas matter," and "I am getting better at writing."

Teachers can also discuss how students can improve their literacy through goal-setting and practice. I used the questions in the Tried and True Strategy example of Literacy Identity Questionnaires to collect students' goals and then grouped them into categories. Some of the most common goal categories from my class are similar to the ones Leigh Hall has found in her work: expand vocabulary, increase reading level, understand hard books, get better at writing, and write more.

The next step in the Literacy Partnership Approach is to connect literacy instruction to the students' goals. For example, in Leigh Hall's (2014) book, the teacher says to students:

> How does this help you with reading? A lot of you have said that you want to be able to read and understand more difficult books. In reading, you have to visualize different ideas and concepts like *survival* and then use those understandings to help you make sense of the story. That's partly what we're working on here—visualizing a concept and showing how we understand it. And then later on, as we read stories about survival, we can visualize different aspects of it to help us understand it better.

In the example, the teacher took the goal of "understand hard books" and created a more specific goal of "understand hard books by visualizing the ideas in the text while reading."

Reading and writing identity can be strengthened through role models who foster a genuine interest in literacy, as well as through a lot of the other C's, such as the next one, providing the right level of challenge for students.

Challenge

Kelly Gallagher (2009) coined a new word to describe what he was witnessing in too many classrooms, *readicide*, defined as:

> read-i-cide: noun, the systematic killing of the love of reading, often exacerbated by the inane, mind-numbing practices found in schools. (p. 2)

If the reading, writing, or learning activities that we are asking students to do are "mind-numbing," then we are not promoting motivation. When it comes to motivation, teachers can employ the Goldilocks principle of not too easy or mind-numbing. And not too hard or frustrating. This doesn't mean that teachers must impart different instruction for each individual student for each lesson, but it does imply that teachers have a sense of what would generally be too easy or too hard for their group of students and to identify the outliers in order to provide tailored support or extra challenge.

The fact of the matter is that students are motivated when they believe that the work is challenging, and as we talked about earlier in this chapter, when they can be successful if they try. The right amount of challenge is motivating (Brandt et al., 2021). Having the right level of challenge builds students' confidence as competent readers and writers. When thinking about the interrelationship between competence and confidence, Zaretta Hammond says,

> We have to instill community habits for growth in learning. Competence precedes confidence. When I'm a competent learner, I have the confidence to engage in intellectual endeavors that might stretch me, might confuse me, or might lead to productive struggle. That's precisely what the science of learning tells us makes the brain grow and allows us to carry a greater cognitive load. (as quoted in Rebora, 2021, para. 8)

Nurturing intellect and high expectations reflect culturally sustaining education.

Providing students the right level of challenge includes "supported struggle" not just leaving students to fend for themselves. Teachers offer support by modeling strategies, chunking difficult tasks into manageable steps, scaffolding reading **comprehension** of complex texts, and providing mentor texts of complex writing. It's important to make sure that we're not constantly putting texts and tasks in front of students that are too hard for them without supporting them. At the same time, it's good to have students learn to grapple with complex text and to be challenged to think critically and creatively when writing.

In addition to supported struggle, teachers can attend to the right level of challenge by being intentional about how they match readers and texts depending on the task. Teachers can attend to the level of challenge by being intentional about how they match readers and texts depending on the task. In other words, teachers can consider the text complexity and difficulty when selecting texts for different instructional purposes. Text complexity refers to both the vocabulary and accessibility of the ideas in the text. Does it have highly technical words? How much inference is required? The difficulty level depends on the reader, as the same text could be difficult for me to read but easy for you.

Research suggests that what effective literacy educators do is select texts based on the reading purpose (Lupo et al., 2025). When we want students to practice *automaticity*, we can choose texts that have common academic words (i.e., words that adolescents need to know because they appear frequently in secondary school) and that have rare words so that students can practice the automaticity skills needed for reading academic vocabulary. For knowledge building, we can choose interesting, relevant texts. For close reading, we can choose short, worthy passages. For textual analysis, we can choose complex texts. And, whenever a text is too much of a stretch for students, there are things we can do to improve the readability.

Some authors go to great lengths to make sure that the reader has everything they need to comprehend the text. Considerate authors supply definitions of difficult words or present graphics to illustrate complex ideas. These authors provide overviews at the beginning and summaries at the end, organizing the middle into sections with headings to increase readability. Teachers can make texts more readable by:

- contextualizing the text and setting it up for the readers,
- previewing the text structure and talking about how the text is organized,
- previewing key vocabulary and providing student-friendly definitions,
- preteaching or providing annotations/hyperlinks for explanations of unfamiliar concepts,
- setting a purpose for reading the text that helps students focus,
- chunking the text into smaller sections,
- creating an abridged version or choosing an important excerpt, and/or
- guiding students through a text by discussing main ideas along the way.

In addition to text complexity and readability, teachers should also consider the maturity level of the texts we ask students to read and the topics that we ask students to write about. We do not want to assign students books that are too babyish for them, as that would not be motivating. We also do not want to provide texts that are too socially mature for our students. Students tend to be more motivated in texts and tasks that are relevant to their current interests and life experiences.

Constructing Meaning

What runs throughout all of the 8 C's is that teaching reading and writing should be in connection to authentic texts with a focus on constructing and communicating meaning. Teaching reading skills should be connected to reading an interesting book or article for the purpose of constructing meaning. Teaching writing should focus on the process of thinking and constructing one's thoughts in order to communicate to authentic audiences in meaningful ways.

Research shows that children are more motivated to read when they believe reading is a chance to construct meaning and build knowledge (Afflerbach, 2022). When thinking about the teaching of writing, a focus on constructing meaning highlights the importance of the process as being as important as the product. Adolescents are way more motivated to write when their audience isn't just the teacher—because let's be honest, pouring your heart into a Google Doc just for Mrs. Krabapel to read during lunch duty isn't exactly thrilling.

Turner and Paris (1995) state the relationship between constructing meaning and motivation as follows:

> Constructing meaning promotes motivation by assisting children in making sense of their learning—the tasks in which they engage and the strategies they employ. They use information gleaned from their daily tasks in literacy to construct purposes for reading and writing and how they may be entertaining, informational, and useful. If children find that literacy allows them to solve interesting problems, they will associate reading and writing with thinking, challenge, and personal growth. If, however, they associate literacy with completing exercises, they may interpret it simply as manipulating symbols or solving abstract puzzles. (p. 669)

A focus on constructing meaning encourages curiosity, autonomy, and engagement. If we want students to be motivated and engaged, then they have to believe that what they're reading and writing is meaningful and useful. They need to see that the instruction you are providing is connected to authentic literacy practices and not just "busy work." Every student, every day should be engaged in critical thinking in connection with authentic texts as they develop advanced literacy skills. Practices that make literacy meaningful include reading for utility and writing for real audiences, as described more below.

Reading for Utility

Research grounded in expectancy-value theory identifies utility value, the belief that reading is useful and relevant, as a powerful driver of student motivation (Eccles & Wigfield, 2020). When students believe reading helps them achieve personal or academic goals—such as understanding real-world issues, solving problems, or mastering content—they invest more effort and engage more deeply. Do students want to learn a new game? Have them read the instructions. Do they want to use **artificial intelligence (AI)** in class?

Have them read how data are stored in the application and the privacy statement. Did your community just experience severe flooding? Have them read an article on local extreme weather trends in order to advocate for a flood-prevention plan.

Writing for a Real Audience

Any time students can write for someone besides the teacher, it is more motivating. Students can write letters to the editor, post book reviews on websites, or give advice to the students they will teach next year. For example, I had my students write a class blog for our young adult literature choice unit. I created the original post and then students hit reply to share their book review. Because students were reading different choices, the other students in the class became an authentic audience. I have also had students use a class blog to discuss shared readings with a class in a different state. Talking with people from other places was very interesting and motivating for my students.

Culturally Sustaining

Most importantly, we want our classrooms to be culturally responsive and sustaining—respectfully reflecting students' lived experiences and actively supporting students' cultural identities, helping them affirm and grow their cultural and linguistic heritage (Muhammad, 2023; Frieson, 2025). When selecting books and texts for the curriculum, it's important to ensure they serve as both *mirrors* and *windows* (Sims Bishop, 2015). *Mirrors* allow students to see their identities, cultures, and experiences represented in what they read. *Windows* offer a view into the lives and perspectives of others, broadening students' understanding of the world.

Curriculum Audit

Conducting a curriculum audit can help educators assess whether the authors, characters, and historical figures included reflect diversity in race, ethnicity, language, gender, ability, and so on. As part of this process, Bryan-Gooden and colleagues (2023) from the Education Justice Research and Organizing Collaborative encourage educators to critically evaluate how people are portrayed in the texts, paying close attention to accuracy, inclusivity, and the presence of stereotypes. It's important to consider whether individuals from marginalized communities are depicted as central, multidimensional people and not as background or token figures. To deepen this analysis, educators should consider whether dominant cultural perspectives are balanced with alternative viewpoints, and whether students are exposed to both historical and contemporary voices from diverse communities. The curricular materials should also acknowledge systemic inequalities—such as colonization, racism, and sexism—and critically examine power dynamics rather than glossing over them. Ultimately, culturally responsive curriculum choices challenge bias and assumptions rather than reinforcing them (see New York University, 2025, in More to Explore for curriculum evaluation resources).

Text Sets

One way to develop or supplement a curriculum that provides multiple perspectives is to curate text sets that bring together diverse voices on a particular issue. For example, the Philadelphia Writing Project has curated text sets on civic arguments that include primary sources from people from marginalized communities and from allies (https://tps.philwp.org/home).

Textual Lineage

Another example of culturally sustaining literacy is to have students share Textual Lineages (Tatum, 2021). The Textual Lineage activity invites students to reflect on the texts (books, articles, songs, speeches, etc.) that have shaped their identities, values, and thinking. The idea is to trace a "lineage" of influential texts that helps students understand themselves as readers and writers and how texts influence their thinking. Students share their Textual Lineage, creating opportunities for connection and discussion. As a side benefit, I have found that students treat the discussions as book recommendations and create a list of what they would like to read. The activity values students' lived experiences and diverse backgrounds by recognizing texts that are meaningful in their lives. Sharing lineages builds empathy and connection among students, fostering a more inclusive and respectful learning environment. I'm grateful to Exley Warren for sharing his textual lineage with us below.

Culturally responsive and sustaining writing instruction is an approach that recognizes and values students' diverse cultural backgrounds, experiences, and linguistic styles, encouraging student voice in the writing process to make learning more meaningful and inclusive. It fosters student engagement, affirms identity, and helps develop critical literacy by allowing students to express their voices authentically. For example, a lesson could involve students writing personal narratives that reflect their cultural traditions while studying an ancient culture or retelling a story from their heritage while practicing storytelling techniques. This validates students' cultural and personal experiences as meaningful components of literacy, particularly important for students from marginalized communities.

Tried and True Strategy by Exley Warren

Lesson: Building Community through Textual Lineages

Context: Class in Normandy, Missouri

Think of Textual Lineages (Figure 6.6) as "my family tree of books and other texts." Textual Lineages are texts that are meaningful and significant to our lives. My mother purchased the *Sports Illustrated* magazine for me around the fourth and fifth grades. I loved reading about the sports world and my heroes through this text. I remember learning about averages from the baseball stats that were published in this magazine. I was so sad when she stopped purchasing this magazine for me. I don't think she realized how this magazine motivated me to be a reader. I looked forward to receiving a new magazine in the mail each month. There is a quote that is inspiring to me by Mark Twain, "The two most important days in your life are the day you are born and the day you find out why." *Long Walk to Freedom*, *Purpose Driven Life*, and *Good to Great* are nonfiction books that were formative to my ideas about leadership.

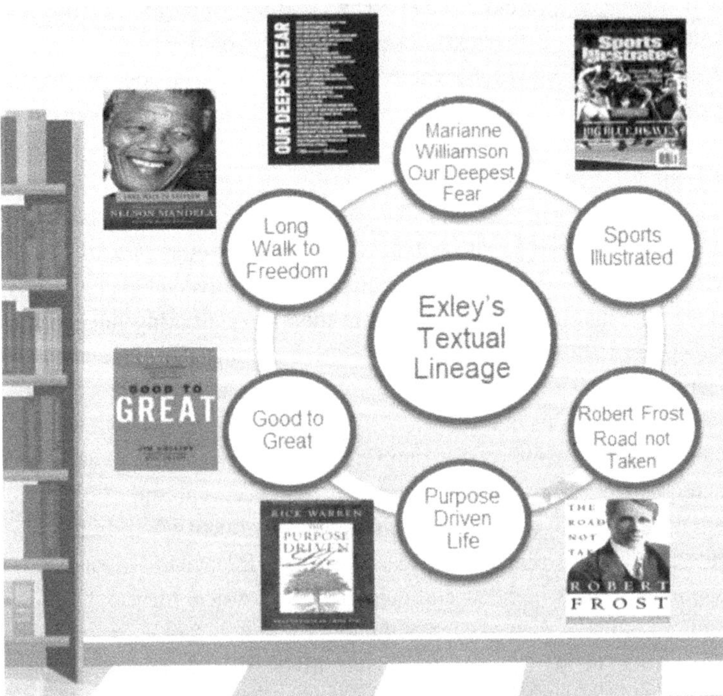

Figure 6.6 Dr. Warren's Textual Lineage.

Another lesson might have students identify different rhetorical styles from various cultures, such as African American oral traditions or Indigenous storytelling, to deepen their understanding of how culture shapes communication. This helps students recognize the power of their own voice and how it has been shaped, encouraging self-expression in their writing and speaking. By incorporating culturally responsive practices, teachers empower students to see their identities reflected in their writing while developing strong literacy skills.

Conclusion

Adolescent students' motivation and engagement with literacy includes cognitive, affective, sociocultural, and critical components of literacy and learning. When learning relates to real life, is meaningful to students, and challenges students to think creatively and critically, students are more likely to be both motivated and engaged. While motivation starts from within the student, teachers can cultivate the right environment where engagement blossoms and literacy takes root and grows.

More to Explore

Hall, L. (2022, March 24). *How reading instruction fails students* [Video]. YouTube. https://youtu.be/Mww43LkV6o0

New York University. (2025). *Culturally responsive curriculum scorecard.* https://steinhardt.nyu.edu/metrocenter/ejroc/services/culturally-responsive-curriculum-scorecards

Parker, K. N. (2023–2024). Literacy for Liberation column in *Educational Leadership.* https://drkimparker.org/publications-podcasts/

Reflect

Reflect on the 8 C's of Motivation Blossom using the Rose, Bud, Thorn reflection routine. The "rose" is something that blossomed in your thinking, the "thorn" is a challenge or frustration, and the "bud" is something you're still curious about or looking forward to learning more about.

Discuss

Questions for discussion to learn from and with each other:

- Why is motivation an important consideration for literacy instruction?
- How do the 8 C's relate to your experiences of being highly motivated to learn something?
- Although intrinsic motivation lies within the learner, the classroom culture that teachers cultivate can nourish or kill motivation. What can teachers do to create an environment in which literacy motivation thrives?
- How would you go about selecting texts for your students to read?
- How would you go about strengthening students' reading and writing identity?

References

Afflerbach, P. (2022). *Teaching readers (not reading): Moving beyond skills and strategies to reader-focused instruction.* Guilford.

Ahmed, S. (2018). *Being the change: Lessons and strategies to teach social comprehension.* Heinemann. https://www.heinemann.com/products/e09970.aspx

Bloom, B. S., Engelhart, M. D., Furst, E., Hill, W. H., & Krathwohl, D. R. (1956). *Handbook I: Cognitive domain.* David McKay.

Brandt, L., Sharp, A. C., & Gardner, D. S. (2021). Examination of teacher practices on student motivation for reading. *The Reading Teacher, 74*(6), 723–31. https://doi.org/10.1002/trtr.1999

Bryan-Gooden, J., Hester, M., & Peoples, L. Q. (2023). *Culturally Responsive ELA Curriculum Scorecard.* Metropolitan Center for Research on Equity and the Transformation of Schools, New York University. https://steinhardt.nyu.edu/sites/default/files/2023-05/CRE%20ELA%20Curriculum%20Scorecard%202023.pdf

Castellano, A. (2024, April 28). The art of annotation: Teaching readers to process texts. *Cult of Pedagogy.* https://www.cultofpedagogy.com/art-of-annotation/

de Bono, E. (2023). *Six thinking hats for schools and families: Inspiring children and young people to think for themselves.* Edward de Bono.

Eccles, J. S., & Wigfield, A. (2020). From expectancy-value theory to situated expectancy-value theory: A developmental, social cognitive, and sociocultural perspective on motivation. *Contemporary Educational Psychology, 61,* 101859.

Fisher, D., Frey, N., & Hattie, J. (2016). *Visible learning for literacy, grades K–12: Implementing the practices that work best to accelerate student learning.* Corwin Press.

Frieson, B. L. (2025). A seat at the table: Black & Latinx teachers reimagining multilingual classrooms as culturally sustaining spaces for Black children. *Reading Research Quarterly, 60*(1), Article e587. https://doi.org/10.1002/rrq.587

Gallagher, K. (2009) *Readicide: How schools are killing reading and what you can do about it.* Stenhouse Publishers.

Guthrie, J. T., & McRae, A. (2017). Motivating and instructing African American students in classrooms. In R. Horowitz & S. J. Samuels (Eds.), *The achievement gap in reading: Complex causes, persistent issues, possible solutions* (pp. 57-81). Routledge.

Hall, L. (2014). *Creating Reading Partnerships.* https://www.amazon.com/Creating-Reading-Partnerships-Leigh-Hall-ebook/dp/B00KGGQM9G

Honore, S. (2025, March 13). Leaving a mark: Annotation strategies for deep learning and discussion. *Social Studies Blog.* https://www.socialstudies.com/blog/leaving-a-mark-annotation-strategies-for-deep-learning-and-discussion/?srsltid=AfmBOop3E-NETnMK-DwVvncyZee6oCM5O7TwFEYfA72dgftVFRXRbHyr

Klein, A. (2022, March 8). Tech fatigue is real for teachers and students: Here's how to ease the burden. *Ed Week.* https://www.edweek.org/technology/tech-fatigue-is-real-for-teachers-and-students-heres-how-to-ease-the-burden/2022/03

Kohn, A. (2022, September 30). Is it enough for learners to be "engaged"? *Alfie Kohn.* https://www.alfiekohn.org/blogs/engagement/

Krebs, D., & Zvi, G. (2020). *The genius hour guidebook: Fostering passion, wonder, and inquiry in the classroom.* Routledge.

Lupo, S., Townsend, D., Knecht, R., & Massey, D. (2025). Recognizing complexity and taking action: Supporting adolescents' foundational literacy skills in culturally and linguistically sustaining ways. *Journal of Adolescent & Adult Literacy, 68*(4), 316–24. https://doi.org/10.1002/jaal.1412

Maslow, A. (1943). A preface to motivation theory. *Biopsychosocial Science and Medicine, 5*(1), 85–92.

Milner, H. R. (2021). *Start where you are, but don't stay there: Understanding diversity, opportunity gaps, and teaching in today's classrooms* (2nd ed.). Harvard Education Press.

Muhammad, G. G. (2023). Culturally and historically responsive education: A policy research brief. *National Council of Teachers of English.* https://ncte.org/wp-content/uploads/2023/05/2023-NCTE-Squire-Office_Culturally-and-Historically-Responsive-Education.pdf

Rebora, A. (2021). Zaretta Hammond on equity and student engagement. *Educational Leadership, 79*(4), 14–8.

Sims Bishop, R. (2015, January 30). *Mirrors, windows and sliding glass doors* [Video]. Youtube. https://www.youtube.com/watch?v=_AAu58SNSyc

Tatum, A. W. (2021). *Teaching Black boys in the elementary grades: Advanced disciplinary reading and writing to secure their futures.* Teachers College Press.

Turner, J., & Paris, S. G. (1995). How literacy tasks influence children's motivation for literacy. *The Reading Teacher, 48*(8), 662–73. https://www.jstor.org/stable/20201530

Literature Cited

Bradbury, R. (1953). *Fahrenheit 451.* Ballantine Books.

Kimmerer, R. W. with Gray Smith, M. (2022). *Braiding sweetgrass for young adults: Indigenous wisdom, scientific knowledge, and the teachings of plants* (N. Neidhardt, Illus.). Zest Books.

Philbrick, W. R. (2000). *The last book in the universe.* The Blue Sky Press.

Boosting Word Recognition and Fluency

7

Adolescent learners may have firm control over foundational reading and writing skills, including word recognition and spelling of thousands of words. However, too many of our students struggle with reading academic grade-level texts. Automatic word recognition of academic grade-level texts is important because as reading becomes more automatic, reading becomes more fluent. Not having to devote as much brain energy to decode words, frees up readers to attend to meaning-making. The same is true with writing. The more automatically students can encode language, the more attention they can devote to the meaning they are trying to communicate.

Literacy Strategy: Anticipation Guide

This Anticipation Guide is designed to help readers activate their background knowledge, challenge misconceptions, and focus on key ideas as they read about the science of reading.

Before Reading
Read each statement below and mark whether you agree (A) or disagree (D). Be ready to explain your thinking.

1 ___ Phonics instruction is essential for all students to become proficient readers.

2 ___ The brain has a natural ability to learn to read without explicit instruction.

3 ___ Early reading instruction can prevent most reading difficulties later on.

4 ___ Reading depends more on background knowledge than on decoding ability.

During Reading
As you read the chapter, look for information that confirms or challenges your initial responses to the statements. Take notes on key evidence or examples provided in the text.

Preview Key Vocabulary

decoding: connecting the graphemes (letters) to the phonemes (sounds)
encoding: connecting the phonemes (sounds) to the graphemes (letters)
morphemic awareness: understanding how parts of words carry meaning
multisyllabic: having two or more syllables

Advanced Phonics

Generally, as young children, we naturally learn oral language through interacting with family. On the other hand, learning written language requires explicit and systematic instruction on **phonics**. Explicit instruction should include modeling on how to decode graphemes (letters) to phonemes (sounds) and an opportunity to practice with feedback. Systematic teaching ensures that all phonetic patterns of English written language are covered in early grades. The University of Florida Literacy Institute (2022) recommends a sequence for phonics instruction, linked in the references and summarized in Table 7.1 (https://ufli.education.ufl.edu/wp-content/uploads/2022/06/UFLI-Scope2.pdf).

What about when working with adolescents? When teaching adolescents, the dosage and duration of phonics instruction, to draw from medical lingo, will be based on the individual student's learning needs. Some students may have gaps in their phonics knowledge that can be remedied quickly, some students might need to review the whole phonics sequence, and everything in between. Some students might not have knowledge gaps but need more time to practice **decoding** and **encoding** words in context.

To assess students' phonics knowledge to inform where to begin instruction with a group of students, teachers can use spelling inventories. According to research, the stages of developing decoding and spelling skills follow along a typical progression. We all pass through each stage, but we do not go through

Table 7.1 Examples of Phonics Skills

Examples of Phonics Skills	
Examples of beginning phonics skills	Consonants → Short vowels → Consonant Vowel Consonant pattern (CVC) → Consonant doubles (e.g., -ff, -ll, -ss, -zz) → Digraphs (e.g., sh, th, ch) → Long-vowel graphemes → Long-vowel CVCe patterns
Examples of advanced phonics skills	Closed and open syllables → Word ending spelling patterns (e.g., -ed, -le) → r-controlled vowels → Common vowel teams → Variant teams → Diphthongs → Silent letters → Other syllable types → Affixes → Suffix spelling changes → Low frequency spellings and variants

these stages at the same pace. The Words Their Way Upper Level Spelling Inventory (2020, pp. 326–9) can be given to the whole class like a traditional spelling test. The inventory is organized to illuminate where a student is along the progression, which identifies what they are ready to learn next.

The authors of the *Teaching Reading Sourcebook* recommend these Do's and Don'ts for teaching **decoding**:

- Do not introduce too many words at one time; there's no magic number but 3–5 decodable or morphologically rich words is typical for a lesson.
- Do introduce new words in isolation before seeing them in texts.
- Do not decode the words for students. Let them practice the patterns they have learned.
- Do point out irregular parts of the word that do not follow expected patterns.
- Do not teach words in isolation only; do read and write connected text. (Honig et al., 2018.)

A playful strategy for practicing phonics is Word Ladder puzzles (e.g., Rasinski & Smith, 2019). Are you ready for some magic? We can turn rain into snow in a matter of minutes. Follow the steps in Table 7.2.

Have students make their own Word Ladder puzzles from dog to cat, short to tall, walk to run, and first to last by replacing, subtracting, or adding one letter or sound at a time to make a new word.

Teachers often ask, is phonics instruction important when teaching multilingual learners? Yes, explicit and systematic phonics instruction of

Table 7.2 Word Ladder Puzzle Example

rain	Replace the initial sound in rain with the /m/ sound. What word does that make?
main	Replace the final sound in main with the /l/ sound.
mail	Delete the initial sound.
ail	Is there a different way to spell ail?
ale	Add an /m/ sound as the initial sound.
male	Replace the long a with a long o sound.
mole	Replace the initial sound with a /h/ sound.
hole	Remove the letter l.
hoe	Replace the /h/ sound with the /sh/ sound.
shoe	What letter do you have to change to turn the word shoe into the word show?
show	Replace the digraph /sh/ with the blend /sn/ sound.
snow	What did you turn rain into?

the English language is beneficial alongside spoken language support for multilingual learners. Claude Goldenberg (2024) of Stanford University offers this advice,

> [W]hen teaching students to read (and write) in a language they are simultaneously learning to speak and understand, teachers need to provide English oral language development instruction that directly supports the acquisition of literacy skills. This will help enable English learners to connect oral English, which they are learning, with written English, which they are also learning. (para. 8)

For example, teachers can integrate oral language, decoding, and encoding instruction during phonics time. This way, students can map the letters, sounds, and meaning. After all, teaching phonics is not the end goal of itself, the end goal is word recognition.

Decoding Multisyllabic Words

The following are ways to support all readers' word recognition by building on their foundational knowledge of phonemic awareness and phonics and focusing on decoding **multisyllabic** words and advanced word study.

Syllable Types

Syllables in the English language are organized around vowels. A syllable is a word or part of a word with only one vowel sound. To figure out how many syllables are in a word, you can try this strategy. Put your hand under your chin, and then say the word you are analyzing. Count the number of times your mouth goes down. That's the number of syllables in that word! This isn't a scientifically based strategy, as it will not work for every word (e.g., comic or problem), but it's a useful way to get started with teaching syllables.

Understanding the syllable division patterns in English can assist in decoding and encoding multisyllabic words. First, we need to understand the different types of vowels in English. You might remember from when you learned to read that there are *short vowels*, represented with a breve ă ĕ ĭ ŏ ŭ, and *long vowels*, represented with a macron ā ē ī ō ū and sometimes y when it makes the ī or ē sound. Say the following words out loud to hear the short vowel sounds: bat, bet, bit, bot, but. The long vowel sounds are the names of the letters that you can hear in the following words: fake, she, time, go, cute, fly.

In addition, the letter "r" affects the sound of any vowel that preceded it creating *r-controlled vowels*. Say the following words aloud to hear the r-controlled vowel sounds: far, fir, fur, fervor. The next two vowel types are often referred to as vowel teams in younger grades because the concept we are trying to convey is about orthographic mapping not necessarily to prepare students to be expert linguists. When students are ready for more advanced **orthography**, they can be exposed to the linguistic terms, which are actually vowel digraphs and diphthongs. The word digraph comes from the prefix di- that means two and -graph that means write. It means two letters written consecutively that make one sound. Diphthong also has di- that means two and -phthong that means sound. It means two letters that blend to make a sliding sound. For some adolescents, using the linguistic terms keeps the phonics instruction from feeling babyish.

The final vowel type is the schwa, which can be spelled with any vowel. It makes the sound /uh/ in an unstressed syllable. Like the first and last *a* in the

Table 7.3 Syllable Types and Vowel Sounds

Syllable Type	Pattern and Vowel Sound	Example
Closed	Ends with a consonant Makes a short vowel sound	KitKat Twix
Open	Ends with a vowel Makes a long vowel sound	Rolo Candy
Vowel–consonant -e	Ends with a silent e Makes a long vowel sound	Mike & Ike Take Five
Vowel digraph or diphthong	Could make long, short, or new vowel sound	PayDay Heath
Vowel-R	Makes r-controlled vowel sound	Starburst Butterfinger
Final stable	Must be the last syllable of a root word Always pronounced the same	Skittles
Unstressed	Sometimes in an unstressed syllable, the vowel makes a schwa sound /uh/	Whatchamacallit

unstressed syllables of banana (bə-**nan**-ə). Students can make a meme using the quote, "I want to be a schwa because it's never stressed" to help them remember this vowel type. There are several free meme generators online that provide easy-to-use templates and popular images.

Here is an example of a lesson that has students use syllable types to decode and pronounce multisyllabic words. This can help them recognize word meanings from their spoken vocabulary knowledge. This lesson could be used before reading the first chapter of *To Kill a Mockingbird* to integrate word recognition practice with connected text.

Tried and True Strategy by Shea Kerkhoff

Lesson: Decoding Multisyllabic Words in *To Kill a Mockingbird*

Context: Grade 9 English class in Knightdale, North Carolina

I start by explaining the rationale of the lesson. I say something like this: "The narrator is an adult sharing memories from her childhood, so her word choice is quite sophisticated. I choose for us to look at these two sentences because they introduce us to the author's style, so we can practice word attack strategies and because the sentences introduce us to the narrator's family."

I then direct students to underline the multisyllabic words in the sentences, meaning words with more than two syllables.

> *We lived on the main __residential__ street in town—__Atticus__, Jem, and I, plus __Calpurnia__, our cook. Jem and I found our father __satisfactory__: he played with us, read to us, and treated us with __courteous detachment__.*

We then move to the next step. "Next, let's use our knowledge of syllables to attack each word one at a time. Place a slash between each syllable making sure that there is a vowel in each syllable and identify the type."

res/id/en/tial

"The first three are closed because they end with a consonant. That makes them say the short vowel sounds. The last is a final stable syllable. You can say the word quietly and listen to see if you recognize it. You might recognize it as a word if I pronounce it rez/i/den/tial. The phonetic pronunciation is close, but not exactly the way I usually say it. That's ok. We will need to be flexible and try different syllable breaks and sounds until we get a word we recognize."

Morphemic Awareness

Morphemic awareness and vocabulary knowledge play a powerful role in supporting advanced decoding and encoding. Morphemic awareness is understanding how parts of words (i.e., prefixes, suffixes, and roots) carry meaning. In early grades, when a reader comes to an unknown word, they decode and then ask themselves if the word they pronounced through decoding makes sense in that context. However, many of the words adolescents come across in grade-level texts will be unfamiliar. Remember our example about digraph and diphthong? Knowing the word parts can help adolescents not only read the word, but figure out what the word means, so they can decide if the word makes sense. Once students know many roots, prefixes, and suffixes, they can use the DISSECT strategy (Figure 7.1) when they encounter unfamiliar multisyllabic words (Woodruff et al., 2002).

Before reading a complex text, have students practice decoding and pronouncing the multisyllabic words that are essential for **comprehension**. See morphemic awareness in action in the lesson scenario titled *Attacking Multisyllabic Medical and Scientific Terms*.

DISSECT

Discover the context
Isolate the prefix
Separate the suffix
Say the stem
Examine the stem
Check the stem
Try the dictionary

Figure 7.1 DISSECT Strategy.

Tried and True Strategy by Shea Kerkhoff

Lesson Name: Attacking Multisyllabic Medical and Scientific Terms

Context: Literacy for Adolescent Learners class in St. Louis, Missouri

Introduction
We are going to be reading a scientific journal article to learn about an innovative idea in medical research. Before we do, we are going to practice decoding multisyllabic words using the DISSECT strategy. The DISSECT strategy is a good strategy to use because a lot of terminology in the medical field comes from Greek and Latin word parts.

First, I will model the strategy. Then, we'll practice together as a whole class. Read the sentence silently. The sentence is from a scientific research abstract by Schwen et al. (2015).

The liver plays a pivotal role for metabolization and detoxification in the mammalian body.

I Do
There are four multisyllabic words. Underline the words with three or more syllables. I'll model with *detoxification*. Use the DISSECT strategy to

isolate the prefix (de) in detoxification, separate the suffix (tion). Are there more suffixes? Possibly but it's hard to tell. We still have many syllables left so let's try the flex strategy.

Here is what we had: de | toxifica | tion

Then underline the vowels or vowel groups: d<u>e</u> | t<u>o</u>x<u>i</u>f<u>i</u>c<u>a</u> | t<u>io</u>n

Separate the syllables so that there is a vowel in each: d<u>e</u> | t<u>o</u>x / <u>i</u>f / <u>i</u>c / <u>a</u> | t<u>io</u>n

Pronounce each syllable: de tox if ic a tion

Do you recognize the word or a part of the word? Maybe you've heard of detox before. Maybe you know that -tion makes a word a noun.

We Do

Now let's practice together. Help me decode *pivotal*, *metabolization*, and *mammalian*.

As for meaning, the nouns *detoxification* and *metabolization* are less familiar words than the related words *detox* and *metabolism*. The adjective form mammalian is less familiar than the noun mammal. *Pivotal* is a precise term for *important* that also adds complexity. We can paraphrase the sentence with the more familiar words: *The liver is important for metabolism and detox in mammals.*

Now that we understand the context a bit better, let's reread the original sentence pronouncing the multisyllabic words. Read aloud with me as I read the sentence: *The liver plays a pivotal role for metabolization and detoxification in the mammalian body.*

Let's check our comprehension: What are the two main roles of the liver?

You Do Together

We are going to read the article "Can Armadillos Show us How to Regrow a Liver?" from the *Biomedical Science Journal for Teens* (Rambukkana et al., 2023). Before we do, work as a small group to decode and pronounce the underlined multisyllabic words in the abstract.

> *What if we could make our body's old or sick cells act young again? Surprisingly, the **bacteria** that cause **leprosy** may show us how. Previously, we discovered that **infecting** cells with leprosy bacteria in a **laboratory** dish "**reprogrammed**" the cells back to an **immature** state. The cells may then be able to produce many different types of cells in the body—and maybe even **regenerate** an organ.*

After students have completed that task, come back as a whole class and review. Ask for volunteers to pronounce and define each word. Go through each of the words, checking for correct pronunciation and meaning before having students read the article independently.

Fluency

Independent reading fluency consists of speed, accuracy, and prosody when reading grade-level texts. Automatic orthographic processing, as discussed in Chapter 2, allows for quick recognition of familiar words, which helps with reading speed. Assuming that the orthographic map that a student has built is accurate, then more automaticity would also lead to greater accuracy. As such, word recognition is an important component of fluency. Prosody means reading with the appropriate expression.

Speed and Accuracy

Assessing speed and accuracy is fairly straightforward. As an **informal assessment**, teachers can have students engage in whisper reading where students read aloud quietly to a partner and then switch who is reading at each paragraph or page. The teacher can walk around and take notes on what they hear. Questions to keep in mind when listening include: Is a student reading slower than natural speech? Is a student guessing at words based on the first few letters or the context? Is the reading monotone without pauses or expression? If the answer is yes to any of these, then the student probably needs fluency practice. Fluency is important because it impacts comprehension.

Read this algebra word problem one word at a time to get a sense of how fluency impacts comprehension. Force yourself to pause after each word before going on to the next. You could even use a piece of paper to cover the words below the line that you are reading so your eyes don't jump ahead!

Pete
has
nickels
and
dimes.
He
has
four
more
nickels
than
dimes.

He
has
eighteen
coins
total.
How
many
nickels
and
dimes
does
he
have?

When students are spending their effort on word reading, they have to read word by word. It's much more difficult to attend to how the words connect and how the ideas relate to one another without fluent reading. Word-by-word reading also slows down reading, meaning that the working memory has to hold information for longer periods of time in order to get to the connections that support meaning-making.

Teachers can also use apps and **artificial intelligence (AI)** to help assess oral reading speed and accuracy (for an AI list, use this case-sensitive link: https://bit.ly/AIlist). It's crucial to keep in mind that the goal of fluency is not speed but comprehension. That's why I use the terms "speed and accuracy" together. We do not want to confuse our students, or ourselves, about the goal. We want to use language that emphasizes accurate word reading and meaning-making of texts. In fact, Hasbrouck and Glaser (2012) define fluency as "reasonably accurate reading, at an appropriate rate, with suitable expression, that leads to accurate and deep comprehension and motivation to read" (p. 13).

That said, assessing fluency includes speed as a variable. First, the teacher selects a grade-level passage of **text** and pastes it into the app. If possible, the teacher adjusts the recording settings to a designated time (usually between 1 and 5 minutes). Then, each student audio records a cold reading of the passage, meaning they read it without looking over it or practicing it beforehand. AI then calculates the correct words per minute to provide speed and accuracy data for each student. Although there are no empirically validated fluency norms for grades 9–12 at the time of this writing, Table 7.4 provides norms for the end of sixth grade and eighth grade (Hasbrouck & Tindal, 2017). According to the International Literacy

Table 7.4 Oral Reading Fluency Norms by Grade Level

Percentile	WCPM sixth grade	WCPM eighth grade
75	173	177
50	146	151
25	122	127

Association, "Researchers generally agree that performance at the 50th percentile of these compiled ORF [oral reading fluency] norms can serve as a reasonable benchmark for determining an appropriate reading rate" (2018, p. 5). I tend to think that if a reader is at or above 151 WCPM in grade 9 or above, they would be doing ok with fluency.

Another way to assess student reading is through timed silent readings. Teachers can give all students a grade-level passage that is 250 words. Let them know that you do not expect them to finish reading the whole passage and that this exercise is not for a grade. Set the timer for a minute and have students read silently. Have them place a mark behind the last word that they read when the timer goes off. You can use this to get a sense of words read per minute for each student. For a more accurate assessment, the Test of Silent Contextual Reading Fluency-2 (Hammill et al., 2006) measure takes three minutes and also can be given to the whole class at the same time. The test consists of reading passages with no spaces between the words (e.g., AYELLOWBIRDWITHBLUEWINGS). Students have to draw a line between as many recognizable words as possible within the three minutes (e.g., A/YELLOW/BIRD/WITH/BLUE/WINGS).

What do you do if you discover that students need to build fluency? One research-based way to build students' fluency is through repeated readings. Providing opportunities for authentic repeated readings can help students focus their attention on word recognition first and then meaning second. The authentic purpose is important in order to respect adolescents, not make it seem babyish or like busy work, and to motivate adolescents to engage in rereading and to do so with dignity. Students could reread in order to practice for a performance, like performing a poem or monologue or a part in readers' theater. Here are two examples of readers' theater scripts for secondary social studies students: "A Deadly Secret: The Lincoln Assassination Conspiracy Trial" (Barchers, 2004) and "Moon Talk from Apollo 11" (Montgomery, 2012). Teachers can utilize AI tools to create a reader's theater script about any curricular topic. Just make sure to fact-check before having students perform.

Prosody

Prosody includes expression, phrasing, and smoothness. Prosody is important for reading because prosody can cause comprehension, such as when students are listening to a fluent reader. Or, prosody can be an effect of comprehension, such as when students understand what the sentence is trying to communicate, then they can add the appropriate expression. Think about the following sentence: I didn't say she stole my money. This sentence can mean seven different things depending on which word you emphasize:

> **I** *didn't say she stole my money.*
> *I **didn't** say she stole my money.*
> *I didn't **say** she stole my money.*
> *I didn't say **she** stole my money.*
> *I didn't say she **stole** my money.*
> *I didn't say she stole **my** money.*
> *I didn't say she stole my **money**.*

In addition to expression, prosody includes phrasing because fluent readers read in phrases. Take that algebra word problem from earlier. If we read it in phrases, it becomes easier to understand.

> *Pete*
> *has nickels and dimes.*
> *He has*
> *four more nickels*
> *than dimes.*
> *He has*
> *eighteen coins*
> *total.*
> *How many*
> *nickels and dimes*
> *does he have?*

Prosody is just as important for public speaking as reading. President Barack Obama was a master of using phrasing to help his audience comprehend what he was communicating. We can help students develop prosody by having them listen to fluent models and direct them to think about phrasing while listening. A lesson idea to practice phrasing is the scooping strategy, as described in the following lesson scenario. The lesson starts by the teaching modeling scooping for the class, and then have them practice by penciling a "scoop" line beneath phrases while listening to President Barack Obama's (2009) National Address to America's Schoolchildren.

Tired and True Strategy by Shea Kerkhoff

Lesson Name: Listening to an Exemplary Model of Public Speaking for Phrasing Practice

Context: Grade 9 English class in Knightdale, North Carolina

Introduction
Today, we are going to work on our reading fluency by listening to President Obama read a very special speech. One of the strategies President Obama uses is phrasing. We are going to practice phrasing using the scooping strategy. I'll go first, and then we will practice together. Here is the first sentence of the speech, after Mr. Obama greets everyone, please read it silently: "I know that for many of you, today is the first day of school."

I Do
I am going to scoop the sentence into phrases. The scoops show where pauses could happen, and the sentence would still sound smooth.

Now, I'll read the sentence pausing at the end of each scoop. As I read, I'll use a scooping hand motion to indicate the phrasing (Birsh et al., 2018). I know / that for many of you / today / is the first day / of school. Did the sentence sound bumpy or smooth? If it sounds smooth, we can keep going. If it sounds bumpy when we read, then we need to try different phrasing placements. (For example, you could take out some of the pauses indicated in my example, if you prefer, to make the reading smoother.)

We Do
We are going to listen to the speech. As you listen, have your copy of the speech and a pencil, so that we can practice phrasing. Scoop with a pencil on your print copy of the speech as you read along. We will stop after the first paragraph for a check-in. (As students are scooping, the teacher is walking around the room and observing how students are doing.)

With a shoulder partner, compare your scoops. Do you have similar phrasing? (Make sure students understand what to do before moving on.) What questions do you have before we keep listening? (The teacher pauses to give students time to ask questions.) Now, we are going to keep listening and scooping. When you hear Mr. Obama say "debate team," we will take a break and check-in again.

You Do
Next, have students practice scooping the next paragraph before listening to it.

And no matter what you want to do with your life, I guarantee that you'll need an education to do it. You want to be a doctor, or a teacher, or a police officer? You want to be a nurse or an architect, a lawyer or a member of our military? You're going to need a good education for every single one of those careers. You cannot drop out of school and just drop into a good job. You've got to train for it and work for it and learn for it.

Have students listen to the paragraph and compare how they scooped the phrases compared to how Mr. Obama did. Pause at the end of the paragraph, and ask students what they noticed. Have them make any revisions to their phrasing to make it smooth. Then, have them read the paragraph silently paying attention to their inner reading voice. Finally, listen to the rest of the speech continuing to notice the phrasing.

To assess students' prosody, have students choose a speech that they will deliver using phrasing and expression. They can choose the Obama speech or select a new speech for an extra challenge. Students will practice phrasing using scooping and reading aloud to listen for smoothness. They will then audio record their reading of the speech.

Teachers can use the recordings to assess prosody through a fluency **rubric**, such as the following adapted from fluency researcher Tim Rasinski (2024). The rubric considers expression, volume, pitch, tone, emphasis, phrasing, rhythm, and smoothness.

Metacognition

Metacognition is thinking about thinking and is connected to fluency. Readers and writers need to think about their thinking when engaging in literacy by self-monitoring to see if the text is making sense and self-regulating to correct errors.

A self-monitoring strategy when reading is called Click or Clunk. Readers pause and ask themself if the reading is clicking, or making sense. If it clicks, then keep going, no need to reread. If the reading is a clunk, or not making sense, then we can apply a metacognitive strategy, sometimes called Fix-Up Strategies, like those shown in Figure 7.2.

Table 7.5 Oral Reading Fluency Rubric

	1	2	3	4
Expression	Reads in a quiet voice as if to get words out. Reading does not sound natural like talking to a friend.	Reading sounds natural in part of the text, but the reader does not always sound like they are talking to a friend.	Reads with volume and expression. However, sometimes the reader slips into expressionless reading and does not sound like they are talking to a friend.	Reads with varied pitch and expression. The reader sounds like they are talking to a friend with their voice matching the interpretation of the passage.
Phrasing	Reads word-by-word in a monotone voice.	Reads in two or three word phrases, not adhering to punctuation, stress, and intonation.	Reads with a mixture of run-ons, mid-sentence pauses for breath, and some choppiness. There is reasonable stress and intonation.	Reads with good phrasing; adhering to punctuation, stress, and intonation.
Smoothness	Frequently hesitates while reading, sounds out words, and repeats words or phrases. The reader makes multiple attempts to read the same passage.	Reads with extended pauses or hesitations. The reader has many rough spots.	Reads with occasional breaks in rhythm. The reader has difficulty with specific words and/or sentence structures.	Reads smoothly with some breaks, but self-corrects with difficult words and/or sentence structures.

Figure 7.2 Metacognitive Strategies for Self-Monitoring During Reading.

Metacognitive strategies when writing include planning, rereading, and asking questions. Metacognitive writers think ahead about what they want to say, making their writing flow more smoothly. Writers can reread their work as they write, noticing when ideas are not clear or words are misspelled and then revising in real time to improve accuracy. Writers can ask themselves questions, helping them become more self-aware over time and write more fluidly with less effort.

Integrating Reading and Writing

Integrating reading fluency, grammar, and sentence-level writing instruction is beneficial for both reading and writing fluency (Baye et al., 2019). Writers communicate phrasing and places to pause through punctuation and emphasis through font formatting. For example, I used italics to indicate what word the reader should emphasize in the sentence: *I* didn't say she stole my money. As readers, we can use these clues to read more fluently. As writers, we can use grammar and formatting to help our work be more readable for our audience.

In intermediate grades, we can talk with students about ending punctuation (e.g., period, exclamation point, and question mark) and that a comma means a short pause, whereas an ending punctuation means a longer pause. As students advance, we can introduce them to more complex sentence patterns and their effect on the reader. Here's an example from Kolln (2003):

1 I loved the book, but I hated the movie.

2 I loved the book; but I hated the movie.

3 I loved the book; I hated the movie.

4 I loved the book; however, I hated the movie.

5 I loved the book: I hated the movie.

The first one we might think of as the basic compound-sentence rule, the comma-plus-conjunction, which puts fairly equal emphasis on the two clauses. The next three, with greater pause the semicolon will give the reader, put more emphasis on the second clause. But there are differences among them, too. Seeing the bare semicolon of (3), the reader will sense a kind of tight finality—no argument, no concessions; the addition of however in (4) adds a note of deliberation, a degree of thoughtfulness in coming to a decision about the movie. The colon in (5) commands special attention: The reader will pause and give even more attention to the word of contrast, *hated*, than in the other four versions (Kolln, 2003, p. 278).

Another way to help students engage in repeated readings to improve fluency is with the Sentence Structure Explicit Instruction Routine. In this protocol, the teacher identifies a complex sentence from the assigned grade-level text. First, the teacher reads the sentence aloud. Second, the teacher and students choral read the sentence. Next, they discuss what made the sentence complex, identifying vocabulary and/or sentence structure, and work together to make meaning of the tricky parts. Finally, students silently read the sentence, focusing on meaning-making of the sentence as a whole.

For example, consider the following sentence from Yaa Gyasi's *Homegoing*: "The family is like the forest: if you are outside it is dense; if you are inside you see that each tree has its own position." Students might notice the use of both a colon and a semicolon and name this structure as what makes the sentence complex. We can rely on our knowledge of phrasing and punctuation to add prosody to our reading and contribute to comprehension.

In addition to building fluency through repeated reading for authentic purposes, the Sentence Structure Direct Instruction Routine also builds knowledge about words and language structure through discussion. Teachers can integrate writing instruction by then having students create sentences

imitating the complex structure. *Being in middle school is like _______:
if _________; if ____________.*

Differentiating for Word Recognition and Fluency

Students may need word work and/or they may need sentence-level intervention in order to be able to access the longer grade-level texts that they need to read and to write without hesitation and with stamina. Word journals, where students collect words that they come across and have opportunities to revisit the words, can provide the multiple exposures that they need for automatic word recognition and for using the word in their writing. They can record interesting words, words they like, and words they hate, to add some novelty.

Sentence-level work can be integrated into whole-class lessons as Bell-Ringers (also called Do Nows or Warm-Ups). Check out this resource by Marcus Luther for a lot of ideas on sentence-level work that can be incorporated as bell-ringers (https://bit.ly/MarcusLuther).

When teaching with longer texts, as a rule of thumb, if I give all students the same text to read, then I will be flexible or differentiate the amount of time that they have to read it. If there is a predetermined amount of time that we have in class to read, then I would differentiate the text by either abbreviating the passage or swapping out above grade-level words for recognizable words. Of course, I would not swap out words that are essential to the content that students need to learn. Likewise, for writing, if there is a certain number of words students need to write, then I am flexible with the amount of time students have to complete it. If it is a timed writing, then I differentiate the number of words required.

Conclusion

By the time children reach intermediate elementary grades, their word recognition skills should be accurate and automatic. These foundational skills then combine with others to help them read fluently and understand what they're reading. As students move through school, word knowledge, reading fluency, and comprehension need to keep improving. Across their day, adolescents should hear fluent reading, read and write a wide range of texts, and engage in meaningful discussions of the texts they read and write. In this way, literacy skills continue to evolve as students advance through the years.

More to Explore

- This article, aptly titled "Supporting foundational skills for adolescents with agency," by Margaret Vaughn and Jessica Masterson is a must read: https://ila-onlinelibrary-wiley-com.ezproxy.umsl.edu/doi/full/10.1002/jaal.1409

- Janée Butler presents *Achieving Adolescent Literacy Proficiency: The Importance of Fluency Instruction* in this video from the 2024 literacy symposium: https://youtu.be/nWlBsu7Bkfo?si=wVWpe45hUXTzlNYu

- David Kearns's video recorded webinar titled *How to Help Students Read Long Words* is available on YouTube: https://youtu.be/NLQ_uDU6dJ8?si=Gb3Hd6NloPqOJIS_

- In this podcast episode 150 of *Melissa & Lori Love Literacy*, the hosts talk with two educators about how they created a successful reading intervention program for secondary students: https://podcasts.apple.com/us/podcast/listen-again-ep-150-science-of-reading-for-all/id1463219123?i=1000678612978

- Check out Tim Rasinski's webpage full of open-access fluency resources: https://www.timrasinski.com/resources.html

Reflect

For this reflection activity, review each statement from the Anticipation Guide and reflect on how your understanding has changed (if at all). For each statement, provide a brief explanation or evidence from the chapter that supports your updated perspective.

Discuss

Questions for discussion to learn from and with each other:

- Which statement from the Anticipation Guide surprised you the most? Why?
- How does the information in this chapter connect to your own experiences with teaching or learning to read?
- How can you apply the science of reading to your teaching and learning?
- Explain the relationships between accuracy and decoding, rate and automatic word recognition, and prosody and comprehension.

References

Baye, A., Lake, C., Inns, A. & Slavin, R. E. (2019). A synthesis of quantitative research on reading programs for secondary students. *Reading Research Quarterly, 54* (2), 133–66. https://doi.org/10.1002/rrq.229

Birsh, J. R., Carreker, S., Moats, L. C., White, N. C., Neuhaus, G., Beckwith, M. C., DeVito, C., Trabucco, G., Berninger, V. W., & Hess, L. E. (2018). *Multisensory teaching of basic language skills*. Brookes Publishing.

Goldenberg, C. (2024, December 3). Research must guide how we teach English learners to read [Substack newsletter]. *We Must End the Reading Wars .... Now*. https://claudegoldenberg.substack.com/p/research-must-guide-how-we-teach

Hammill, D. D., Wiederholt, J. L., & Allen, E. A. (2006). Test of Silent Contextual Reading Fluency-2. https://www.proedinc.com/Products/13805/toscrf2-test-of-silent-contextual-reading-fluencysecond-edition.aspx

Hasbrouck, J., & Glaser, D. R. (2012). *Reading fluency: Understanding and teaching this complex skill*. Gibson Hasbrouck.

Hasbrouck, J., & Tindal, G. (2017). An update to compiled ORF norms (Technical Report No. 1702). Behavioral Research and Teaching, University of Oregon. https://www.readingrockets.org/sites/default/files/2023-08/2017_ORF_NORMS.pdf

Honig, B., Diamond, L., Gutlohn, L., & Cole, C. L. (2018). *Teaching reading sourcebook* (3rd ed.). CORE.

International Literacy Association. (2018). *Reading fluently does not mean reading fast*. https://www.literacyworldwide.org/docs/default-source/where-we-stand/ila-reading-fluently-does-not-mean-reading-fast.pdf

Kolln, M. (2003). *Rhetorical grammar: Grammatical choices, rhetorical effects* (4th ed.). Longman.

Rasinski, T. (2024). Multidimensional fluency rubric. http://www.timrasinski.com/presentations/multidimensional_fluency_rubric_4_factors.pdf

Rasinski, T., & Smith, M. C. (2019). *Daily word ladders: Content areas grades 4+*. Scholastic. https://shop.scholastic.com/teachers-ecommerce/teacher/books/daily-word-ladders-content-areas-grades-4-6-9781338627442.html

University of Florida Literacy Institute (UFLI). (2022). Scope and sequence at-a-glance: All concepts (K–2). https://ufli.education.ufl.edu/wp-content/uploads/2022/06/UFLI-Scope2.pdf

Woodruff, S., Schumacher, J. B., & Deshler, D. D. (2002). *The effects of an intensive reading intervention on the decoding skills of high school students with reading deficits* [Research Report]. https://eric.ed.gov/?id=ED469293

Words Their Way. (2020). Upper Level Spelling Inventory. *Savvas*. https://mysavvastraining.com/assets/files/documents/WTW6e_Inventories_04202021_1619457927.pdf

Literature Cited

Barchers, S. I. (2004). *Judge for yourself: Famous American trials for readers theatre*. Teacher Ideas Press.

C-SPAN (2009, September 8). *Pres. Obama national address to students* [Video]. YouTube. https://youtu.be/3iqsxCWjCvI?si=ULWwCOb_FbziwgvF

Gyasi, Y. (2016). *Homegoing*. Penguin Random House.

Lee, H. (1960). *To kill a mockingbird*. J. B. Lippincott.

Montgomery, C. (2012, July 17). *Moon talk—From Apollo 11 (quick version) (R = 5.8)*. Readers Theater All Year Round. https://www.readerstheaterallyear.com/articles/20120718

Obama, B. (2009, September 8). Remarks by the president in a national address to America's schoolchildren [Transcript]. The White House

Office of the Press Secretary. https://obamawhitehouse.archives.
gov/the-press-office/remarks-president-a-national-address-americas-
schoolchildren

Rambukkana, A. and others. (2023). Can armadillos show us how to
regrow a liver? *Biomedical Science Journal for Teens.* https://www.
sciencejournalforkids.org/wp-content/uploads/2023/05/armadillo_article.pdf

Schwen, L. O., Schenk, A., Kreutz, C., Timmer, J., Bartolomé Rodríguez,
M. M., Kuepfer, L., & Preusser, T. (2015). Representative sinusoids
for hepatic four-scale pharmacokinetics simulations. *PLoS One, 10*(7),
e0133653. https://pmc.ncbi.nlm.nih.gov/articles/PMC4519332/

Wis, R. (Director). (1965). *The sound of music* [Film]. Twentieth Century
Fox; Argyle Enterprises.

Building Vocabulary and Knowledge

8

Can you figure out what is going on in this passage?

Rohit who made a fine 83 at Lord's, was the only Indian batsman who looked in control, but he fell for 19 when he mishooked a looping bouncer from Overton to Ollie Robinson at mid-on. Prior to getting dismissed, the opener had witnessed both Rahane and Rishabh Pant perish on either side of lunch.

The knowledge that a learner brings to a **text** and their cultural experiences impact their ability to make meaning. The passage above is about a cricket match between India and England (*Anderson, openers humiliate India as England dominate Day 1*, 2021). I am not knowledgeable about the sport of cricket and could not decipher what was going on. Growing up in the United States, baseball—not cricket—was part of my cultural experience. I know what "turn two" and "protect the plate" mean, but I do not know what "looping bouncer" or "lunch" mean in a sports context.

There is a renowned experiment by Recht and Leslie from 1988 about reading and baseball. The primary aim of the study was to find out what had a bigger difference: reading level or background knowledge. The findings revealed that children well-versed in baseball performed well, regardless of whether they were labeled as proficient or struggling readers. Notably, those children labeled as "struggling" but possessing extensive knowledge about baseball outperformed some of their classmates labeled as "good" readers but lacking familiarity with the sport. It is important to note that this study was with a small sample, which means that the findings are not meant to be generalized to a larger population. You could replicate the study in your own classroom to see what you learn.

One takeaway from the study is that teachers should select texts that reflect a variety of cultural backgrounds and diverse lived experiences. Another is that

Literacy Strategy: Alphaboxes

As you read, you can use the Alphaboxes strategy to keep track of ideas from the chapter. Make a table with six rows and four columns (see Table 8.2). When you come across a new word or important concept, add it to the table beside the corresponding first letter. For example, aerodynamics would be added to the first box because it starts with the letter A. For the last box, it can be a word that starts with X, Y, or Z. It's ok if you do not fill out all of the boxes. Here is a free download for your use (https://bit.ly/alphaboxestemplate).

Preview Key Vocabulary

background knowledge: what a reader knows about a topic, concept, or the world that helps them make sense of a text
cognitive overload: too much information for the brain to process
reciprocal: two-way relationship
retrieval practice: actively recalling information
synonym: a word that means the same or almost the same as another word

teachers can encourage students to draw upon their background knowledge and experiences to make meaning from texts. And, we can support students' reading **comprehension** when we help build their knowledge.

Reciprocal Relationship of Reading and Writing

Reading and knowledge have a **reciprocal** relationship. The more words you know, the more texts you will be able to comprehend; and the more texts you read, the more words you will learn. Likewise with content and cultural knowledge. The more scientific concepts, historical facts, and cultural experiences you can draw from, the more texts you will be able to comprehend. And the more you read, the more knowledge you gain about the world.

Building Word-Level Knowledge

A lot of research has been done on teaching and learning vocabulary in grades 4–12, offering teachers valuable insights about rich vocabulary instruction across content areas. One key takeaway is that expanding adolescents' breadth and depth of vocabulary is essential for meeting the literacy needs of secondary school across disciplines. In fact, the number of **multisyllabic** words that students encounter in school makes a steep climb starting in grade 4. From this point on, almost all new words students encounter in school are multisyllabic (Kearns, 2024).

While students have been dutifully copying dictionary definitions for generations, research shows that memorizing definitions does not significantly improve students' understanding of the words (Krishnan et al., 2025). Here are three reasons why focusing solely on definitions falls short:

1 Words can have different meanings depending on the context. One definition might not apply in every situation.

2 Definitions often don't give students enough information to use the words correctly or to transfer the knowledge of what that word means to words with similar word parts.

3 Students will encounter over 100,000 new words over the course of their schooling, making direct instruction of all of these words just not possible.

In reality, we need multiple opportunities for **engagement** with new words and concepts. Research suggests that at least ten exposures are needed to learn a new word, and some students may need twenty-five or more exposures (Cervetti et al., 2023). Students gain stronger recall and deeper understanding of vocabulary when they encounter words within reading contexts and actively use those words in writing.

In order to provide multiple exposures and opportunities to deepen knowledge, students need to see, hear, speak, spell, and write new words. And students need to be able to try to speak and write with new words in a low stakes, safe environment, like the example in the Tried and True Strategy by Mr. Kerkhoff from Indiana.

Tried and True Strategy by Jordan Kerkhoff

Lesson: Vocabulary Comics

Context: Sixth-grade elementary class in Otterbein, Indiana

Being the comic nerd that I am, one approach I like to use is to have students make a short comic strip that uses one of our vocabulary words. Sometimes I have the students write a short story in comic form where they have to use a certain number of vocabulary words correctly. Other times, we'll structure it in a way where the students are trying to establish enough context in one panel without actually using a word from our list. Then, we share and guess as a class, sort of like a Pictionary game approach. We often use a website called www.pixton.com that allows the students to utilize an extensive library of backgrounds and characters.

We can build students' word knowledge both through direct instruction of individual words that are connected to the texts they will be reading and through word-learning strategies. I talk about each of these in the following two sections.

Teaching Individual Words before Reading

Before reading, teachers have to analyze texts and consider which words to directly teach before reading. Too many words can cause **cognitive overload**, which hinders learning. But leaving students to fend for themselves can lead to confusion. I recommend focusing on about five words per lesson.

Typically, words that are part of students' everyday language, also referred to as Tier 1 words, are not necessary to teach. But books and language at school have **academic language**, referred to as Tier 2. Academic language contains structures and words that are new to students. We should explicitly teach Tier 2 words from a text that are common in academic language as these have high leverage across content areas. Tier 3 words are terms particular to a discipline or the terminology has a different meaning in a content area than the meaning of the word in everyday speech. We should teach Tier 3 words that are essential to being able to comprehend the text or essential to being able to speak and write about the concept being taught (Beck et al., 2013; Graham et al., 2016).

The Vocabulary Decision-Making Model in Table 8.1 charts types of Tier 2 and Tier 3 vocabulary types with considerations and examples for choosing vocabulary to explicitly teach (Graves et al., 2014).

- Essential—crucial technical term or concepts needed for understanding the text students are reading
- Valuable—of broad, general utility for students' reading and writing and thus of enduring importance in academic discourse beyond this particular lesson
- Sophisticated **synonyms**—accessible words that are synonyms for known concepts or concrete ideas that can easily be explained
- Multiple meaning—**homonyms** are the same word that has multiple meanings, and could be confusing if students do not understand that the word means something different in the disciplinary context than in common usage

Vocabulary Explicit Instruction Routine

Teachers can use an explicit instruction routine for teaching individual words where students See it, Hear it, Say it, and Write it. This word-learning routine integrates reading, listening, speaking, and writing to exponentially increase students' recall. I start the direct instruction by projecting the spelling and a student-friendly definition. For all students, but especially when teaching students for whom English is not their first language, I pronounce the word and have students echo me several times. Next, I provide an image along with a sentence using the word in context—after all, a picture is worth a thousand words. I then ask *Would you rather* or *Have you ever* type questions to have the students actively process the word and the meaning. For example, with the focus word consoled, *Would you rather be consoled by an enemy or a friend?* or *Have you ever consoled a friend? What did you do?* I have students use the word in their responses. For students who need a scaffold, I would provide Sentence Stems to help them form their responses, such as *I would rather ....*

Frayer Model

A popular vocabulary strategy is the Frayer Model. The Frayer Model puts the focus word in the center of a graphic organizer. The Frayer Model uses four boxes around the focus word for students to add (1) the definition in their

Table 8.1 Vocabulary Decision-Making Model

	Types	Examples	Questions	Considerations
Tier 3	Essential and technical terms	rhombus protagonist abolitionist magma cataclysm	Is the word a label for an idea that students need to know?	Words that do not typically occur in everyday conversation and are critical to this particular lesson.
Tier 3	Words with multiple meanings	meter delta net voice table	Does the word have a different meaning in a different content area or in everyday talk?	Everyday words that have a different meaning in this content area or across content areas, which could cause confusion.
Tier 2	Valuable academic language	elaborate analyze infer apply critique	Will the students come across the word often in school?	The word will be used in group discussion or in a writing task. The word is commonly used in other content areas, too.
Tier 2	Sophisticated synonyms	saunter: walk vertigo: dizzy beneficial: good effervescent: bubbly jubilant: happy	Is the concept represented by the word important to understanding the text?	The word has a similar, more common synonym that can easily be told to students and the word is important to comprehending the text.

own words, (2) characteristics or features of the term to help students identify it, (3) examples of the word, and (4) nonexamples. This strategy works really well for science and mathematics terms. Linked is a free download for a digital version (https://bit.ly/digitalfrayer).

Digital Tools for Word Building

Digital tools offer ways to visualize words and gamify word learning. Several free websites offer word relationship webs, some display synonyms, and others display related parts of speech. Word cloud generators offer another way for students to visualize words and add their creative touches. Online dictionaries (such as wordhippo.com and mathwords.com) provide student-friendly definitions, audio pronunciations, example sentences for context, visualizations, and even translations to other languages all in one place. In addition to the affordances of acquiring work knowledge, digital tools can be used to communicate word knowledge through images, audio, and text. Flashcard-building websites help students get repeated exposure by first making the flashcards and then practicing with them. There are many websites that offer vocabulary games for general word building through play (such as play.freerice.com).

Word-Learning Strategies

Although we know that reading a lot is a way to grow a broad and deep vocabulary, in order to be able to learn new words through reading, readers need to be able to use Context Clues when they encounter a word that they can decode but are not sure what the word means (Cervetti et al., 2023). We can teach students five ways to use Context Clues to figure out the meaning of words that they do not know (Beers, 2023):

1 Definition or Explanation Clues are the most direct of the Context Clues types. The author defines the word for the reader, generally in the same sentence offset by commas.

2 Restatement clues, the next clue type, are when the author provides a synonym or restates the word in multiple contexts. These clues may not appear in the same sentence, so look for signal words that point to the clue.

3 On the other hand, Contrast Clues are when the author offers an opposite meaning or antonym.

4 With Example Clues, the reader must infer the word meaning by the example, illustration, metaphor, or simile.

5 Gist Clues are the most subtle type of clue. Readers must infer the word meaning by the passage or even read ahead before they understand the word in context.

Figure 8.1

To learn more about Context Clues and read examples, view the free download linked by scanning the QR code in Figure 8.1 or linked here: http://bit.ly/3QmiVoo. When Context Clues are not enough or when a text does not provide clues, students need to know how to use text features like boldface words and the glossary to make meaning.

Building Linguistic Knowledge

Research confirms that advanced linguistic knowledge (i.e., morphology, grammar, and **syntax**) is related to reading comprehension in adolescence (Pearson et al., 2020). A research-based instructional strategy for building linguistic knowledge is the Teacher Think Aloud. Fisher and Frey (2015) explain that expert teachers frequently model how they apply their linguistic knowledge by pausing when reading aloud to demonstrate the following:

- Word Reading: Breaking the word into word parts, using **phonics**, and determining the meaning of unknown words using morphology and context clues.

- Text Features: Naming parts of a text, such as the table of contents, index, and glossary. Using features that are added to a text to aid understanding, such as headings, captions, and bold words.

- Text Structure: Thinking about the ways in which the author structured the text, ranging from the functions of words in a sentence to the macro level.

Understanding Morphology

Morphology is the study of how words are formed through parts, called morphemes. Teaching morphology in grades 4–12 focuses on learning word parts, specifically roots, affixes, and suffixes. Understanding morphology can strengthen word recognition and word solving. Take this sentence from Chapter 7 as an example: "The liver plays a pivotal role for metabolization and detoxification in the mammalian body" (Schwen et al., 2015, abstract). As for word recognition, the words *detoxification* and *metabolization* have the -ation suffix to make them nouns. These nouns are less familiar words than the related words *detox* and *metabolize* or *metabolism*. The adjective form *mammalian* is less familiar than the noun *mammal*. Understanding that the suffixes *-tion* and *-ian* change the part of speech but not the root meaning, we can make an educated guess as to what the words are communicating.

This strategy, depicted in Figure 8.2, is called Semantic Mapping. The focus word is placed in a bubble, and then the word parts are written inside the bubbles that extend from the oval containing the focus word. Students can add words in the same family, related words, and examples. Students can add words and images to their Semantic Maps to help make the word meaning more concrete and easier to understand. Depending on the particular focus word, other categories could be added to the map, such as cognates, synonyms, and antonyms. Semantic Mapping can be completed individually or collaboratively, using paper and markers or digital tools. I made the following figure in Canva using a template for mind maps, but you could also insert a diagram in Google Slides or bubbl.us.

Playing review games—like Pictionary and Bingo—taps into principles of learning science by promoting **retrieval practice** (i.e., actively recalling information). These games also increase **motivation** and engagement through immediate feedback and friendly competition. What's more, review

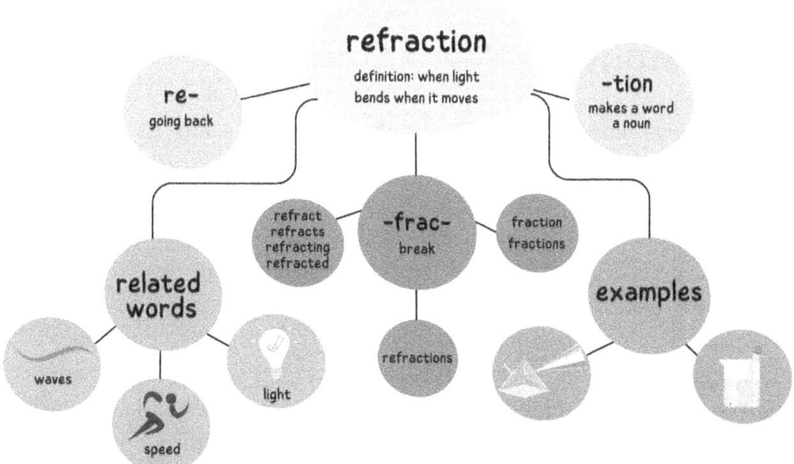

Figure 8.2 Semantic Map Example.

Tried and True Strategy by Diana Hammond

Lesson: Morphology Jenga for Prefixes, Suffixes, and Roots

Context: High school class in Kirkwood, Missouri

I was inspired by a colleague to consider what "word work" looked like in a secondary classroom. That led us to adapt some games for use in our classroom. One example we used was Jenga blocks to support practice with prefixes, suffixes, and roots. Initially, we wrote the terms on the blocks using a dash before, after, or on both sides to indicate what function it served. When playing the game, a student would have to come up with a word that used the prefix, suffix, or root they selected before placing it on top of the stack. Later, we worked smarter and numbered the Jenga blocks and provided a corresponding numbered handout. This allowed us to adapt the strategy for a variety of purposes (e.g., writing prompts, student interviews, and synonym challenge).

---

games provide the repeated exposure and spaced practice needed for long-term retention. Research in cognitive science confirms that retrieval and spaced practice are effective strategies for reinforcing learning (Agarwal & Bain, 2019). As a fresh take on a familiar favorite, Ms. Hammond reimagined Jenga for her high school students to review morphemes. Want to see the Morphology Jenga directions? Here's a free download: https://bit.ly/morphologyjenga, and the Tried and True Strategy above shows how the game played out in real life.

Understanding Word Origin

Have you ever wondered why in a spelling bee, contestants ask for the word origin? Word origin acts like a clue because knowing where a word comes from can reveal helpful patterns in pronunciation and spelling. For example, words borrowed from France often have silent letters. The word ballet is pronounced "bal-lay" because of the French spelling rule, and some people pronounce "croissant" as "krwah-sahn" (silent "t") in keeping with French.

During a unit on the Holocaust, my students and I had to pronounce a lot of German words from the texts that we were reading. The teacher next door had taken German in high school, and shared this trick with us. Although in English, when two vowels go walking, the first one does the talking (e.g., the ē in lie), the German saying is, the first vowel walks and the second vowel talks, like the ē in Liesl and Friedrich from *The Sound of Music*. While this pattern has many exceptions in English, it's pretty stable for -ie- and -ei-digraphs in German, and helped us pronounce and spell *reich* (rike), *heil* (highl), and *Elie Wiesel* (EL-ee vee-ZEL). When the word *diesel* came up, we noticed that it followed the German pronunciation pattern, so we checked the dictionary and, sure enough, it traced back to German origins.

Learning the origin of words can support adolescents' spelling skills, word recognition, pronunciation, and vocabulary development. What can be tricky about learning morphemes is that letter combinations aren't always morphemes, or might have different meanings based on the word origin. For example, the Latin root *-homo-* means *human*, but in Greek, the prefix *homo-* means *same*. So, even though they look identical, they come from different origins and have different meanings. Here are some other curveballs:

- Latin *di-* = apart, away (as in divide, divergent)
- Greek *di-* = two, twice (as in dilemma, dioxide)
- Latin *bi-* = two, twice (as in bicycle, bilingual)
- Latin *pre-* = come before (as in precede, pretest)
- Latin *pro-* = forward (as in proceed, progress)
- Greek *proto-* = earliest, first (as in prototype, protoplasm)

Depending on what class you teach, there might be borrowed words from French, such as in the culinary arts, or Italian, such as in music. Making students aware of patterns and morphemes from languages that commonly appear in your content area can help build their vocabulary.

Understanding Syntax

In order to help students grow their knowledge about language and literacy, we can have them play with sentences. Sentence Unscramble is a strategy that helps students think about the function of words by requiring them to reconstruct a meaningful sentence from a set of jumbled words. This activity encourages students to think carefully about word order and sentence structure, helping them understand how words serve different functions and work together to create meaning. Take a look at this example—it teaches how lists are structured and where adjectives belong, while also reinforcing content knowledge about the food chain.

Directions: *Unscramble the sentences to reveal an important idea about food chains.*

> **Scramble**: *plants/provide/to/Green/carnivores/energy/herbivores/omnivores/and*
>
> **Possible Answer**: *Green plants provide energy to herbivores, carnivores, and omnivores.*
>
> **Scramble**: *producers/supply/to/Primary/energy/grass/birds/algae/insects/cats/consumers/and/and/such as/such as*
>
> **Answer**: *Primary producers, such as grass and algae, supply energy to consumers, such as insects, birds, and cats.*

This kind of activity connects vocabulary, sentence structure, and content understanding in a low-stakes, interactive way.

Sentence Revising is another strategy that helps students develop their understanding of syntax by encouraging them to manipulate and improve sentence structure for clarity, emphasis, or flow. By working with authentic examples, either their own writing or mentor texts, students gain hands-on practice recognizing how word order, punctuation, and grammatical choices shape meaning. Sentence Revising builds syntactic awareness, but it also boosts students' confidence in unpacking complex sentences they read and crafting more effective sentences in their own writing. See the Tried and True Strategy for a lesson that connects the novel students are reading in class with Sentence Revising.

Tried and True Strategy by Shea Kerkhoff

Lesson: Teaching Pronouns and Antecedents through Sentence Revising

Context: Grade 9 English class in Knightdale, North Carolina

I do this mini-lesson during our reading of *To Kill a Mockingbird*. The following isn't a script that I follow word by word, but it gives an idea of the nature of the direct instruction and questions I would implement.

The novel *To Kill a Mockingbird* begins with the adult narrator reflecting back on her childhood. As the adult narrator, the author begins with a complex style of writing. Using this complex style helps to show the difference in perspective between the adult perspective of the narrator in the present and the child perspective of her character in the past. Read these first two sentences from *To Kill a Mockingbird*, "When he was nearly thirteen, my brother Jem got his arm badly broken at the elbow. When it healed, and Jem's fears of never being able to play football were assuaged, he was seldom self-conscious about his injury."

To make the writing more clear to us as readers, let's match the pronouns to the antecedents. The first pronoun is *he*. Highlight it in green. Who is the word *he* referring to? Highlight your answer in green. The second pronoun is *it*. Highlight *it* in yellow. Also, highlight in yellow what *it* is referring to. When we want our writing to be clear, we should not use a pronoun before naming the antecedent. Rewrite the sentence to be more clear.

Possible answers:

When my brother Jem was nearly thirteen, he got his arm badly broken at the elbow.
My brother Jem got his arm badly broken at the elbow when he was nearly thirteen.

The second sentence breaks the same rule. Highlight the pronoun *it* in yellow. Also, highlight in yellow what it is referring to. When we want our writing to be clear, we should not use a pronoun before naming the antecedent. Rewrite the sentence to be more clear.

Possible answers:

When his injury healed, and Jem's fears of never being able to play football were assuaged, he was seldom self-conscious about it.
When Jem's elbow healed, and Jem's fears of never being able to play football were assuaged, he was seldom self-conscious about it.

Now, try to match the pronouns to the antecedents in these sentences where the author introduces her other loved ones to us. "We lived on the main residential street in town—Atticus, Jem and I, plus Calpurnia our cook. Jem and I found our father satisfactory: he played with us, read to us, and treated us with courteous detachment." How would you rewrite the sentences using a clear and concise style? What do the different styles of writing affect you as the reader? What is lost and what is gained?

Reading and Writing to Build Knowledge

In order to gain broad and deep vocabulary knowledge, students need to read a lot, access new knowledge through multiple modalities, and engage in talking and writing about new concepts. Although the main idea of this book has been to teach reading and writing, reading and writing are also tools to learn new concepts. Let's look at both reading and writing in turn.

Reading is a way to build knowledge, but only if the reader can access the text. Before reading complex, content-rich texts, teachers can preview vocabulary, build **background knowledge**, set a purpose for reading, and model a strategy that students can use when reading. During reading, teachers can provide scaffolds to support students' knowledge-building. After reading, students can write, talk, and reflect to extend their thinking and reinforce their learning.

Before

Too often, students are given instructions like this. Read the following passage and answer the questions.

> Two statistics that are frequently used to identify specific areas of misfit in a model are standardized residuals and modification indices. A residual reflects the difference between the observed sample value and model-implied estimate for each indicator variance and covariance (e.g., the deviation between the sample covariance and the model-implied covariance of indicators X1 and X2). Modification indices should be used as a guide and not the sole basis for eliminating areas of misfit in a model.

1 What statistics can identify misfit in a model?

2 How should modification indices be used?

Were you able to answer the questions? Did this help you understand the content? You might be able to answer the questions, but you probably didn't learn anything from the passage. We want to provide learners with opportunities to use words in context in a way that actually helps them understand the concepts behind the words. Previewing and talking about words before reading helps students build background knowledge, make connections, and better understand the text as they read.

Like the example above, my experience in school was reading the assigned text and answering the questions at the end. About halfway through high school, I discovered that if I read the questions first, that helped me set a purpose for reading, and I could answer the questions with greater understanding. I now know that this is a research-based strategy. As teachers, we can scaffold students' meaning-making by setting a purpose for reading and pointing students' attention to the most important parts.

Here are a few before-reading strategies you can use to help students tap into what they already know and get clear on *why* they're reading—both key steps for knowledge building.

Anticipation Guide

An Anticipation Guide is an instructional strategy that helps students make connections with the text. The Anticipation Guide presents statements related to the text, some of which may be true and others may not. Students decide whether each statement is true or false with no consequence for being wrong. The goal isn't to get the right answers before reading, but rather to set a purpose for reading. The Anticipation Guide activates prior knowledge by prompting students to take a stance on key ideas and builds curiosity about how the text will challenge or confirm their thinking. See an example of this strategy in Chapter 7.

Quick Write

In a Quick Write, students are free to write their initial thoughts about a question or prompt. The idea is not to worry about grammar or spelling, but to activate knowledge and make personal connections to what they will be learning. Quick Writes usually range from two to five minutes. Students then share what they wrote, providing the opportunity to use vocabulary words in writing and speaking. Because students bring a variety of experiences and knowledge to the class, sharing what they know helps expand and enrich everyone's background knowledge.

Concept Map

Similar to Semantic Mapping, a Concept Map (sometimes called a Mind Map) is a visual tool that shows relationships between ideas, usually organized with a main concept in the center that is connected to related terms. It helps students organize their thinking and make connections between the terms and concepts that they're learning. As a vocabulary- and knowledge-building activity, I would have the class co-create a Concept Map together. Either I would record their ideas and connections on the whiteboard or have students come to the board whenever they thought of an idea so that they could add it themselves. Creating the Concept Map as a whole class provides opportunities for students to remember prior learning or gain the background knowledge needed to better understand new content and make meaningful connections as they read.

Frontloading with Images

Frontloading with Images is a strategy where teachers introduce key concepts or vocabulary through carefully selected visuals before diving into a text or lesson. This approach taps into students' visual processing strengths, builds background knowledge, and sparks curiosity—especially for those who might struggle with language alone and for multilingual learners. Research shows that pairing visuals with words improves comprehension by activating prior knowledge and supporting information processing through both verbal and nonverbal systems (Paivio, 2014; Saletta, 2018). It's a simple move that can make complex content more accessible and memorable for all learners. For example, to introduce a unit on jazz, the teacher shows photos of iconic jazz musicians performing, along with images of their instruments and venues

Tried and True by Lynne Petersen

Lesson: Building Knowledge about Weather through Frontloading with Images

Context: Seventh-grade science class in Raleigh, North Carolina

When teaching seventh-grade science to striving readers, I would spend the first day of a new unit trying to activate prior knowledge to help with new vocabulary. This would include a Gallery Walk of pictures from the unit. Students had to look at all the images, state what they thought the image was, and if it was connected to any other images on the walk. For example, when teaching weather, I placed photos of weather occurrences (tornado, hurricane, water cycle, clouds, weather map). After the Gallery Walk, the students had five minutes with a partner to compare notes about their Gallery Walk. We would then review each item as a class. I would state the word, show the picture on the board, and ask: Who has heard this word before? Where have you heard it? Do you recognize any prefixes, suffixes, or root words? Do you have an example of the word? What do you think a good definition could be? Students would share their answers. I then gave them a vocabulary sheet with columns: word, student definition, teacher definition, example, and picture. Next, they filled out their definition. Once they were finished, I shared my definition, which they wrote on the sheet. They completed the rest of the vocabulary chart, taped it in their interactive notebooks, and folded the chart to only be able to see the word. Each day, we added two to four new words to the chart until we had all the vocabulary for that unit. We also reviewed our previously learned words. Students worked together to quiz each other.

like the Cotton Club, to pique students' interest and set the historical and cultural context. For an example from a science classroom, see the Tried and True lesson from Ms. Petersen in North Carolina.

Possible Sentences

With this strategy, the teacher gives students key words from the text, and students make predictions about what they think the text will be about. For example, if I gave you the words spacecraft, lunar, crater, and orbit, what do predict the text is about? The teacher can start by projecting the words for the whole class to see and model the prediction steps. The first couple of times a class tries this prediction strategy, the teacher can think aloud as they make connections between the words to create a sentence by saying things like: *This makes me think of ...* so *I think the text is going to be about ...* Then, students volunteer their predictions, using the words in their sentences.

For more practice, the students can be placed in groups of three or four, and each person in the group given a different quote from the text that contains one of the key words. Each student reads their quote and jots down a possible sentence using Sentence Stems such as *I predict ... because the text/ author ...* Students then talk in their small group, and the teacher can monitor the conversations to make sure there are no misconceptions that could lead students down the wrong path when they begin to read. View these slides for an example of Possible Sentences as well as other strategies in practice by following the QR code in Figure 8.3 or this link (https://bit.ly/beforereading).

During

It's no surprise that active reading enhances our ability to learn from text. Did you know that writing about texts also enhances our ability to learn? The following strategies help students engage with the words, texts, and ideas for knowledge building.

Alphaboxes

Alphaboxes act as a notecatcher for words while reading. For example, when reading "Forces on a Baseball" on NASA's Aerodynamics of Baseball website, I filled in the boxes shown in Table 8.2. My objective was not

Figure 8.3

Table 8.2 Alphaboxes Example

Acceleration—speeding up	Ballistic—science of projectiles	C	Drag—force that acts opposite of motion and slows an object down
Experimental and experimentally—determined by an experiment	Force—push or pull	Gravitation - force that pulls objects toward center of Earth	H
I	J	Knuckleball	Lift—perpendicular to motion
Mass—amount of matter	Newton's law of motion	O	Perpendicular—lines that look like this + or this T
Quantity—amount	Rotation—turning	Symmetric—same	Trajectory—path
U	Velocity—speed	Weight—force exerted on an object pulling it toward Earth's center, related to mass and gravity	XYZ

necessarily to fill in all of the boxes, but to record words that I would want to remember so that I could use them in a class discussion about the text. Check out the Tried and True Strategy by Sharon Wright on the next page for a different way to use this versatile strategy.

Word Journal

Keeping a Word Journal is an approach to learning vocabulary that invites students to self-select the words that they are interested in learning. Students

Tried and True Strategy by Sharon Wright

Lesson: Alphaboxes for Final Exam Prep

Context: Seventh-grade math in Chalmers, Indiana

I have my students use Alphaboxes to review the vocabulary for the year before the final exam. I have them work in groups of three, and each group has a paper with the four by six ABC's table. They add as many vocabulary words as they can in ten minutes, but only one word per box. They can use their notes, their textbook, and any resource they can find. For added fun, we use the Scattergories point system, where it doesn't count if another group has the same word or double points for alliteration (e.g., order of operations, adjacent angle). The group with the most points wins a prize.

can identify words from texts, both in and out of school, and collect the words in a personal journal. There are digital templates available or an old-school composition book works just fine (https://sites.google.com/mpsaz.org/slideprojects/digital-journal). Some teachers may be concerned about giving students control over their own vocabulary learning, but a research study in a middle school found: "Regardless of reading ability, students seemed to be capable of self-selecting critical terms while reading an expository passage" (Harmon et al., 2008, p. 45).

It Says / I Say

This strategy integrates reading and writing by having students make a T-Chart. On the left side, they label the column "It Says," and they take notes about the important ideas in the reading using the discipline-specific terms from the text. On the right side, they label the column "I Say" and respond to the text by interpreting the ideas into their own words, making connections, and drawing conclusions. Students can turn and talk with a partner about what they are writing at checkpoints throughout the reading.

Sketch and Label

During reading, students can draw a visual representation of the concepts in the text and then label the drawing using both the vocabulary words from the text and their own understanding. Students can sketch a model, a picture, or something similar to a Concept Map to support sense-making while

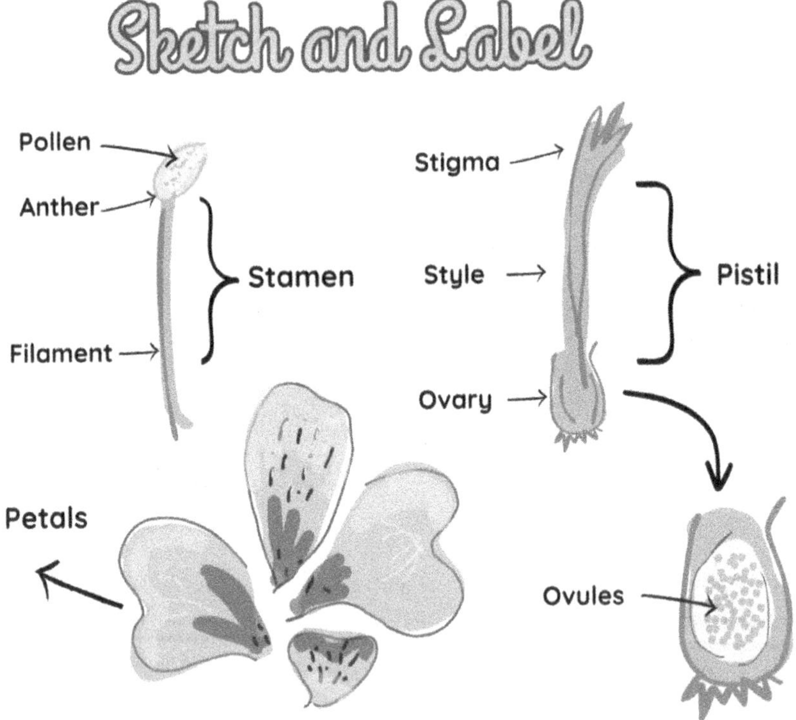

Figure 8.4 Sketch and Label Example.

reading (Hattan et al., 2024). Sketch and Label works well for short texts, like a mathematical word problem, as well as with longer texts, like a science chapter describing plant parts and functions (see Figure 8.4 for an example). I've also used this strategy in English to have students sketch the setting in "The Most Dangerous Game" and label the different parts of the island.

After

After reading a complex, content-rich text, students can engage in writing and talking in order to extend their thinking further.

List, Group, Label

It's no surprise that this strategy begins by having students collaboratively list all of the important features, characteristics, or ideas about the focus word. The focus word can be a technical term or the main idea of the text. The students then group words from their list to form categories and label each category. The purpose is not to select the "right" words but on the conversations, reasoning, and synthesis of ideas that emerge throughout the process.

Engaging in discussions about vocabulary encourages students to draw connections between words, deepen their understanding, and gain new insights. This type of meaning-making enhances comprehension and strengthens retention of information. Additionally, as teachers observe these discussions, they can provide clarification and check for understanding.

Word Tournament

The Word Tournament routine engages vocabulary from a text in an interactive way. Students begin by choosing 15–20 significant words from the text. In small groups, they collaborate to narrow their list down to eight words, which are positioned on the far left side of a tournament-style bracket. Through discussion, they determine which four words will move to the next round, followed by selecting two finalists, and ultimately, a single "winning" word. Each group then shares with the whole class the reasoning behind their final choice. As with List, Group, Label, there are no right or wrong words to choose. The purpose is to have discussions about the content using the discipline-specific vocabulary.

Conclusion

Learning vocabulary is more than just memorizing definitions—it's about seeing, hearing, and using words in meaningful ways. Research shows that students benefit from explicit vocabulary instruction on word meanings when that instruction is contextualized to the reading, listening, speaking, and writing happening as part of the content learning objectives. In addition to direct teaching of word meanings, rich vocabulary instruction includes students using vocabulary words in discussions and writing, and learning word solving strategies that they can transfer to other texts. It's important to remember that accumulating a vast vocabulary is not the goal of education. It's a means to an end. The goal is for students to have the language needed in order to build knowledge about the world and to express their knowledge and their experiences with others.

More to Explore

- Listen to this Classroom Caffeine podcast about language development with secondary students: https://www.classroomcaffeine.com/guests/dianna-townsend

- Check out linguist Lyn Stone's video on Morphology: https://www.youtube.com/watch?v=Sjf9G_KtHj4

- This blog by a middle-grades teacher in Singapore has great ideas for teaching vocabulary that are low prep: https://www.middleweb.com/46708/low-prep-and-no-prep-vocabulary-activities/

- AdLit.org has even more strategies to learn about: https://www.adlit.org/in-the-classroom/strategies

Reflect

Look over your Alphaboxes. Which words/concepts are new to you? Choose one of the new words/concepts, and use the Frayer Model or Concept Map to explore the word in more depth.

Discuss

Questions for discussion to learn from and with each other:

- What are some do's and don'ts for teaching vocabulary?
- What is the relationship between knowledge and reading? How can you apply your understanding of the relationship between knowledge and comprehension?
- What strategies did you learn that you intend to use in your reading or teaching?

References

Agarwal, P. K., & Bain, P. M. (2019). *Powerful teaching: Unleash the science of learning*. Jossey-Bass.

Beck, I. L., McKeown, M. G., & Kucan, L. (2013). *Bringing words to life: Robust vocabulary instruction* (2nd ed.). Guilford.

Beers, K. (2023). *When kids can't read: What teachers can do* (2nd ed.). Heinemann.

Cervetti, G. N., Fitzgerald, M. S., Hiebert, E. H., & Hebert, M. (2023). Meta-analysis examining the impact of vocabulary instruction on vocabulary knowledge and skill. *Reading Psychology, 44*(6), 672–709. https://doi.org/10.1080/02702711.2023.2179146

Fisher, D., & Frey, N. (2015). Teacher modeling using complex informational texts. *The Reading Teacher, 69*(1), 63–9. https://doi.org/10.1002/trtr.1372

Graham, S., Bruch, J., Fitzgerald, J., Friedrich, L., Furgeson, J., Greene, K., Kim, J., Lyskawa, J., Olson, C.B., & Smither Wulsin, C. (2016). *Teaching secondary students to write effectively* (NCEE Report 2017-4002). National Center for Education Evaluation and Regional Assistance (NCEE), Institute of Education Sciences, U.S. Department of Education. https://ies.ed.gov/ncee/WWC/PracticeGuide/22

Graves, M. F., Baumann, J. F., Blachowicz, C. L. Z., Manyak, P., Bates, A., Cieply, C., Davis, J. R., & Von Gunten, H. (2014). Words, words, everywhere, but which ones do we teach? *The Reading Teacher, 67*(5), 333–46. https://doi.org/10.1002/trtr.1228

Harmon, J. M., Wood, K. D., Hedrick, W. B., & Gress, M. (2008). "Pick a word—not just any word": Using vocabulary self-selection with expository texts. *Middle School Journal, 40*(1), 43–52. https://doi.org/10.1080/00940771.2008.11461664

Hattan, C., Alexander, P. A., & Lupo, S. M. (2024). Leveraging what students know to make sense of texts: What the research says about prior knowledge activation. *Review of Educational Research, 94*(1), 73–111. https://doi.org/10.3102/00346543221148478

Kearns, D. (2024, December 11) *How to help students read long words* [Video]. YouTube. https://youtu.be/NLQ_uDU6dJ8?si=Gb3Hd6NloPqOJIS_

Krishnan, J., Friedrich, L., Sailors, M., Cole, M., & Howlett, H. (2025). Meaning-based, code-based, and vocabulary-based instruction in middle and high school classrooms: The case for attention to all three. *Journal of Adolescent & Adult Literacy, 68*(4), 400–7. https://doi.org/10.1002/jaal.1410

Paivio, A. (2014). Intelligence, dual coding theory, and the brain. *Intelligence, 47*, 141–58. https://doi.org/10.1016/j.intell.2014.09.002

Pearson, P. D., Palincsar, A. S., Biancarosa, G., & Berman, A. I. (2020). Reaping the rewards of the Reading for Understanding Initiative. *National Academy of Education.*

Recht, D. R., & Leslie, L. (1988). Effect of prior knowledge on good and poor readers' memory of text. *Journal of Educational Psychology, 80*(1), 16–20. https://psycnet.apa.org/doi/10.1037/0022-0663.80.1.16

Saletta, M. (2018). Reading disabilities in adolescents and adults. *Language, Speech, and Hearing Services in Schools, 49*(4), 787–97. https://doi.org/10.1044/2018_lshss-dyslc-18-0005

Literature Cited

Anderson, openers humiliate India as England dominate Day 1 | India tour of England, 2021. (2021, August 25). https://www.cricket.com/news/anderson-openers-humiliate-india-as-england-dominate-day-1-1629915308841

Connell, R. (1924). *The most dangerous game.* Collier's.

Lee, H. (1960). *To kill a mockingbird.* Lippincott.

NASA. (n.d.). *Forces on a baseball.* Glenn Research Center. https://www1.grc.nasa.gov/beginners-guide-to-aeronautics/forces-on-a-baseball/

Schwen, L. O., Schenk, A., Kreutz, C., Timmer, J., Bartolomé Rodríguez, M. M., Kuepfer, L., & Preusser, T. (2015). Representative sinusoids for hepatic four-scale pharmacokinetics simulations. *PLoS One, 10*(7), Article e0133653. https://pmc.ncbi.nlm.nih.gov/articles/PMC4519332/

Making Meaning Through Text

9

According to the National Assessment of Education Progress (NAEP) 2022 Reading Framework, reading comprehension is a complex process shaped by cognitive, social, and cultural influences, including readers' abilities to:

- Engage with **text** in print and **multimodal** forms;
- Employ personal resources including foundational reading skills, language, knowledge, and motivations; and
- Extract, construct, integrate, critique, and apply meaning in activities across a range of social and cultural contexts.

However, in 2022, just thirty-one percent of eighth-grade students performed at or above the proficient level on the NAEP reading assessment, indicating that a large percentage of adolescents are below proficient in reading. This statistic propels headlines, like this one in the *Scientific American* that says "Kids Can't Read" (Blank, 2023). However, what would be more accurate would be to say that the majority of readers are not able to extract, construct, integrate, critique, and apply meaning from texts across contexts. Readers might be able to say all of the words in a text, but not be able to comprehend what the text is saying. This indicates a need for educators across grade levels and content areas to engage students in more and better comprehension instruction.

And, there is hope! Research illuminates promising practices. To improve comprehension, **meta-analysis** research has found that instruction should include experiences that increase both *word* knowledge and *world* knowledge and that engage adolescents in meaningful discussions about texts (Vaughn et al., 2022). In other words, when students read and talk about interesting, content-rich, complex texts, their comprehension improves! We'll dig into more specifics throughout this chapter.

Literacy Strategy: Sketchnotes

Taking notes while reading is one way to monitor your understanding and to be able to summarize the reading along the way, two important skills that support comprehension. Another skill that supports comprehension is visualizing what you read as you are reading. A great strategy that combines note-taking with visualizing is called Sketchnotes. Sketchnotes combine drawing and writing to create a visual representation of the reading. You can use handwriting fonts, arrows, symbols, doodles, and colors in a way that is creative and personalized to you. For students who are multilingual, I encourage them to use multiple languages in their Sketchnotes. If that applies to you, you are invited to use your full linguistic repertoire!

Preview Key Vocabulary

comprehension: making meaning of written, spoken, or viewed text
comprehension strategy: a tool that assists readers in making meaning
multimodal: made up of more than one mode: written, visual, and/or audio
schema: mental network of information

What Is Reading Comprehension?

Helping students engage with and make sense of content-rich, complex texts is at the heart of building strong reading **comprehension**. The famous RAND model (Snow, 2002) describes comprehension as "the process of simultaneously extracting and constructing meaning through interaction and involvement with written language" (p. 11). We define reading comprehension as the making of meaning through textual, visual, and/or graphic communication between four components: interaction of the reader, the text, and the activity within the sociocultural context (Figure 9.1).

The Reader

The cognitive processes within the reader's mind include foundational reading skills (e.g., word recognition and fluency), knowledge

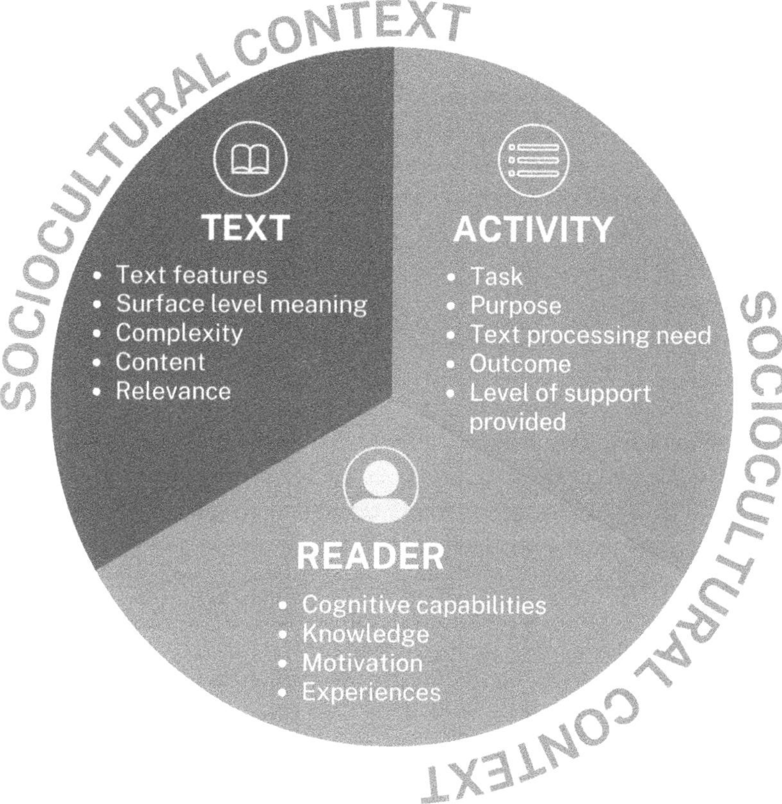

Figure 9.1 Reading Comprehension.

(e.g., **background knowledge**, content knowledge, and knowledge about texts and reading), and executive function (e.g., memory, attention, and retrieval). Reading is influenced not only by cognitive processes but also by physical, emotional, and sensory experiences. The concept of the reader as *embodied* suggests that reading comprehension isn't just happening in the mind—it's a full-body experience. Research shows that posture, movement, and even the tactile experience of holding a book can shape how readers engage with and make meaning from a text (Glenberg, 2011). For example, physically interacting with text—such as highlighting, annotating, or turning pages—can enhance memory and understanding. Similarly, emotional states and bodily sensations can affect attention and **motivation**. The reader may feel healthy and energized or sick and tired, impacting their capability to read.

The Text

The text refers to what is being read, whether it's a short story, a science article, or a math word problem. Some texts are straightforward and considerate to the reader, whereas others are complex with tricky text structure, unfamiliar vocabulary, and abstract ideas. These features can make comprehension easier or harder depending on the reader. For example, a student might breeze through a graphic novel but struggle with a dense informational article.

The text also refers to the modality—whether print, digital, or multimodal. Research shows that online reading comprehension involves more than just traditional reading skills—it also requires students to navigate hyperlinks, evaluate sources, and integrate information from multiple digital texts. Skilled online readers must be able to locate relevant information, determine its credibility, and synthesize it to build understanding. Because digital environments often include distractions and nonlinear structures, students need strong critical thinking and **self-regulation** strategies to comprehend effectively online. Because print texts have a stable layout and physical structure, readers can use visual–spatial memory to recall where information appears on a page—such as remembering that a key idea was on the top-left of a right-hand page—which may support comprehension and information retrieval for some individuals (van Moort et al., 2025; Mangen et al., 2013).

The Activity

Now let's zoom in on the activity—the purpose and task behind the reading. The activity is all about *why* students are reading and *what* they're expected to do with the text. It can be externally imposed or internally generated. Are they reading to find specific information? To enjoy a story? To compare two authors' perspectives? The purpose shapes how a reader approaches the text and which strategies they use. For example, skimming a webpage for a quick fact is different from analyzing a poem for theme and tone. When students know why they're reading, they're more likely to stay engaged and get something meaningful out of it. However, if the reader does not fully accept the mandated purpose or finds no relevance in the text, they may not read purposefully, impacting comprehension. In this way, the reader, text, and activity components are **reciprocal** in relationship.

The Sociocultural Context

The sociocultural context is basically everything swirling around a reader's life that shapes how they make sense of a text—culture, community values, lived experiences, and even what's been trending in their corner of TikTok. It's the backdrop that influences not just what students know, but how they interpret what they read and which connections they make. Ignoring it is like trying to understand a joke without knowing the punchline's cultural reference—it just falls flat. Here's a joke that lands in Australia but usually gets blank looks in the United States:

> **Q**: *Why did the kangaroo stop drinking coffee?*
> **A**: *Because it made him too **jumped-up**!*

Australians use the slang "jumped-up" to mean over-excited. Americans don't use this slang, so the humor feels a bit contrived. When we recognize the role of sociocultural context, we can choose texts, prompts, and discussions that connect to students' worlds, making comprehension more than just **decoding** words—it becomes making meaning that actually *means* something to them.

In the RAND model, comprehension is dependent on all four components, meaning that in order to answer the question, *Did the reader comprehend this text?* We would need to know the activity and context in order to say yes or no. As the RAND model shows, reading is an interaction between social and cognitive elements, where students' understanding of texts evolves from their personal experiences to a broader understanding of the world around them. It's crucial for students to move past learning isolated literacy skills and to see how these fit into their real-life experiences. Research by Langer (2002) discovered that the best literacy programs link students' lives and background knowledge to the texts they read and encourage conversations among students to build these connections. These conversations and connections help students build comprehension and build a mental network of information, called **schema**.

Let's break down each of the four components in the RAND model with an illustration to show how this works. Let's say that the reader is David, who has solid foundational reading skills but little prior knowledge about the activity he is about to attempt—cooking. The activity component refers to the task or purpose for reading. In our illustration, David is reading a recipe for enchiladas that he wants to prepare with his mother for family dinner. Because the literacy activity is happening in the context of preparing for that night's dinner, there is a motivation and sense of urgency for David to make meaning from the text. Because it is something that he volunteers to do, not something assigned to him by a teacher or boss, this is an internally generated activity. The text is a handwritten recipe with measurements and technical terms organized as a process of steps, with no images.

The larger sociocultural context is that David and his mother came from a wealthy background where they did not cook and never observed other people cooking either. They now find themselves having to learn with little schema to draw from. David can read every word on the paper, but he is not able to complete the activity because he is unfamiliar with the technical terminology, particularly the phrase, "fold in the cheese," which he interprets as meaning to fold slices like paper and isn't sure what he is supposed to do with the "broken" (that is, shredded) cheese that his mother bought.

Sound familiar? You might recognize this hilarious scene from the series *Schitt's Creek*. Without having had the experience of seeing someone cook enchiladas, David had no knowledge from which to draw a conclusion about what fold might mean in this instance. Comprehension being tied to technical vocabulary or content-specific processes is quite common in the context of adolescents reading academic texts too.

In grades 4–12, students are reading and writing to build knowledge about the world across a variety of subjects. As students read grade-level academic texts, they retrieve and build on the knowledge they already have (i.e., background knowledge) in order to build new knowledge in the content area they are studying. Readers store knowledge in a web-like mental framework, called schema, which connects and organizes information in a way that can be retrieved when called upon.

What is tricky about background knowledge is that sometimes an author assumes readers have knowledge that they do not. When this is the case, teachers can provide strategies and scaffolds to help students access the text. Students with a strong knowledge base and well-developed **comprehension strategies** are able to more easily use literacy as a tool for learning, which means they keep building more and more knowledge that becomes a bigger and bigger storehouse of background knowledge. The bigger their knowledge base, the more complex texts they can access.

Scaffolding Content Area Texts

The first step in being able to scaffold content area texts is to identify the difficult or tricky parts of the text. I find the Complexity Rubric for Informational Texts helpful for this step. The **rubric** outlines four dimensions of text complexity: (a) text structure, (b) language, (c) author's purpose, and (d) knowledge demands (see rubric at https://achievethecore.org/content/upload/SCASS_Info_Text_Complexity_Qualitative_Measures_Info_Rubric_2.8.pdf.pdf; CCSSO, n.d.).

- Text Structure—How is the text organized? Are the text structures used easy to discern? Are there clear connections and transitions between ideas or does the reader have to do more work to connect the ideas? How closely do the text features, illustrations, and graphics align with the main text? Do they act as a companion to the text or do they add new information?

- Language Features—How closely does the text adhere to students' everyday language? Is the language more contemporary and conversational or is it more archaic or discipline specific? Is the language explicit and straightforward or does it include abstract, ironic, or figurative language? How complex is the sentence structure?

- Author's Purpose/Meaning—Is the purpose explicitly stated or must it be inferred? Is there a single, well-defined purpose or are there multiple levels of meaning that may be more abstract?

- Knowledge Demands on the Reader—What sort of experiential knowledge and/or subject-specific knowledge would be necessary to understand the text? What cultural knowledge, world knowledge, or literary knowledge is required? How advanced is the vocabulary?

Then, depending on what makes the text complex, we can alert students to the difficult parts ahead of time and model how to tackle the text.

Exposing Text Structure

For example, sequential or chronological are the simplest text structures because it's the way we naturally tell stories: "First he said that he was going to pick me up, but then he never showed, so I texted him, and you will not believe what he said next." Sometimes authors play with structure in order to add interest to the story, and this may or may not need to be previewed with your students depending on whether it would ruin the enjoyment of the reading. At other times, however, the subject matter is just too complex to use a simple structure, and therefore, the author needs to use a more complex structure or even a combination of structures in order to best communicate the information.

Figure 9.2

For example, a typical peer-reviewed research article in a scientific journal uses at least three organizational structures. The introduction usually uses a problem/solution organizational structure by presenting a problem and then explaining how the research will solve that problem. The methods section usually describes the sequence of steps the researcher undertook. The results section might utilize cause and effect or compare and contrast or even both to organize what the researchers discovered. The conclusion could harken back to the problem and solution structure introduced in the beginning.

Before reading a scientific article, I first chunk the larger text into these sections for the students. We preview the structure that the author is using to organize the section before we read. We review what students know about that organizational structure, activate their schema, and build reading knowledge about what to look for in that section. In the methods, for example, the reader should look for transparency as to what steps the researcher took. To review **patterns of organization** that create common text structures, view these slides by scanning the QR code in Figure 9.2 or following the link (https://bit.ly/textstru).

Previewing Language, Vocabulary, and Sentence Structure

If the tricky part of the text is the language (e.g., conventionality, vocabulary, or sentence structure), then I would preview the language structure instead of organizational structure. Although it is not necessary to preview every word students might not know in the text, it is important to preview the essential vocabulary needed to understand the content objective for the lesson. As for sentence structure, choosing a couple of tricky sentences to unpack before reading can help model how to approach other complex sentences they encounter during the reading.

For example, I would project a sentence from a letter from Abigail Adams, and have the class work through it together using the Juicy Sentence Protocol (Whole, Part, Whole; Cucchiara, 2019) by first asking, *What do you see in this sentence as a whole that makes it complex?*

I have sometimes been ready to think that the passion for Liberty cannot be Eaquelly Strong in the Breasts of those who have been accustomed to deprive their fellow Creatures of theirs. (Massachusetts Historical Society, n.d.)

Students might notice that there are words with capital letters, that equally is spelled weird, and that it is a long sentence. We would then check to see if there were any introductory phrases or any clauses that we could separate from the rest of the sentence, and figure out what each part says literally. Next, we would read the sentence back together as a whole to talk about what the author means, taking into consideration figurative or abstract language.

In Abigail Adams' letter, "strong in the breasts" is figurative language referring to a deep-rooted passion and "their fellow Creatures" is abstract but considering the context probably refers to women (Massachusetts Historical Society, n.d.). As to previewing the vocabulary, students might not be familiar with the meaning of the word *deprived*, and that word is essential to being able to comprehend the sentence, so I would supply a student-friendly definition.

Preparing for Author's Purpose

At the risk of oversimplification, determining the author's purpose can be as easy as P.I.E. (persuade, inform, or entertain). What can be particularly difficult about complex texts is that the authors' purpose is not explicit. To scaffold texts where the authors' purpose is implicit, teachers can read the texts together with students in chunks, pausing at the end of each chunk to discuss what the purpose and main idea of the section is. Students can then practice creating headings collaboratively to continue building their comprehension skills.

Tried and True Strategy by Shea Kerkhoff

Strategy Name: Creating Headings for Complex Texts

Context: Literacy for Adolescent Learners class in St. Louis, Missouri

Our class read the *Washington Post* article "We Mythologize Highways but They've Damaged Communities of Color" by Ryan Reft. What makes this article complex is that the author's purpose and main ideas are not explicit, and there are no text features that help illuminate the purpose. Specifically, there are no headings or subheadings.

To scaffold comprehension of the text, I prepared for the lesson by chunking the article into manageable sections. I also copied and pasted the article into a Google Doc, with a hyperlink to the original, so that we could manipulate the sections. To introduce the article, I began by connecting the article to students' lives by asking *What does getting your driver's license mean to you? What does it represent?* I then connected the answers of "independence" and "freedom" to the word "mythologizing" in the author's title, explaining that other words for mythologizing are *idealizing* and *exaggerating.* I then point to the text feature that names the genre of the article as "perspective" and ask students to predict what the author's perspective about highways is going to be.

I explain that I have chunked the article into smaller sections that we will read and discuss one at a time to determine what the author's purpose and main ideas are. Students silently read the first section and then to prompt discussion I ask: *What is the author trying to tell us here? What is the main purpose of this section?* After class discussion, students turn to a shoulder partner to create a heading for that chunk of text that makes the main idea explicit. I walk around, checking the headings to make sure that students are catching on, and ask a pair to share out their particularly compelling heading. The students then read the next section silently, and then I ask: *How does this connect to what the author said earlier? What is the author trying to tell us here?* Then, students partner to write a heading, and we continue in this fashion through the article. Example headings created include: *Cars Became Symbol of Freedom* and *Families of Color Displaced by Highways.*

After reading and discussing the article, each student completes an exit ticket with the following:

> Go back to your original prediction. Were you correct? Rewrite your sentence here as a summary sentence, correcting anything from your prediction that was not in the article. As an option, you can use the following Sentence Stem: The purpose of this article was to [persuade, inform, or entertain] the reader about …

For students who need more scaffolding, the teacher can create headings for each chunk that name the main idea, and students can create subheadings for each paragraph or even hashtags if writing hashtags connects to a literacy the student already possesses.

What's especially complex is when an author purposely tricks readers by using the conventions of a **genre** traditionally used for informational purposes to persuade or entertain the reader. Take this November 30, 2005 headline, "CIA Realizes It's Been Using Black Highlighters All These Years." The headline is from *The Onion*, which plays with the journalism genre in an ironic way with the purpose of being funny, but it takes the ability of the reader to think critically or to have the background knowledge that the publication is satirical to realize what is happening. Although the teacher should not take away the pleasure of figuring out what is going on, they can alert students by reminding them to pay attention to the author's purpose when reading.

Activating and Building Background Knowledge

As mentioned earlier, sometimes the author—myself included—assumes that the reader will have background knowledge that they do not have. That means that there may be topics in this book that I breeze over that you wish I would have explained in more depth.

As teachers, we can frame this as an author problem, not a reader problem, which can shield our students from some embarrassment if they are not able to meet the knowledge demands of the text. Before reading a text that I believe students may not have sufficient background knowledge to comprehend, I draw a Concept Map (also called a Mind Map) on the board with the topic in the middle. I have students volunteer to add what they already know about the topic. Because students bring different background knowledge to the table, discussing the topic activates schema and gets everyone on the same page before we begin reading. Activating schema is helpful, but it's easier to show you than to tell you why. Read the following passage:

> With the hocked gems financing him our hero bravely defied all scornful laughter that tried to prevent his scheme. Your eyes deceive he had said. An egg, not a table, correctly typifies this unexplored planet. Now three sturdy sisters sought proof. Forging along, sometimes through calm vastness, yet more often through turbulent peaks and valleys, days became weeks as many doubters spread fearful rumors about the edge. At last, from nowhere, welcome winged creatures appeared signifying momentous success. (Dooling & Lachman, 1971, p. 217)

It's hard to comprehend. Take another look at the paragraph, but this time I'll activate your background knowledge by telling you it's about Christopher Columbus.

Without that context, the passage probably seemed confusing. While you might have understood the vocabulary and sentence structure—and maybe even guessed it described an exploration—you likely missed many of the deeper references. But once you knew it was about Columbus, you could use your background knowledge to go back and make sense of it. The "hocked gems" are Queen Isabella of Spain's jewelry. The "unexplored planet" is Earth that is round like an egg not flat like a table. The "three sturdy sisters" are the boats named the Nina, Pinta, and Santa Maria.

Knowing the topic activates your schema about Columbus. That means you're mentally prepared to retrieve and process information related to him. Think of it like an operating system. When you launch an app, the operating system loads only the drivers and libraries that app needs. When you encounter a topic like Columbus, your brain "loads" the Columbus schema, activating bits of knowledge about ships, sponsors, and geography. Activating schema not only prepares you for what you're about to read, but it also helps you make connections that deepen understanding and improve overall comprehension.

Reading Comprehension Strategies

We can teach students comprehension strategies that work across different texts in the content areas. Whereas scaffolding is what teachers do to help students access grade-level texts, comprehension strategies are actions readers can transfer to other texts to help make meaning. The goal with strategies is that teachers will explicitly explain and model the strategies, provide supported practice, and eventually, students will have a toolbox of strategies and the ability to apply the right strategy at the right time whenever they need them. Although there are hundreds of strategies to choose from, high-leverage strategies engage students in the following active reading skills: questioning, summarizing, visualizing, monitoring understanding, and talking about texts. In each of the sections below, I highlight a few evidence-based strategies that have worked in my classroom and across content areas.

Questioning

Questioning as a **comprehension strategy** includes asking and answering questions in order to transform reading from a passive activity into an active exploration. Writing their own questions before reading sets a purpose for reading, during reading signals confusion and prompts readers to seek clarification, and after reading promotes discussion and evaluation of texts. Answering questions helps readers process and explain ideas in their own words, reinforcing comprehension.

Discussion Cubes

Discussion Cubes bring an element of fun and chance to answering questions. Teachers can make Discussion Cubes out of cardstock or buy soft photo cubes with pockets in which to insert the questions. In pairs or small groups, students roll the cube like a die and have to answer the question rolled. They take turns rolling until time runs out.

Question the Author

Question the Author is a simple strategy that invites students to discuss the text in a way that disrupts the idea that authors have all the right answers. The researchers (Beck et al., 1996) who developed the strategy describe it as follows:

> The kind of narrow, retrieval-based questions that traditionally accompany school lessons serve more to limit than to activate meaning-getting. The queries used in Questioning the Author are designed to invite "understanding, interpretation, and elaboration" by having students explore the meaning of what is written in the texts they read. The intent of interrogating the ideas in a text through dialogue with the author is to "depose" the authority of the text by actualizing the presence of an author as a fallible human being. (p. 387)

The teacher begins by initiating discussion with queries like *What is the author trying to say?* The teacher can then push the discussion to focus on meaning with a question like, *That's what the author says, now what does it mean?* Or revisit the text because there has been a misunderstanding with a question such as *Does the author explain it clearly? What information is missing that we need in order to understand what the author is trying to tell us?* Teachers then extend the discussion to analyze the text with questions like *What is the author doing here?* and *Is there anything that suggests the author might have a personal bias?* It's best to have queries prepared in advance of the class discussion, but also be flexible to move the discussion in the way that best supports students in collectively making meaning.

Summarizing

Summarizing is a skill that is often found on reading comprehension assessments because it requires the reader to recognize the main ideas. What makes summarizing difficult with grade-level texts for adolescents is that the main idea is often implicit, and students have to use their inference skills to make determinations. Also, the ideas in complex texts are often complex themselves, meaning that the relationship or interaction of several essential ideas may be a more accurate description of what the author is describing rather than one main idea.

Gist Statement

A Gist Statement summarizes the main idea of a text in just a sentence, helping readers focus on the core message without getting lost in details. A Gist Statement is built from a set of questions that students can routinely ask in order to get to the gist, in other words, to summarize the main idea concisely. The first question is to illuminate the subject: *Who or what is the text about?* The next is to get at the most important details, *Did what? When/Where? Why/ How?* Finally, students write a summary sentence. The Gist Statement works well at the paragraph or section level when reading complex texts.

Two Dollar Summary

A Two Dollar Summary is a fun and low-stakes strategy to help students write concise summaries of what they've read. The idea is that each word costs ten cents, so students are allowed to spend only two dollars, or twenty words total, to summarize the main points of a text. First, they identify words and phrases that are important ideas. They then write a twenty-word summary that captures the most essential point of the important ideas. Both of these summary strategies encourage careful word choice, synthesis of information, and focus on key concepts.

Visualizing

Visualizing turns words into mental models and/or pictures. Allan Paivio's (2014) Dual Coding Theory posits that the brain processes information through both verbal and visual systems. By engaging both systems, individuals can create stronger, more memorable mental representations, leading to better recall and understanding. When the reader pictures what's happening in the text, it's easier to understand what's going on and remember it later. I like to draw pictures when encountering word problems in mathematics class. Take the following algebra problem:

> *Two trains leave cities that are 480 miles apart and travel toward each other. One train travels at 60 miles per hour, and the other at 80 miles per hour. How long will it take before the two trains meet?*

I need to just make sense of what is happening before I start thinking about the numbers and equations, so I drew the following in Figure 9.3.

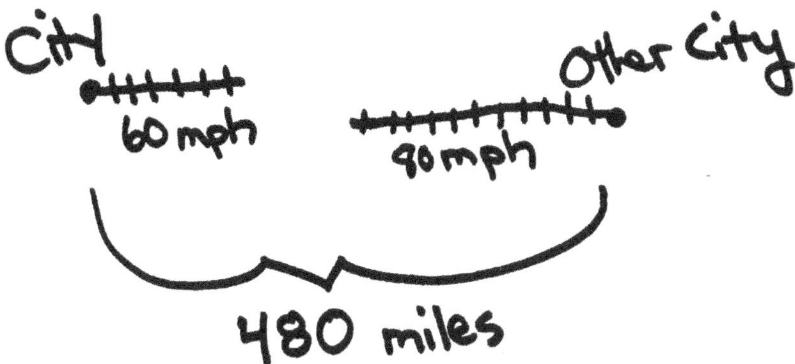

Figure 9.3 Drawing a Word Problem Example.

Storyboard

Visualizing helps reading comprehension because the reader sees the story or information like a movie. Storyboards were originally used by movie directors to plan camera shots for a film but can also be used by students to encourage them to make a movie in their minds as they read. Many digital whiteboards have Storyboard templates. Or, take it old school and have students fold their paper in half horizontally (i.e., hot dog bun fold), then trifold vertically (i.e., brochure fold), unfold and they have six panels to illustrate the text as they read. Especially the first time using this strategy, the teacher can preassign each panel to a chunk of text, explicitly explain to students how visualizing improves reading comprehension, and model the first panel for the class with a focus on ideas behind the pictures not on creating perfect artwork.

Graffiti Wall

A small- or whole-group activity that encourages students to visualize is called a Graffiti Wall. On a Graffiti Wall, students combine words, images, symbols, colors, and their full linguistic and visual repertoires to explore a concept or theme from a text. It's like Sketchnotes but on a grander scale! Teachers can hang a bulletin board or chart paper on the wall and ask students to make the paper messy, filling the paper up with every thought and picture in their heads. Digital whiteboards also have collaboration options, but the physical version adds movement, which is a plus.

Monitoring Understanding

Monitoring understanding helps reading comprehension by allowing readers to recognize when something doesn't make sense and use strategies to repair their understanding.

Click or Clunk and Fix-Up Strategies

Click or Clunk and Fix-Up Strategies are reading comprehension tools that help students monitor their understanding as they read and take action when they get confused. Students are encouraged to pause regularly and ask themselves: *Did that make sense? Was that a click or a clunk?* A click means the reading makes sense. The reader understands what the words are saying and what's going on. For example, "The Civil Rights Act of 1964 outlawed segregation." *That clicks, I get it!* A clunk means something doesn't make sense—it could be a tricky word, a confusing sentence, or an unclear idea. For example, "The economic implications were unprecedented." *That's a clunk, what does* implications *mean?* When readers hit a clunk, they use these Fix-Up strategies to fix confusion and keep going:

- Reread the sentence more slowly.
- Look ahead or behind for clues in the text.
- Break the word apart (prefix, root, suffix).
- Check a dictionary or glossary.
- Think about what they already know about the topic.
- Summarize the last part they *did* understand.
- Ask for help from a peer or teacher.

Together, these strategies help students stay actively engaged, recognize when they're confused, and take steps to repair comprehension—essential skills for becoming independent readers. Click here for a free download of a Fix-Up Strategy bookmark (https://bit.ly/3FLCGE6).

Color-Coded Annotations

Annotating the text with symbols, codes, color, and notes helps the reader actively monitor comprehension. How to annotate is a matter of personal preference, for the most part, but teachers can provide models and ideas to support students in active reading. Color-Coded Annotations using highlighters or sticky notes integrates active reading with the strategy of visualizing, too. In math, readers can highlight the variables in the word problem for the *x*-axis green and for *y*-axis yellow. Just remember that "color coding" doesn't mean using every highlighter in the pack until the page looks like it's been attacked by a rainbow with a grudge.

Or, if the class is using a book that cannot be marked up, small sticky notes can be used. For instance, when reading a history textbook, students can use sticky notes to indicate points in the text where they make text-to-self, text-to-text, and text-to-world connections, with a separate color and code for each type of connection: T-S yellow, T-T pink, and T-W blue (Harvey & Goudvis, 2007).

Talking about Texts

Teachers should provide regular opportunities for students to discuss what they are reading. Talking helps readers process information and practice using new words in context. Likewise, writing about reading also helps students process and provides the added benefit of helping students prepare for discussions. Listening to other students helps readers consider different interpretations and learn from diverse perspectives.

Sentence Frames

Sentence Frames give students the language structure they need, freeing them to focus on building ideas about the text—much like a house frame

---

Tried and True Strategy by Michele Hicks

Lesson Name: Sentence Frames with Romeo and Juliet

Context: English I ESL class in Durham, North Carolina

My students use Sentence Frames to generate ideas as they engage with the graphic play of *Romeo and Juliet*. I provide students with fill-in-the-blank sentences to answer in writing. Students who need additional support can work with a partner. As an after reading activity, students can use the Sentence Frames as they communicate about the play.

Example: Juliet is_________________. She says to the Nurse, "_________________" on page 92.

Juliet is _________________. I can tell this by_________________ because_________________.

holds the structure so the builders can focus on creating the rooms inside. See how Dr. Hicks uses Sentence Frames for multilingual learners to process their thinking about the text and to prepare for a whole class discussion. Giving students a chance to write using Sentence Frames before discussion also gives students a chance to process the reading and collect their thoughts.

Text Rendering

Text Rendering is a strategy to help students get to the essence of a dense text through discussion. As students read, they highlight ideas that they think are important. When they finish reading, they choose what they feel is the most important sentence, phrase, and word of the piece—one of each. They do three rounds of discussion, first sharing their sentences, then phrases, then words. It's okay if something is repeated. During the final round, a scribe records each word (for large groups, it can be helpful to have two scribes). Then, the group choral reads this new text, meaning that they all read it aloud together. Choral Reading gives adolescent readers a chance to actively practice fluency and expression with the support of a group, while allowing them to blend in and build confidence without the pressure of reading aloud alone, but older grades may prefer to read silently instead. Text Rendering ends with the group discussing what fresh insights they gained about the text by looking at it in this way.

Save the Last Word

The *Save the Last Word* protocol is a structured discussion strategy designed to promote thoughtful dialogue and deep **engagement** with a text. In this protocol, students discuss in small groups of three to five. Each participant selects a meaningful quote and shares it with their group explaining why they chose it. I like to have students post on our online discussion board as I find quieter students and extroverted students alike find small group discussion boards engaging. The other group members then take turns responding to the quote—sharing their interpretations, reactions, or connections. After everyone has replied, the original participant synthesizes what the others said and has "the last word." This structure ensures that all voices are heard, encourages active listening, and helps students reflect more deeply on both the text and their peers' perspectives. Who doesn't like having the last word?

Putting It All Together: Reading Guides

So far, we have learned about strategies that support questioning, summarizing, visualizing, monitoring understanding, and talking about texts. In order to guide students' practice of these strategies, teachers can create a Reading Guide. The first step is to determine what makes the text complex and where students might have difficulty with comprehension. Then, determine what scaffolding and strategies would help support student success. Rather than taking away all of the need for students to problem solve, grapple with ideas, and think critically, a Reading Guide would support students in accessing the text and pointing students to the most important information in the text so that they *can* think critically while reading. Reading Guides can be independent work, but are most effective when they are interactive with partners or a small group. Reading Guides can also be differentiated, providing more or less support to different students, such as providing a word bank or sentence stems for multilingual learners.

A typical Reading Guide template would introduce the text in a way that activates background knowledge by connecting the text to students' lives or to previous learning, and then set a purpose for reading to help focus students' attention on what you would like for them to get out of reading the text. For example, read this informational text in order to learn how glaciers shaped our state and to practice the reading strategies we learned this week. Reading Guides then chunk the text and walk students through a reading strategy to use to make meaning during that chunk, such as a visualizing strategy or summary strategy. Although the reading strategies in this book can be used with different texts, they should not be applied at random. Teachers should choose a strategy that aligns with the purpose for reading and supports students with what makes the text complex.

Reading Guides often end with a series of text-dependent questions. Text-dependent questions require students to go back to the reading to support their answers with textual evidence. Revisiting the text and answering questions can support meaning-making (Vaughn et al., 2022). Text-dependent questions include recall, or right-there questions that students can point to the answer in the text. These questions help point students to the most important ideas, but should not be the only type of questions. Questions should encourage readers to go beyond surface-level facts. When readers analyze, infer, and connect ideas, that leads to deeper comprehension. Other types of text-dependent question–answer relationships include think-and-search, where students have to synthesize information or connect examples from multiple places in the text, and author-and-me, where the students have to think about what they learned from the text or make inferences connecting the words to their own experiences to answer the question. See an example template at the case-sensitive link (https://bit.ly/ReadingGuideTemplate).

Conclusion

As we wrap up this chapter on reading comprehension, it's important to remember that teaching adolescents to understand what they read goes beyond strategies and worksheets—it's about sparking their curiosity and helping them see reading as a tool for thinking. When we engage students' thinking before they even open a book—by activating what they already know, inviting them to make predictions, and setting clear purposes—we lay the groundwork for meaningful reading. As teachers, it's essential to be intentional about the texts and activities we assign because clear, purposeful tasks with rich texts help students focus their learning and deepen their knowledge. But it doesn't stop there. Extending their thinking after reading is just as crucial. When students are encouraged to make connections, synthesize new ideas, and apply their understanding across subjects, active reading becomes more than a classroom task—it becomes a habit of mind. Our job is to help students see reading as a way to think deeply, learn widely, and connect their ideas to the world around them.

More to Explore

American Museum of Natural History. (2016). *Using the interactive reading guide*. https://www.amnh.org/learn-teach/curriculum-collections/integrating-literacy-strategies-into-science-instruction/interactive-reading-guides

Fisher, D., & Frey, N. (2020). The skill, will, and thrill of comprehending content area texts. *The Reading Teacher*, *73*(6), 819–24. https://doi.org/10.1002/trtr.1897

TextProject. (n.d.). *Texts for high school readers*. https://textproject.org/teachers/free-texts/teens/

Vlog Brothers. (2025). *Do audiobooks count as reading?* [Video]. YouTube. https://youtu.be/80SCl6n0TEo?si=uolSRJ5RYLbjhbOd

Reflect

For this reflection activity, use your Sketchnotes to Question the Author. What was the author's message? What did the author think that you knew that you did not? What was the muddiest point? Also, create questions of your own. Then, take a stab at trying to answer the questions yourself. As you use writing to think, you might find that you come to more understanding. If you are part of a course or book club, bring your questions to the group. Through talking, you might hear different perspectives that enhance your understanding further.

Discuss

Questions for discussion to learn from and with each other:

- What questions would you ask the author?
- What questions do you have for each other?
- What do you identify as the components of reading comprehension and how do the components relate to each other? What is the difference between decoding words and understanding what is read?
- What makes a text complex, and how can teachers scaffold reading comprehension of complex texts?
- What strategies do you use to help you make meaning from complex texts?
- How would you apply one of the strategies from this chapter to your classroom?

References

Beck, I. L., McKeown, M. G., Sandora, C., Kucan, L., & Worthy, J. (1996). Questioning the author: A yearlong classroom implementation to engage students with text. *The Elementary School Journal, 96*(4), 385–414. https://doi.org/10.1086/461835

Blank, M. (2023, September 26). Two thirds of American kids can't read fluently. *Scientific American.* https://www.scientificamerican.com/article/two-thirds-of-american-kids-cant-read-fluently/

Council of Chief State School Officers (CCSSO). (n.d.). *Text complexity: Qualitative measures rubric, informational texts.* https://navigatingtextcomplexity.kaulfussec.com/Learn_the_Ropes.html

Cucchiara, M. (2019). Language of learning: Content-rich texts build knowledge and skills. *The Learning Professional, 40*(2), 32–6. https://learningforward.org/journal/april-2019-vol-40-no-2/language-of-learning-content-rich-texts-build-knowledge-and-skills/

Dooling, D. J., & Lachman, R. (1971). Effects of comprehension on retention of prose. *Journal of Experimental Psychology, 88*(2), 216–22. https://doi.org/10.1037/h0030904

Glenberg, A. M. (2011). How reading comprehension is embodied and why that matters. *International Electronic Journal of Elementary Education, 4*(1), 5–18.

Harvey, S., & Goudvis, A. (2007). *Strategies that work: Teaching comprehension for understanding and engagement* (2nd ed.). Stenhouse Publishers.

Langer, J. (2002). *Effective literacy instruction: Building successful reading and writing programs.* National Council of Teachers of English.

Mangen, A., Walgermo, B. R., & Brønnick, K. (2013). Reading linear texts on paper versus computer screen: Effects on reading comprehension. *International Journal of Educational Research, 58,* 61–8. https://doi.org/10.1016/j.ijer.2012.12.002

National Assessment of Educational Progress (NAEP). (2022). *National achievement-level results, Grade 8.* https://www.nationsreportcard.gov/reading/nation/achievement/?grade=8

Paivio, A. (2014). Intelligence, dual coding theory, and the brain. *Intelligence, 47,* 141–58. https://doi.org/10.1016/j.intell.2014.09.002

Snow, C. E. (2002). *Reading for understanding: Toward an R & D program in reading comprehension.* RAND Corporation. https://www.rand.org/pubs/monograph_reports/MR1465.html

van Moort, M. L., de Bruïne, A., & van den Broek, P. (2025). Reading comprehension in an online world: Challenges, opportunities, and implications for education. *The Reading Teacher, 79*(1), Article e70006. https://doi.org/10.1002/trtr.70006

Vaughn, S., Gersten, R., Dimino, J., Taylor, M. J., Newman-Gonchar, R., Krowka, S., Kieffer, M. J., McKeown, M., Reed, D., Sanchez, M., St. Martin, K., Wexler, J., Morgan, S., Yañez, A., & Jayanthi, M. (2022). *Providing reading interventions for students in grades 4–9* (Report No. WWC 2022007). National Center for Education Evaluation and Regional Assistance (NCEE), Institute of Education Sciences, U.S. Department of Education. https://whatworks.ed.gov/

Literature Cited

CIA realizes it's been using black highlighters all these years. (2005, November 30). *The Onion.* https://theonion.com/cia-realizes-its-been-using-black-highlighters-all-thes-1819568147/

Massachusetts Historical Society. (n.d.). *Letter from Abigail Adams to John Adams, 31 March—5 April 1776.* https://www.masshist.org/digitaladams/archive/doc?id=L17760331aa

Read, D. W. (Writer), Levy E. (Writer), Levy D. (Writer), & Ciccoritti J. (Director). (2016, March 16). Family dinner (Season 2, Episode 2). In E. Levy, D. Levy, F. Levy, A. Barnsley, B. Feigin, & K. White (Executive Producers), *Schitt's creek.* Not a Real Company Productions; CBC; Pop TV.

Reft, R. (2023, January 19). We mythologize highways, but they've damaged communities of color. *Washington Post.* https://www.washingtonpost.com/made-by-history/2023/01/19/interstate-highways-black-neighborhoods/

Communicating Meaning Through Text

10

Make a quick list of all of the writing you did this week.

Here's my list. Grocery list, thank you note, text messages, professional emails to colleagues, email to my Senator, a personal story and service project description for a fundraising site, revisions of instructions for a course assignment, request for advice on a social media site, photo captions on Instagram, notes on a presentation I attended, a journal entry, edits for a previous chapter, and the draft of this chapter.

Some of these writings were just for me. The grocery list was an aid to help me remember everything that I needed to buy, the notes on the presentation were to help me actively listen and provide a resource to come back to remember my key takeaways, and the journaling was a tool for me to process my thoughts and feelings. Others were for an audience, including the general public, specific individuals, and you!

In school, this is the case too. This chapter includes strategies for writing for self, writing to learn, writing to demonstrate learning, and writing for an authentic audience. The chapter is organized in three sections: Writing to Learn, Learning to Write, and Writing Process. The categories do not represent a sequence or progression. Rather, they are all part of a comprehensive writing curriculum and should happen across content areas. **Meta-analysis** research in grades 4–12 consistently shows that students benefit from explicitly teaching on the features of effective writing (Graham & Perin, 2007; Graham et al., 2025) and from opportunities for extended writing across content areas (Graham et al., 2020).

> ## Literacy Strategy
>
> *Annotate with Relate and Apply*
> As you are reading, think about yourself as a writer and about yourself as a teacher of writing. Mark the text and make notes in the margin for ideas that you relate to as a writer. And, mark the text and make notes in the margins for ideas that you want to apply in your classroom.

> ## Preview Key Vocabulary
>
> **dialogic:** an approach to teaching that values open-ended dialogue
> **mentor text:** an exemplary text that students can use as a model and imitate
> **patterns of organization:** structures that authors use to organize texts or sections of texts
> **worked example:** working through a process step-by-step together

Writing to Learn

The purpose of writing to learn includes to process information, uncover hidden insights, and clarify one's thinking. Meta-analysis research has found that when students wrote about what they read—especially responding with personal reactions and interpretations, writing summaries and notes, and answering questions in writing—it improved **comprehension** and learning (Graham & Hebert, 2011; Graham et al., 2020). Incorporating opportunities for students to write to learn increases the tools in their toolbox for information processing and makes writing a routine part of their day. Writing to learn activities should be framed as low risk, and although what students write can allow teachers to check for understanding of the content, these activities should not be graded for grammar or spelling as that is not the purpose of writing to learn. This type of writing also does not go through the full writing process from planning to revising; rather, the focus is on recording one's thinking at that moment in time, like the Quick List we made in the introduction of this chapter. Students need time to practice writing, and making writing a routine part of each class gives students the number of opportunities that they need to become fluent writers without the pressure of a perfect product looming overhead.

Writing into the Day

At the beginning of this chapter, I asked you to create a list of everything you had written this week. Beginning a learning experience with writing is referred to as Writing Into the Day. Here's how high school teacher Den'ja Pommarane describes it: "Writing Into the Day is an activity where students spend a slice of time (usually seven to 10 minutes) writing at the beginning of the period" (2018, para. 4). Writing acts as a way of centering everyone in the room, helping them transition from whatever was happening before and preparing them for learning. Pommarane says she never mandated that students had to stick to the prompt or share their work with peers because sometimes "they had something more pressing on their mind—maybe they had failed a math test the period before English or had a fight with their parents the previous night and needed time and space to process" (para. 5). What is required is that students write the whole time with the reasoning that nonstop writing helps build fluency (Datchuck, 2017). I encourage students to write whatever comes to their mind and not to worry too much about spelling or grammar. I advise them to try not to edit in their head, just concentrate on getting the idea down on paper. If they don't know what to write, I tell them to record their stream of consciousness, *I am not sure what to write, so I am just writing these words until an idea comes to me.*

The writing prompt can be a question, a quote, an image, or anything that sparks thinking. The purpose can be to review a previous lesson, tapping into the learning science principles of retrieval and rehearsal. Or the prompt can relate a component of the content to their lives, tapping into the evidence base of culturally responsive pedagogy. Here are some sample prompts:

- Woodworking or Construction: Think about a time when you fixed or built something. What did you learn about yourself in the process?

- Agriculture: Think about a place you've spent time, like a yard, park, or field. How might the quality of the soil there affect what grows and how people use the land?

- Physical Education: Describe a physical activity you enjoy. How does it affect your mood or energy level?

- Music: Think of a song that means something to you. What emotions or memories does it bring up, and why do you think music has that power?

- Family and Consumer Sciences: What is one meal or recipe that's important in your family, and what does it say about your culture or traditions?

Dialogic Journal

Students can keep a journal or notebook to hold the routine writing they do in your class in one place. This enables them to be able to go back and see how their thinking has evolved or to build on an idea they wrote about last month. In addition to students being able to read their own writing, a journal can facilitate communication between the teacher and students. When teachers and students communicate with each other in a journal, this is called a Dialogic Journal. **Dialogic** is related to the word dialogue, which indicates the two-way nature of communication, and is an approach where students and teachers build knowledge together through questioning, listening, and responding.

Similar to Ms. Pommarane's experience, in my experience, the journal entries range from questions about curricular content to sharing personal experiences. It's important to note that before I ask students to write, I let them know who will be reading their writing. So, in the case of a Dialogic Journal, that would be me, their teacher. And I share how teachers are mandatory reporters, meaning that if I am worried that someone is being harmed or is going to hurt themselves or others, that I have to report it to the authorities. Students usually understand that, but it's always good to be upfront. The way the Dialogic Journal is structured varies. Sometimes I would write back at the end of the entry or in the margins. But sometimes writing on their page seemed like an invasion or there just physically wasn't room, so sticky notes work well too (see Figure 10.1). Dialogic journals are powerful because they provide a space for reflection, dialogue, and deeper meaning-making.

Take a Line for a Walk

This writing to learn strategy incorporates reading, writing, and walking! It's a great way to incorporate movement in the classroom. Similar to dialogic journals, this strategy encourages dialogue and co-construction of knowledge, but rather than between the student and teacher, these written conversations happen with peers. High school teacher Marilyn Yung uses this strategy with students in conjunction with reading a text. She says with her juniors, "we used the activity to review and establish prior knowledge about World War I in preparation for our reading later this week of Ernest Hemingway's short story 'In Another Country'" (2020, para. 5). Here are the steps Ms. Yung uses:

1 After students are finished reading, ask them to find a line—a sentence or two will do—and write it down, word for word, at the top of a clean piece of paper. Write about why the line stood out to them, what surprised them, what they noticed, or however they would like to respond.

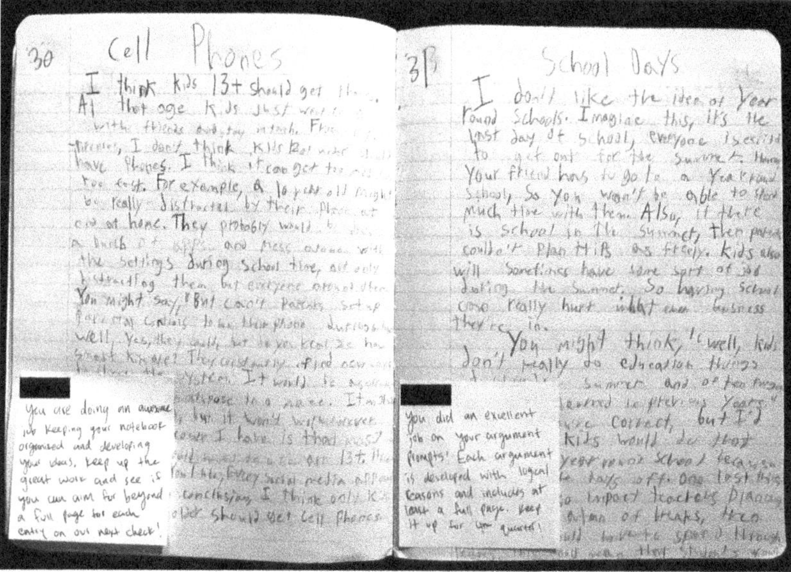

Figure 10.1 Dialogic Journal Example.

2 Then, have students stand up, leave their own page at their desk, grab their pen, and move to another desk.

3 From here, they continue the conversation that's been started on the page at their new desk. Do they agree with the thoughts? Disagree? Have a connection? Have a question? The goal is to keep writing for one minute in response.

4 Repeat about three more times, and then return to their original seats and skim through the writing that has been collected.

5 Ask a few students to share their written conversations, including any especially interesting or insightful comments.

Learning to Write

This section explains the foundational writing knowledge and skills that research shows require explicit instruction (Sedita, 2023; Graham et al., 2025). Although this section is organized from part to whole—sentences, paragraphs, essays—adolescent students should have regular opportunities to write extensively with sentence level and paragraph level work in service of more substantial writing, including essays and other **genres**.

Composing Sentences

The science of writing shows that when students work with sentence-level **syntax**, in other words, playing with how sentences are built and structured, they become stronger writers *and* readers. Learning to expand, combine, and rearrange sentences helps students see how language works to shape meaning. This kind of hands-on practice doesn't just improve their grammar, it helps them write with more clarity, variety, and voice. And because reading and writing are so connected, the benefits go both ways. Students who understand sentence structure are better equipped to unpack complex sentences when they read, leading to stronger comprehension and more confident communication across the board.

Sentence Expansion

A developmental sequence for sentence expansion, shown in Table 10.1, starts with a simple sentence and builds to include additional information. Teachers explicitly teach the function of words in a sentence within the context of expanding students' sentences to include more details. Teachers can provide students with an organizer like in Table 10.1 and can use the 5W+H questions (i.e., Who, What, When, Where, Why, How) as a scaffold as students are learning parts of speech and their functions. Students can then practice sentence expansion by writing captions for a photo starting with the subject and what the subject is doing, and answering more questions to add any details relevant to the photo. Photos can come from your curriculum or educational websites. For example, the organization Visual Thinking Strategies has an Image of the Week webpage (https://vtshome.org/weekly-image/) and *The New York Times* has a weekly What's Going on in the Picture? (https://www.nytimes.com/column/learning-whats-going-on-in-this-picture).

A sentence expansion strategy that also supports content learning is Because, But, So. This strategy works well with content about a change, transformation, or result, like an event in history or a cause–effect relationship in science. The teacher provides a sentence stem related to the content that can be expanded by using because, but, and so. Then, students write three sentences using three conjunctions The Civil Rights Movement was a turning point in American history ___.

- **Because** it challenged deeply rooted systems of racial injustice.
- **But** it faced fierce resistance from individuals and institutions.
- **So** it led to landmark legislation like the Civil Rights Act of 1964 and the Voting Rights Act of 1965.

Table 10.1 Development of Sentence Expansion

		Who or what?	Doing or did what?	
1. Writing a complete sentence: Subject and predicate		Noun	Verb	
		My dog	jumps.	

	What kind?	Who or what?	Doing or did what?	
2. Expand the Subject	Adjective	Noun	Verb	
	My cute	dog	jumps.	

		Who or what?	Doing or did what?	How?
3. Expand the Predicate		Noun	Verb	Adverb
		My dog	jumps	eagerly.

	When?	Who or what?	Doing or did what?	Where? Why?
4. Adding prepositional phrases and dependent clauses	Phrase/clause	Noun	Verb	Phrase/clause
	In the morning	My dog	jumps	on my bed because he wants me to play.

5. Put it all together!	Phrase/ clause	Adj.	Noun	Verb	Adverb	Phrase/ clause
	In the morning	my cute	dog	jumps	eagerly	on my bed because he wants me to play.

6. Writing a complete sentence: Subject and predicate			Who or what?	Doing or did what?		
			Noun	Verb		
			My dog	jumps.		

7. Expand the Subject	What kind?		Who or what?	Doing or did what?		
	Adjective		Noun	Verb		
	My cute		dog	jumps.		

8. Expand the Predicate		Who or what?	Doing or did what?	How?	
		Noun	Verb	Adverb	
		My dog	jumps	eagerly.	

9. Adding prepositional phrases and dependent clauses	When?	Who or what?	Doing or did what?	Where? Why?
	Phrase/clause	Noun	Verb	Phrase/clause
	In the morning	My dog	jumps	on my bed because he wants me to play.

10. Put it all together!	Phrase/ clause	Adj.	Noun	Verb	Adverb	Phrase/ clause
	In the morning	my cute	dog	jumps	eagerly	on my bed because he wants me to play.

For an extra challenge, students can attempt to revise the three sentences to write one compound-complex sentence: **Because** it challenged deeply rooted systems of racial injustice, the Civil Rights movement faced fierce resistance from individuals and institutions, **but** it led to landmark legislation like the Civil Rights Act of 1964 and the Voting Rights Act of 1965, **so** The Civil Rights Movement was a turning point in American history. Because almost all characters in literature experience a transformation, the strategy works well as a way to integrate reading and writing instruction. For example, Cyrano helped Christian marry Roxanne **because** of his desire for her happiness, **but** he secretly loved Roxanne, **so** he trapped himself in silent heartbreak. Roxanne wanted to marry Christian **because** she thought he was the one writing her love letters, **but** it was actually Cyrano, **so** she was unknowingly caught in the same trap.

Sentence Combining

When we speak, we naturally use simple sentences, and we add information by using compound sentences. Compound sentences are two complete ideas joined by a coordinating conjunction (i.e., for, and, nor, but, yes, so that make the acronym FANBOYS). Even young children will speak in compound sentences. Take this example from a 4-year-old: *I want to go to the park, and I want to go to McDonald's, but I want to go see my aunt.* However, as students progress through school, they will be expected to be able to read and write complex sentences.

Instruction on combining sentences should reflect the developmental progression of oral language by starting with compound sentences. Teachers can provide explicit instruction on what simple and compound sentences are as well as examples of each. Example sentences can come from a content area textbook to reinforce content knowledge or from students' writing to increase authenticity. After practicing a couple together as a class, partners can practice writing compound sentences by combining two simple sentences and using a word bank of conjunctions. As a closing, each student can choose one of the sentences to imitate to create their own compound sentence.

The next sentence type to introduce would be complex and then compound complex. After learning the types, it's important to give students the opportunity to use sentence combining in their own writing because sentence combining is not the goal for learners, the ability to write sophisticated sentences is the goal.

Sentence Unscramble

There are many different ways to write complex sentences, so I recommend using the Sentence Unscramble instructional strategy as a way to help adolescents deconstruct and construct complex sentences. In addition, complex sentences are not often used in everyday speech, so providing instruction is necessary. Provide students a model sentence, and a sentence that uses the same structure but is cut into pieces. Have students put the pieces together following the structure in the model. Model sentences can include appositive phrases, adjectival clauses, and relative clauses, to name a few. This activity not only helps students write complex sentences, it helps them deconstruct complex sentences when they encounter them in reading, too!

Imitation Writing

Imitation Writing can be used in combination with another strategy, like Sentence Combining and Unscramble discussed above, or on its own. It can also be used for practice writing sentences or paragraphs. Just like it sounds, students use an example to imitate. Students can find their own example or

Tried and True Strategy by Ben Vessa

Lesson Title: Imitating Other Writers

Context: Twelfth-grade English class in Knightdale, North Carolina

I would get frustrated when I returned essays to students with all my helpful corrections and suggestions, and they would only look at their grade. Now, I have them interact with their graded essays in a variety of ways. I started using the Imitating Other Writers strategy after attending a district workshop. First, the students collect data of their own writing, charting the first four words of each sentence from their first two body paragraphs. I want them to see if each sentence begins subject–verb or if there is a variety of sentence beginnings. Second, I have them count the number of words in each sentence to see if they vary in lengths (short, medium, long). Last, I supply them with sample sentences from famous writers and have them rewrite sentences from their own paper imitating the syntactic structure of those authors. Free download here (https://bit. ly/imitatingwriters).

the teacher can provide them. For example, the teacher could ask students to find an effective sentence and then discuss as a class what makes the varied examples effective. Students then practice imitating what made the writing effective. Or, the teacher can provide examples that demonstrate a specific technique in order to focus a lesson, as in the Tried and True lesson from North Carolina.

Producing Paragraphs

Typically, by upper elementary, students have learned how to produce paragraphs. As they advance through upper elementary and secondary school, the complexity of their writing should also be advancing. What's more, the style that is expected in each discipline is different, so students need to see models and have conversations about what effective writing looks like in each class. For example, science prioritizes a clear and concise writing style and expects a claim as the topic sentence with evidence and reasoning as the supporting details. In English, the topic sentence is the main idea and textual evidence, analysis, and commentary are expected for supporting details. The following strategies can help students learn to write effective paragraphs across the curriculum.

Anchor Chart

An Anchor Chart is a visual support created with students that captures key concepts, strategies, or steps for a particular skill—in this case, writing paragraphs. Anchor Charts can serve as a reference tool to reinforce expectations for strong paragraph writing, such as including a clear topic sentence, supporting evidence and details, and an ending sentence (sometimes called a closing or linking sentence). Teachers might co-construct an Anchor Chart using a model paragraph, color-coding each part, and annotating the function of each sentence based on the expectations of the discipline, as shown in Figure 10.2. The Anchor Chart is then displayed as a go-to guide to writing organized, coherent, and well-developed paragraphs.

Teachers could also co-construct an Anchor Chart about transition words and phrases to link sentences for different **patterns of organization**, as shown in Figure 10.3. Connecting transitions to patterns of organization helps students better understand how to structure their own paragraphs when writing and recognize these words as signals to an author's organizational strategy when reading.

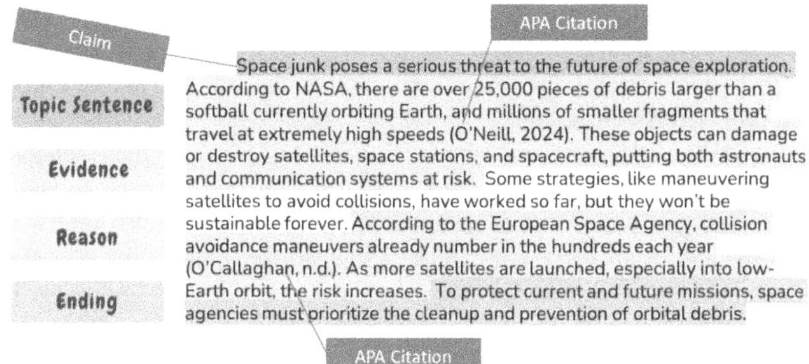

Figure 10.2 Paragraph Writing Anchor Chart Example.

TRANSITION WORDS
for Informative Writing

TIME /SEQUENTIAL

Firstly, secondly, thirdly, lastly
First, next, then, finally
To begin, after, in the end

CAUSE & EFFECT

As a result	For this reason
Because	Consequently
Thus	Therefore
So	Accordingly
Due to	Ultimately

COMPARE & CONTRAST

Similarly	Although
Like / unlike	Likewise
In comparison to	Similar to
In contrast to	On the other hand
However	

DESCRIPTION

For example	We see this when
For instance	This is clearly shown
Specifically	Such as
To illustrate	An example being
To be specific	Looks like

Figure 10.3 Transition Word Anchor Chart Example.

Partner Reading with Paragraph Shrinking

Finding the main idea and knowing how to sum things up aren't just tools for better reading, they pull double duty in writing, too. Although these strategies are often praised for boosting reading comprehension, teaching students to identify main ideas and to summarize comes in handy for writing topic sentences as well. Partner Reading with Paragraph Shrinking is a strategy with evidence from grades 2 to 12 that helps all students, and especially students with learning disabilities and multilingual learners develop these two skills (IRIS Center, 2025).

Teachers partner students heterogeneously by ability, so that each pair has a high-performing reader. That said, each student takes turns being the reader and the coach. Student A, arranged by the teacher ahead of time to be the high-performing reader, reads for five minutes, and Student B serves as the coach. Student A stops at the end of each paragraph to summarize, and the coach provides support for the summary with the following prompts:

- Name the most important *who or what.*
- Tell the most important thing about *who or what.*
- Say the main idea in ten words or less.

As the reader is reading, the coach reads along. If the reader makes an error that impedes understanding, the coach says, "check it." If the reader needs more help, the coach pronounces the word. If the reader incorrectly summarizes the paragraph, the coach says, "check it." If the summary is more than ten words, the coach says, "shrink it." If the reader needs more help, the coach gives the correct summary. At the end of five minutes, Student A becomes the reader, Student B becomes the coach, and they continue the process.

Harris Moves

In younger grades, students write opinion paragraphs primarily based on their own experiences. Around fourth grade, students begin to learn about argument writing with evidence-based claims rather than personal opinions. They begin to find and use information from texts as evidence. But using evidence effectively and providing commentary on one's reasoning are difficult for writers of any age. The Harris Moves are a set of rhetorical strategies developed by Joseph Harris (2017) to help students with just that. These "moves" include the techniques of illustrating, authorizing, extending, and countering as shown in Table 10.2. Instead of simply adding quotes from texts as the evidence in a paragraph, Harris Moves encourage students to strategically use evidence and explain their reasoning, helping them craft more analytical paragraphs.

Table 10.2 Examples of Harris Moves

Name	Move	Example
Topic sentence: Single-use plastics should be banned because they harm the environment.		
Illustrating	Providing an example	For example, goats in Kenya were eating plastic bags and getting sick or even dying (https://www.npr.org/sections/goatsandsoda/2023/08/09/1190211814).
Authorizing	Using a well-respected authority figure or expert to raise credibility	According to the National Geographic Society, millions of tons of plastic waste enter the ocean every year, causing serious damage to marine life.
Topic sentence: There are better options we can use than single-use plastics.		
Authorizing and Illustrating	See above	Leticia Soares, who is a researcher at the National Aviary, says that little changes can make a big difference, like saying no to plastic straws at restaurants.
Extending	Putting a new spin on the source's point or adding your own insight	In addition, we can bring our own reusable water bottle to school and reusable bags to stores.
Countering	Offering a different point of view	Some people say plastic is more affordable than other options, but just because something is cheap doesn't mean it's worth the cost to the planet.

Revising for Sentence Variety

While early readers appreciate the predictability of repeating sentence patterns like what follows, it's pretty boring for more advanced readers. Compare the following two fourth-grade paragraphs on bats. Which do you find more interesting to read?

> Version 1
> Fruit bats are not scary. Fruit bats are helpful. Fruit bats like sweet fruit. Fruit bats eat bananas. Fruit bats eat mangoes. Fruit bats drop fruit seeds when they fly. Fruit bats help new fruit plants grow.
>
> Version 2
> Fruit bats are not scary. They are helpful! Fruit bats eat bananas, mangoes, and other sweet treats. Then, fruit bats drop seeds as they fly and help new plants grow. This makes bats important for a healthy forest. Next time you see a bat, remember they're being helpful!

In the example about bats above, the student used the following strategies to revise in order to combine sentences and vary the sentence beginnings. Both of these strategies improve coherence by taking choppy sentences and making them flow.

- Revise sentence beginnings by using pronouns (e.g., they, you, it)
  - Original: Fruit bats are not scary. Fruit bats are helpful.
  - Revised: Fruit bats are not scary. They are helpful!
- Revise sentence beginnings by adding transition words (e.g., then, next)
  - Original: Fruit bats eat bananas, mangoes, and other sweet treats. Fruit bats drop seeds as they fly.
  - Revised: Fruit bats eat bananas, mangoes, and other sweet treats. Then, fruit bats drop seeds as they fly.
- Combine sentences by creating parallel lists with a conjunction (e.g., and, or)
  - Original: Fruit bats like sweet fruit. Fruit bats eat bananas. Fruit bats eat mangoes.
  - Revised: Fruit bats eat bananas, mangoes, and other sweet treats.
- Combine sentences by combining predicates with a conjunction (e.g., and, so, yet)
  - Original: Fruit bats drop fruit seeds when they fly. Fruit bats help new fruit plants grow.
  - Revised: Fruit bats drop seeds as they fly and help new plants grow.

- Revise sentence beginnings and combine sentences by using an adverbial phrase at the beginning.
  - Original: Remember, bats are helpful when you see a bat.
  - Revised: When you see a bat, remember they're being helpful!

My ninth-grade English teacher, Mr. Korty, taught us Sentence Combining and sentence variety by introducing a technique a week. He would start on Monday by showing us examples of the compound or complex sentence type we would be practicing and walking us through the parts. He would give us sentences to revise using the new technique. Tuesday, we would work with partners to write our own sentences using the examples as models. When we had a writing assignment draft, we would take time at the end of the week to revise our drafts using any one of the techniques we had learned up to that point. I still use the techniques I learned from Mr. Korty, such as starting a sentence with the word *when*.

When it comes to teaching students how to write strong paragraphs, the Science of Writing reminds us that it's not just for early learners. Often, adolescents need explicit instruction on how paragraphs work: they should understand the purpose of a topic sentence, how to develop ideas with evidence and examples, and how to wrap things up with a concluding sentence. Routine practice, feedback, and revisiting foundational sentence-level skills—like syntax and transitions—help students compose paragraphs fluently. It's also crucial to model the thinking behind writing—like how to make our writing coherent and interesting for our readers—to compose well-developed paragraphs.

Writing Essays

The word essay comes from the French language and means "to try." I like that framing—to try—when thinking about the purpose of writing essays in school. The hope is that students try to explore a topic, think deeply about an issue, and come to a greater understanding than they would have without writing. Teachers assign essays in school in order for students to engage in writing to learn, to demonstrate learning, and to express their ideas to an audience. This section explains how to teach the technical skills of essay writing in a way that reduces cognitive load, allowing students to focus more energy on generating ideas and thinking critically.

Shared Writing

The Shared Writing instructional strategy is where a teacher leads the class through creating a piece of writing and thinks aloud about the decision-making and problem-solving needed for each step. This instructional strategy is backed by learning science research. Walking students through a process step-by-step, called a **worked example**, helps reduce the cognitive load on students by reducing the thinking needed for idea generation and allowing them the cognition to focus on learning the writing skill, strategy, or technique (Renkl, 2023). Shared Writing is also an opportunity for teachers to think aloud about **self-regulation**. This teaches students to monitor where they are in the process and choose appropriate strategies for the task.

Along the way, the teacher can fade out the thinking aloud and transition to asking students questions about what they would do or say next. The teacher can also probe students for explanations, so that the students become the ones thinking aloud. Shared Writing aligns with the Gradual Release of Responsibility instructional method as teachers begin by modeling writing moves and self-regulation and then eventually give students the **autonomy** to manage the writing process in the way that works best for them (Graham & Harris, 2018).

Mentor Texts

A **Mentor Text** is a piece of writing that serves as a model for students to learn specific writing techniques, structures, or styles. Teachers use Mentor Texts to highlight strong examples of craft, such as word choice, syntax, or organization. These texts can be published works, student writing, or teacher-created examples. By studying and imitating Mentor Texts, students develop their own writing skills more intentionally (Graham et al., 2019; Graham & Perin, 2007). In my class, I have used Gloria Anzaldúa's "How to Tame a Wild Tongue" as a Mentor Text to explore style and voice, specifically how she blends genres and languages and how she uses specific details and imagery. After reading the Mentor Text, students worked in small groups to identify examples of the five senses in Anzaldúa's essay. My students completed Table 10.3 on a shared doc. They then each created their own table to brainstorm vivid imagery and specific details that they could add to their own essays, using the languages of their choice.

Kernel Essay

A Kernel Essay is a simple, structured framework that helps students organize their thoughts before diving into a full piece of writing. The concept was

Table 10.3 Sensory Details Example

	See	Hear	Touch	Smell	Taste
Group 1	"pulling out all the metal from my mouth"	"Silver bits plop and tinkle into the basin."	"hot steaming tamales"	family cooking	"The wilderness has dried out our tongues."
Group 2	Pushing out wads of cotton, pushing back drills, the long thin needle	bolero, rancherita, and corrido music, norteno music, conjuntos, bajo sexta	"That was good for three licks on the knuckles with a sharp ruler."	the stench of the dental operation	"My mouth salivates at the thought of hot steaming tamales I would be eating if I were home."
Group 3	Like an ear of corn—a female seed-bearing organ—the mestiza is tenacious, tightly wrapped in the husks of her culture. (p. 82)	Hot, sultry evenings when corridos … Reverberated out of cheap amplifiers from the local cantinas	"We speak with tongues of fire" (p. 80) "My fingers move sly against your palm" (p. 81)	"The stench of cow manure and the yellow patches on the ground"	"My sister Hilda's hot, spicy, menudo, chile colorado, making it deep red, pieces of panza"

Table 10.4 Kernel Essay Outline Example

	1. I think…	2. I thought this because…	3. For example…	4. This matters because…	5. In conclusion…
1.	I think invasive species can seriously damage ecosystems.				
2.	I thought this because they often outcompete native species.				
3.	For example, zebra mussels have spread through US waterways and hurt native fish populations.				
4.	This matters because it disrupts food chains and biodiversity.				
5.	In conclusion, managing invasive species is important for protecting natural environments.				

developed by Gretchen Bernabei, a veteran teacher who saw the power of giving students a clear, repeatable format to launch their ideas. Think of a Kernel Essay like a blueprint—it doesn't do all the writing for students, but it gives them the structure they need to get started confidently and stay focused.

Each Kernel Essay is built around a series of prompts or stems that guide students through the logic or flow of their thinking. For example, a classic Kernel Essay for expository writing might follow this structure: *I think … I thought this because … For example … This matters because … In conclusion …* Students write one sentence for each part, and just like that, they've created the seed of their essay. From there they can grow their ideas. Let's say students in a middle school science class studying ecosystems are asked to write a Kernel Essay on the impact of invasive species. It might look like Table 10.4.

With the Kernel Essay scaffold, students are ready to expand, revise, and turn their ideas into a strong, well-organized essay. See more examples of Kernel Essay structures here (https://bit.ly/kernelessay).

Writing Process

Comprehensive writing instruction provides ample opportunities for students to write for authentic audiences in order to communicate meaning to others. Although not all of my writing goes through a multistep process, when I write for authentic audiences, I begin by planning, usually in some sort of concept map. Then, I start drafting. After I get my initial thinking down, I think about how to best organize the ideas for my audience and purpose. Digital composing makes it fairly easy to cut and paste entire sections using a trial-and-error approach, but sometimes I create an outline and then paste my drafted sections into the outline. After this, I run spell check, because that's easy. Then, I revise and edit by reading what I wrote from top to bottom. I'm pretty good at grammar, so I can revise and edit at the same time. But, when I publish, there is a final proofreading step where I double-check for any errors before sending to print. When my piece is published, I share it with others. After all, if it's not on the Gram, it didn't happen! My process isn't exactly the same every time, and it's iterative in that I might go back and repeat steps before moving forward.

I say all this to say, if my own process isn't the same every time, I can't expect each of my hundreds of students to use the same process every time for every piece of writing. On the other hand, I do have a process that I can articulate, and my process has evolved by learning strategies from other writers who have articulated their process. In addition, my experience as an educator has taught me that students appreciate both structure and flexibility when it comes to writing. My approach has always been to explicitly teach students a process, but to allow flexibility for students to make the process their own. Along the way, I show students strategies that I use and strategies that I have picked up from someone else (i.e., the way I do this is ... and another way to do this is ...).

An approach that I find helpful and has a strong evidence base is the Self-Regulated Strategy Development (SRSD) approach for teaching writing in elementary and secondary grades (Graham & Harris, 2018; What Works Clearinghouse, 2017). SRSD uses the acronym POWRE to summarize the writing process: Plan, Organize, Write and say more, Revise, and Edit. For each phase, teachers begin with discussing what the strategy is and why it works, teachers model the strategy and support students through scaffolded practice, and end with students applying strategies independently in writing when they determine a need. Specifically, the SRSD Gradual Release of Responsibility sequence is

1 activate it,

2 discuss it,

3 model it,

4 memorize it,

5 support it, and

6 independent performance.

Research demonstrates that students benefit from explicit teaching of strategies and collaborating with peers within each phase, framed within a process view (Graham & Harris, 2018). Below are some examples of what this can look like in practice, organized by the phases of the POWRE writing process.

Plan

A strategy for the planning phase of the writing process is RAFT. Yes, another acronym. RAFT stands for Role, Audience, Format, and Topic. The acronym can help students dissect a writing prompt to understand what they are being asked to do or to help students plan the kind of writing that they want to do. To scaffold, teachers can provide students a graphic organizer to fill out. When making a decision about their role, writers determine whether they want to take an objective approach for the purpose of informing their audience, tell a personal approach and speak from their heart, or choose from an infinite number of possible angles and purposes. The role they take might depend upon the intended audience or format. For example, if my purpose is to persuade my audience about the dangers of vaping, then if I am writing to children, I might choose to tell a personal story to illustrate my point and approach the writing from my point of view as a mother. But if I am writing a grant proposal, I might choose to write a synthesis of the empirical evidence from my point of view as a researcher. The audience and the format also inform writer's decisions related to formality of language. In the example above, I would use informal language with children and formal language for a grant proposal.

When considering the topic, writers need to narrow the topic to the point that the ideas will be able to be well-developed but not narrowed so much that there isn't much to say. The topic should be like a camera zoom: zoomed in enough to see the details clearly, but not so close that you lose the full picture. If the topic is too zoomed out, it's like trying to take a picture of the whole world—you can't capture much detail. But if you zoom in too far, like on just one pixel, you lose the context. Just the right zoom makes the writing equally clear and interesting.

Organize

Strategies for organizing include the Anchor Chart and the Kernel Essay ideas in the Essay Writing section. Also, the text structure graphic organizers in Chapter 9 provide support in helping students use patterns of organization in their writing. Too often, adolescents generate a lot of great ideas before writing, but then those ideas do not always transfer to their drafts. Organizing at the paragraph level and the essay level can help alleviate this problem. With the Single Paragraph Outline (Hochman & Wexler, 2017), students outline one paragraph at a time with a complete topic sentence that states the main idea, supporting details written as phrases or notes, and a concluding sentence that summarizes the paragraph or links back to the topic sentence. When writing a multiple paragraph composition, the paragraph outlines can be arranged in the order that makes the most sense to create an organized whole.

Revise

Ready for another acronym? The RADaR acronym introduced by Anderson and Gallagher (2012) walks students through considerations for revision. The letters stand for Replace, Add, Delete, and Reorder (Table 10.5).

Another effective strategy for the revision phase is to have students color code both the **rubric** and their own writing. Start by assigning a different color to each criterion on the rubric, such as:

- Claim (GREEN)
- Evidence (YELLOW)
- Giving credit to the source (PINK)
- Reasoning and commentary on the evidence (ORANGE)
- Transitions (BLUE)

Then, have students go through their own writing and highlight each part that corresponds to those criteria. This visual alignment helps students see which parts of the rubric they have met and which parts may be missing or underdeveloped and in need of revision. This simple technique builds

Table 10.5 Replace, Add, Delete, and Reorder

Replace	Add	Delete	Reorder
Words that are not specific	New support	Off-topic ideas	To flow better
Words that are overused	Descriptive adjectives and adverbs	Repetitive words or phrases	So details support main ideas
Sentences that are unclear	Rhetorical or literary devices	Unnecessary details	So most important points are last

---

Tried and True Strategy by Tracy Brosch

Strategy Name: Writing Buffet

Context: Sixth-grade class in St. Louis, Missouri

I learned the Writing Buffet strategy at a Writing Project event and have used it with my students in middle grades through university level ever since. The strategy can be used in many ways, but I've most often incorporated it when writers are ready for feedback during the writing process. Each writer brings in a piece (often in draft form) and staples a piece of colored paper to the back of the writing. All of the various pieces of writing are set on a buffet table. The group passes through the buffet line and picks up a piece of writing. As a responder, they read the piece and provide feedback on the colored sheet. When finished, the responder takes the piece back to the buffet table, dropping it off and picking up a new piece. Repeat. At the end, each writer retrieves their piece and enjoys the varied responses. I use this strategy to highlight writing successes with the intention of imploring students to see that the purpose of revision is to lift all parts of their writing to the level where their craft choices are noticeable. Additionally, writing communities need opportunities for feedback from a varied audience and to read the writing of their peers.

---

self-awareness, supports metacognition, and turns the rubric into a meaningful tool rather than just a score. Peers and teachers can also use the same color-coding system to highlight parts of a student's writing, making it easier to give targeted feedback and have focused conversations about strengths and areas for revision. Watch fifth-grade teacher Bob McLaughlin from Massachusetts in the linked video (https://youtu.be/H1jZCKaVgJM?si=_I47cap-yYcJNZ3y). Check out another way to approach revision in the above Tried and True Strategy.

Edit

Two super simple strategies that I use all the time and have taught students for editing are to change the size and font on my document and to read aloud. When I have been looking at a document for a long time, my eyes start to skip punctuation, letters, and even whole words because my brain thinks it already knows what is there. Making the size larger and changing the font means my eyes no longer recognize the writing. Reading the piece aloud also forces my brain to slow down. With these two strategies, I am better able to catch mistakes.

Praise, Question, Polish, often referred to as PQP, is a peer editing protocol where students first praise something specific in a peer's work, then ask questions to clarify the meaning of words or sentences that are unclear, and finally offer a suggestion on what could be polished to improve the writing. It encourages respectful, balanced feedback and helps students develop both their writing and critique skills.

Editing is also the phase where I use **artificial intelligence (AI)**. I prefer AI tools that give an explanation rather than just making the changes, so that I can learn from my mistakes. It's important to recognize that AI is already embedded by default into word processing, search engines, and other composing tools. Autocorrect, grammar and spell checking, and predictive text are just a few examples. So, to tell students that they cannot use any AI isn't realistic. Instead, I suggest having conversations with students about appropriate use. For example, my niece's sophomore English teacher explained to her class that it was okay to use the free version of Grammarly, but not to use the paid version because it changed too much and made the writing lose the student's voice. My niece thought that was reasonable, and followed that advice.

Conclusion

Like assembling IKEA furniture, teaching writing might come with a few mysterious parts, several missing screws, and enough coffee to count as a personality trait—but in the end, something useful (and possibly even stylish) comes together. So trust the process and remember to celebrate the moments of success. After all, teaching students to write at the sentence, paragraph, and essay level isn't just about grammar rules and graphic organizers—it's about helping them find their voice, build their ideas, and share them with the world.

More to Explore

- Check out the National Writing Project Resource Hub: https://teach.nwp.org/
- Explore even more strategies in Read, Write, Think's Strategy Guide for Teaching Writing: https://www.readwritethink.org/professional-development/strategy-guide-series/teaching-writing

- Watch expert teachers model writing strategies on the SRSD in Action on The Science of Writing webpage: https://srsdonline.org/srsd-in-action/

- In this episode of Melissa and Lori Love Literacy, researcher Steven Graham talks all things writing: https://literacypodcast.com/podcast?podcast=Buzzsprout-16247500

Reflect

Reflect on your learning by reviewing your annotations. Set an intention for how you will apply your learning. If you'd like, you can use the Sentence Stems *I learned … I will …*

Discuss

Questions for discussion to learn from and with each other:

1 How can teachers use writing to learn in the classroom?

2 What does the research say about teaching writing?

3 Consider this quote from Katherine Bomer (2010): "As a writer and a reader, I am happiest with surprising, fresh ways of using language and shaping texts. I am uncomfortable when language is forced to fit into formulas determined by notions of correctness and acceptability in school settings and does not reflect how people writing outside of schools use language and genre to convince and move readers, to open eyes, to discover through the act of writing, or to express beauty and deep emotion" (p. 3). How does the author's philosophy compare to your philosophy of teaching writing?

4 Consider this quote from EdWeek, "Participants, mostly undergraduate and graduate students, who constructed essays with the assistance of ChatGPT exhibited less brain activity during the task than those participants who were asked to write on their own. The AI-users were much less likely to be able to recall what they had written and felt less ownership over their work. Independent evaluators who reviewed the essays found the AI-supported ones to be lacking in individuality and creativity" (Schwartz, 2025, para. 4). How does this research finding impact your philosophy of using AI when writing?

References

Anderson, J., & Gallagher, K. (2012). *Writing coach: Writing and grammar for the 21st Century*. Prentice Hall.

Bomer, K. (2010). *Hidden gems: Naming and teaching from the brilliance in every student's writing*. Heinemann.

Datchuk, S. M. (2017). A direct instruction and precision teaching intervention to improve sentence construction of middle school students with writing difficulties. *Journal of Special Education, 51*(2), 62–71. https://doi.org/10.1177/0022466916665588

Graham, S., & Harris, K. R. (2018). Evidence-based writing practices: A meta-analysis of existing meta-analyses. In R. Fidalgo, K. R. Harris, & M. Braaksma (Eds.), *Design principles for teaching effective writing: Theoretical and empirical grounded principles* (pp. 13–37). Brill.

Graham, S., & Hebert, M. (2011). Writing to read: A meta-analysis of the impact of writing and writing instruction on reading. *Harvard Educational Review, 81*(4), 710–44. https://doi/10.17763/haer.81.4.t2k0m13756113566

Graham, S., & Perin, D. (2007). *Writing next: Effective strategies to improve writing of adolescents in middle and high schools* [Report]. Alliance for Excellent Education.

Graham, S., Kiuhara, S. A., & MacKay, M. (2020). The effects of writing on learning in science, social studies, and mathematics: A meta-analysis. *Review of Educational Research, 90*(2), 179–226. https://doi.org/10.3102/0034654320914744

Graham, S., Bruch, J., Fitzgerald, J., Friedrich, L., Furgeson, J., Greene, K., Kim, J., Lyskawa, J., Olson, C. B., & Smither Wulsin, C. (2019). *Teaching secondary students to write effectively* (NCEE Report 2017-4002). National Center for Education Evaluation and Regional Assistance (NCEE), Institute of Education Sciences, US Department of Education. https://ies.ed.gov/ncee/WWC/PracticeGuide/22

Graham, S., Cao, Y., Kim, Y.-S. G., Lee, J., Tate, T., Collins, P., Cho, M., Moon, Y., Chung, H. Q., & Olson, C. B. (2025). Effective writing instruction for students in grades 6 to 12: A best evidence meta-analysis. *Reading and Writing, 38*(4), 1–46. https://doi.org/10.1007/s11145-024-10539-2

Harris, J. (2017). *Rewriting: How to do things with texts* (2nd ed.). University Press of Colorado.

Hochman, J. C., & Wexler, N. (2017). *The writing revolution: A guide to advancing thinking through writing in all subjects and grades*. John Wiley & Sons.

IRIS Center. (2025). *PALS: A reading strategy for grades 2–6*. https://iris. peabody.vanderbilt.edu/module/pals26/cresource/q1/p01/

Pommarane, D. (2018, September 20). The benefits of writing into the day for a whole year [Blog]. *Literacy Now*. https://www.literacyworldwide. org/blog/literacy-now/2018/09/20/the-benefits-and-gains-from-writing-into-the-day-for-a-whole-year

Renkl, A. (2023). Using worked examples for ill-structured learning content. In C. E. Overson, C. M. Hakala, L. L. Kordonowy, & V. A. Benassi (Eds.), *In their own words: What scholars want you to know about why and how to apply the science of learning in your academic setting* (pp. 207–24). Society for the Teaching of Psychology. https:// www.unh.edu/teaching-learning-resource-hub/sites/default/files/ media/2023-06/itow-using-worked-examples-for-ill-structured-learning-content-renkl.pdf

Schwartz, S. (2025, June 26). Brain activity is lower for writers who use AI. What that means for students. *Education Week*. https://www.edweek. org/technology/brain-activity-is-lower-for-writers-who-use-ai-what-that-means-for-students/2025/06

Sedita, J. (2023). *The writing rope*. Brookes Publishing.

What Works Clearinghouse. (2017, November). *Self-regulated strategy development*. Institute of Education Science, US Department of Education. https://ies.ed.gov/ncee/WWC/Intervention/1292

Yung, M. (2020). ELA Brave and True. https://elabraveandtrue. com/2020/03/10/try-this-low-stakes-writing-activity-called-take-a-line-for-a-walk/

Literature Cited

Anzaldúa, G. (2007). *Borderlands/la frontera: The new mestiza* (3rd ed.). Aunt Lute Books.

Digging Into Digital Literacy

11

Even in the digital age, we continue to have disparities related to digital literacy, which are driven, at least in part, by the digital divide. The digital divide is a term used to describe the differences in access to technology, including access to the hardware (e.g., actual devices), software (e.g., programs that make devices work, such as apps), and infrastructure (e.g., high-speed, reliable internet access). These differences play a role in digital literacy development inside and outside of the classroom. Not all districts are on equal footing when it comes to resources, so while some students swipe through multimedia resources on tablets, others are left flipping through outdated books. Similarly, families may not have access to high-speed Internet, which means even students with a tablet may not be able to use the apps at home.

What's more, with technology evolving at lightning speed—some estimates say digital tools become outdated every three years—gaining access is only half the battle. Schools must constantly adapt just to keep up. In order to help students succeed in the ever-changing world of technology, educators need strategies that will continue to be useful even as the digital landscape changes rapidly. In this chapter, you will learn more about digital literacy and strategies you can use to confidently support your students even as you continue to learn alongside them.

Literacy Strategy: Circle of Perspectives

While reading this chapter, use the Circle of Perspectives thinking routine from Harvard Project Zero to practice perspective-taking. Consider the following perspectives as you think about how digital literacy has and will change over time.

- From the perspective of yourself as a student
- From the perspective of a practicing teacher
- From the perspective of a student who hasn't been born yet

Preview Vocabulary

artificial intelligence (AI): use of technology to accomplish tasks that typically require human abilities

AI literacy: knowledge, skills, and dispositions needed to engage productively with artificial intelligence

critical media literacy: knowledge, skills, and dispositions needed to engage analytically and critically with social and mass media

digital citizenship: knowledge, skills, and dispositions needed to engage responsibly with the world through the internet

digital footprint: all information about a person posted online intentionally or unintentionally

Defining Digital Literacy

When we consider digital literacy, a variety of things are likely to come to mind, such as teaching students how to build a spreadsheet or use search engines. Digital literacy is an umbrella term that includes critical media literacy, AI literacy, digital citizenship, online research, **multimodal** digital composition, and other literacies related to the capability to consume, curate, and create digital texts (Beach et al., 2026). In essence, it encompasses the same literacies we need to read and write print texts. For example, to read an article online, we have to decode the words, connect our knowledge about the world together with the ideas in the **text** to make inferences, and question the credibility of the information.

But, oftentimes in the digital literacy space, these skills are amplified. In traditional newspaper publishing, articles go through an editorial process with fact-checking and a review by an editor. Of course, this doesn't guarantee accuracy, but we could trust that stories went through a process. With the internet, there is a greater opportunity for self-publishing. On one hand, this offers pathways to more diverse perspectives that may not have been open through the traditional publishing process. On the other hand, this means that readers must do their own fact-checking. Digital spaces require students to become more critical consumers and creators of digital texts, carefully considering the messages that they read and that they put out into the world.

Critical Media Literacy

Critical media literacy is the ability to access, evaluate, and create media and online texts with the skills necessary to critically analyze purpose, biases, and merit in media messages (von Gillern et al., 2022). Educators Darren Hudgins and Jennifer LaGarde (2021) use the analogy of being a digital detective to explain critical media literacy to students. As digital detectives—fedora optional, but highly encouraged—the Internet is their crime scene. Their mission? Evaluate the credibility and reliability of what they find online. With this analogy, students learn not only practical skills to help them navigate the Internet but also the critical dispositions to be curious, cautious, and conscientious.

Teachers can help students develop their investigative toolkit: checking for an author's credentials, looking for evidence over emotion, and examining the tone of the content. Teachers encourage curiosity and questioning. Is the author an expert or just someone's uncle with strong opinions and a YouTube channel? We also teach them to be cautious and skeptical of claims that sound too good to be true, like sites that promise miraculous results with a single click. Because in the world of online info, not everything is as innocent as it looks—and even that grumpy cat might be up to something.

Teachers model being conscientious by examining bias. Bias in general shapes how information is created, framed, and interpreted, which is exactly what critical media literacy trains us to spot. Readers analyze bias in sources by questioning the author's intentions, determining facts versus opinions, identifying loaded language, looking at selection and omission of information, and considering whose interests are served by the message being communicated.

Readers also interrogate their own bias by being aware of confirmation bias and implicit bias. Confirmation bias is when we tend to notice and believe things that agree with what we already think, and overlook anything that doesn't. It's like wearing glasses that only let us see what we already believe and can impact the sources we choose and the evidence we accept. Implicit bias is when we unknowingly hold attitudes or stereotypes that influence how we see others. Recognizing and challenging these hidden biases is a key part of critical media literacy, because it helps us question whose perspectives are being shown and whether representations are fair. To mitigate bias, teachers demonstrate how to explore multiple perspectives, ask *what am I missing?*, and focus on the evidence instead of just being right.

The following Digital Detective Routine is adapted from Hudgins and LaGarde's (2021) book.

- Ask questions: Stay open and curious as you search for clues about trustworthiness.
- Investigate forensics: Look for the date of publication, **digital footprint** of the author, links to other sources, and other evidence.
- Uncover bias: Separate fact from opinion, beware of confirmation bias, and look for corroborating evidence.

The detective's job is to collect clues to detect the truth (not prove they are correct), or what Peter Adams from the News Literacy Project refers to as approaching the world with "intellectual humility" (Watson, 2021). An open mind with a healthy dose of humility and skepticism can protect adolescents from clickbait and deepfakes, equip them with the skills to make informed decisions, and empower students to create responsible and truthful media.

Critical media literacy also looks at how media messages are constructed and how media messages influence perception. Writers from a critical media literacy lens consider whose voices are represented and whose are missing, and they create media texts that responsibly and ethically engage with audiences. This awareness becomes even more crucial in our fast-changing media environment, where technology continually reshapes how information is created, shared, and consumed. With the speed of internet publishing, the speed of information sharing, and the speed of **artificial intelligence (AI)** innovation, today's students need strong critical media literacy to navigate and shape the digital world with awareness and agency.

AI Literacy

One of the most rapidly changing aspects of digital literacy is **AI literacy**. What was once limited to computer science class is now becoming a part of nearly every field of study—including healthcare, journalism, and finance. *Forbes* magazine projects that AI will replace 97 million jobs in the United States. But it's not all loss—AI is expected to create 170 million new jobs just as quickly (Marr, 2025). A unique element of teaching digital literacy is that we, as educators, might often be learning how to use new technology along with our students. AI, and especially generative AI and large language model (LLM), is a perfect example of how technology is changing the shape of literacy teaching and learning day by day.

In preparing for writing this chapter, I decided to use a chatty LLM to get me thinking about ways to begin. In the first prompt, I asked for ideas for "an intro for a chapter on digital literacy," which generated three options with short examples for each and reminders to adapt it for my specific audience. Although the results were relevant and answered the prompt, they felt too generic for my purpose. So, I revised the prompt: "please suggest some engaging hooks for a chapter on digital literacy for 4th–12th grade teachers and preservice teachers." This resulted in three ideas—focus on real-world relevance and student impact, highlight the challenges and opportunities for educators, and start with a question or intriguing scenario—with much more detailed examples, like this one: "Digital literacy isn't just about using devices; it's about empowering your students to become responsible digital citizens who understand the power and permanence of online interactions." But, although technically well-written, the examples provided fell short of the real-world impact and challenges teachers face when working with adolescents in online learning spaces.

Although using LLMs for writing isn't able to produce texts better than humans can—yet—it is increasingly on teachers' minds. Whether concerns about cheating or excitement about possibilities to enhance instruction, both lines of thinking lead to the question: *What are the appropriate uses of AI in education?* We must first recognize common uses of AI before we can determine the appropriate role and boundaries for AI in our classrooms. AI permeates our lives perhaps in ways we may not even be aware of.

Put simply, AI can be categorized into three types: reactive, predictive, and generative (ASCD et al., 2023). As illustrated in Figure 11.1, robots,

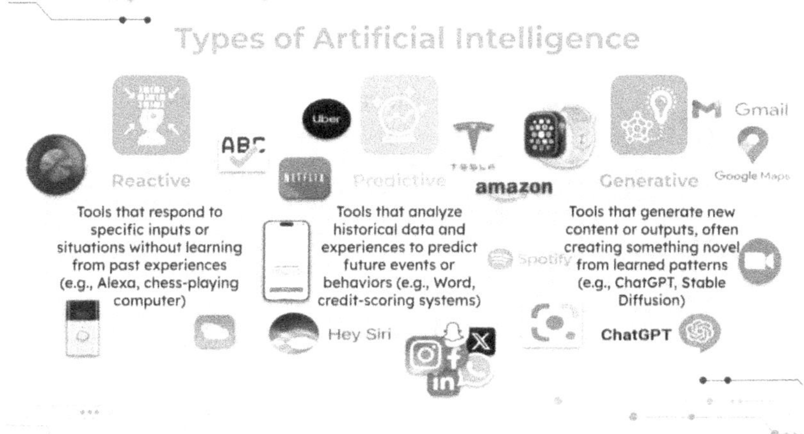

Figure 11.1 Types of AI.

spellcheck, and chess-playing computers are applications of reactive AI that provide output based on input. Second, word-processing software and search engines use algorithms to create predictive text and suggestions. The third type of AI, generative, creates new content from learned patterns and continues to learn and improve.

According to educational research, AI that scaffolds literacy by providing instant feedback or models of effective writing can be helpful for learning. When working with high school writers, researchers found that students productively used ChatGPT to give examples of hooks or counterarguments and that "no students copied and pasted ChatGPT's specific examples into their developing draft" (Levine et al., 2025, p. 451). AI is equipped to give real-time feedback on a writer's word choice, **syntax**, clarity, and coherence, and provide feedback on a reader's pronunciation, fluency, and vocabulary knowledge.

Interestingly, **meta-analysis** research has found that intelligent tutoring systems can improve reading by identifying gaps in **comprehension** and adjusting questions accordingly to purposely target gaps (Xu et al., 2019). Intelligent tutoring systems can also adapt text complexity of selections in real time, providing opportunities to challenge students to read even more complex text. In addition, studies have found that talking about books with AI chatbots familiar with the content helps keep students engaged in reading (Liu et al., 2022). For a list of AI tools, follow this case-sensitive link or scan the QR code in Figure 11.2 (https:// bit.ly/AIlist).

However, AI that does the thinking for students is troublesome. According to an *Education Week* article, research in neuroscience shows that the use of AI while writing an essay can reduce brain activity and create conflict in terms of writing ownership (Schwartz, 2025). Specifically, the research found that students who relied on ChatGPT while writing an essay showed low brain activity during the various important steps of the writing process as compared to those who used other online resources or only their own brain. Moreover, the group using ChatGPT weren't able to easily recall what they wrote or confidently view themselves as authors of the essay. The way that AI is incorporated into essay writing—and more specifically the timing—is important.

Generative AI is not going away. That's why teachers need to be AI literate

Figure 11.2

and ready to help students make the most of what AI can do, while steering clear of its negative side effects. AI literacy includes skills and knowledge, such as building prompts, understanding that machines are tools not people, and that machines can generate false statements called hallucinations. AI literacy also includes ethical considerations, such as academic honesty and climate concerns.

In addition, it's important for teachers not to fall for the detection illusion—there's currently no software that can reliably detect AI-generated text. In fact, these tools often flag human writing as AI (false positives), which can unfairly penalize students. One way to bring students into the conversation about AI is by co-creating a class code for how and when it's okay to use AI. The goal? A clear understanding and student ownership of appropriate AI use. Together with the teacher, students co-create a shared definition of what "appropriate AI use" means in class. They establish clear criteria for when AI use is allowed, when it must be cited or appended, and when tasks should reflect purely human work. The next step is to test their definition and criteria against potential uses—clarifying whether AI is okay for brainstorming ideas, editing drafts, creating images for presentations, and so on—and revising criteria as needed. This process promotes transparency, raises AI literacy, and empowers students to self-regulate their use of tools aligning expectations around both learning goals and academic integrity. A helpful resource for this discussion is the AI Assessment Scale, a flexible framework ranging from "No AI" to "AI-Assisted" to "Full AI" (Furze, 2024). Here is an example from a school district in Washington that used the scale to spark discussion about acceptable use (https://bit.ly/AIclassmatrix).

Another important reason to have conversations with students about AI is that it plays a complicated role in the digital divide. AI can either widen gaps or help close them, depending on who has access and how it's used. That makes it all the more critical to bring these issues into the classroom. Božić (2023) argues, on one hand, that AI can contribute to increasing the digital divide through various means: it can be hard to access the infrastructure that is required for AI to run, AI requires specific skills and education to operate it effectively, bias baked into the models can perpetuate oppression, AI surveillance may contribute to discrimination, and all of this may increase socioeconomic gaps. On the other hand, AI has the potential to narrow the gap in different ways: improving accessibility, contributing to differentiated learning, providing information to those who would otherwise be unable to access it, mitigating the tendency for human bias to contribute to decisions, and providing new economic opportunities. It is up to us to increase the potential benefits while limiting negative impacts. And, as teachers, we are in an important position to teach students how to use AI effectively, ethically, and safely.

Digital Citizenship

Digital citizenship involves engaging safely and responsibly with the world through the internet. As adolescents gain more access to digital platforms, like social media, they also face new risks and responsibilities. That's why Maqsood and Chiasson (2021) highlight several key areas of digital citizenship to focus on with adolescents:

- Cyberbullying: Help students recognize harmful behaviors like spreading rumors, sharing embarrassing photos, or using intimidation online.
- Data privacy: Teach students how apps collect their data, why location permissions and targeted ads matter, and how to take control of what they share.
- Digital footprint: Encourage students to think about the permanence of what they share online, reflect on the pressure to overshare, and protect themselves from impersonation.
- Ethics: Discuss the importance of getting consent before sharing someone else's content, understanding copyright rules, and respectful discourse even when we disagree.

These lessons go beyond just staying safe. They build lifelong habits for navigating the digital world responsibly and ethically.

As students grow in their understanding of social responsibility, teachers can help them see how technology can be a force for good. Advocacy is a powerful form of digital citizenship—and it's something we can actively teach. Sam von Gillern and colleagues (2022) emphasize that students need support in critically examining the social and civic issues that matter to them. That means helping them build critical media literacy skills like evaluating sources, thinking critically, and understanding multiple perspectives that we discussed earlier in this chapter in order to be informed on the issues. From there, students can move into creating their own messages—applying their digital writing skills to something meaningful. The final step? Sharing their work with an audience. At that point, it's essential to revisit lessons about online responsibility and safety so students understand how to advocate as empowered digital citizens.

How Do We Teach Digital Literacy?

Although some literacy skills used with print texts transfer to digital spaces, there are some unique skills that we need to teach into. The strategies below offer practical ways teachers can guide students through the process of researching and writing using online resources.

Online Research

First things first—don't assume students know how to write a solid research question. They often need some direct instruction here. Otherwise, they'll type something vague into Google, get hit with 1,000+ results, panic-scroll, and grab the first link they see (hello, random blog from 2009). By helping students craft clear, focused questions from the start, teachers are not just saving them from the search spiral, they're setting them up to find sources that actually *answer* the question they're trying to explore. Teachers can kick off a discussion about compelling questions by presenting students the criteria in Table 11.1. After students have drafted a research question, they can give each other feedback using the criteria before moving on to the next step of the research process.

Once students have a solid question, it is important to instruct them on how to find credible and reliable sources. To be honest, I start with Wikipedia

Table 11.1 Creating Research Questions

Compelling research questions should:	Compelling research questions should not:
• Spark the researcher's curiosity • Be able to be answered through research • Consider the possibility of multiple perspectives	• Lead to a yes or no answer • Already be definitively answered (e.g., Is Earth a planet?) • Be overly broad • Be too narrow
Research question revision process:	
Topic: Artificial Intelligence First version, already definitively answered: What is generative AI? Second version, too broad, not researchable: Is generative AI good or bad? Third version: Does generative AI help more than it harms when it comes to the environment?	

to build **background knowledge** and get an overview of my topic. When teaching students how to get started, we can explain to them that Wikipedia and YouTube are okay places to start, but that we shouldn't stop there. Show students to use Boolean operators (e.g., AND and NOT) and quotation marks to narrow their online searches; for example, *AI AND "environmental racism"* gives results that include both terms, whereas *AI NOT robots* helps filter out unrelated topics.

Teachers can guide students to search across multiple sources and points of view for corroboration of information. There are a variety of strategies to help students learn this skill set. Three of my favorites are Reading Sideways, introduced to me by Bryan Gaskill and described in the Tried and True section below, Lateral Reading, and Horizontal Reading. Are sideways, lateral, and horizontal really different strategies, you ask? Yes—just like lounging, reclining, and resting are technically different ways to avoid folding laundry.

Tried and True Strategy by Bryan Gaskill

Strategy Name: Reading Sideways

Context: Class at Marshall High School in Missouri

One of the strategies I have students practice is creating mind maps to visualize and track their thinking as they read digitally. Students begin with a single term—sometimes assigned, sometimes chosen from a shared text, or selected independently—which they write in the center of their page in their Writer's Notebooks. Using a digital encyclopedia such as Wikipedia, they skim the surface of the topic with the goal of identifying connections, exploring the breadth of the subject, and posing questions for deeper inquiry. While reading online, they create analog mind maps in their Writer's Notebooks. Each time they click a link, they add another term to their web of thinking and draw lines to show clustering and connection. This mapping process builds students' comfort with navigating beyond a single text to seek new information. It fosters curiosity, develops context and background knowledge, and promotes individuality and agency. The mind maps serve as anchors for peer, small-group, and whole-class conversations. The process of creation is more important than the product, but it makes the students' invisible decisions and associations observable. We often end the activity by posing a few questions that are focused, complex, and arguable. At some point, students return to these questions for further investigation.

Lateral Reading

Lateral reading is the practice of checking a site's credibility before investing time in close reading. Instead of staying on one site, readers open new tabs to investigate who created the source, what others say about it, and whether it's trustworthy—just as professional fact-checkers do. This approach comes from research from Stanford History Education Group comparing how students, professors, and fact-checkers evaluate online information (Wineburg & McGrew, 2019). Many students and professors read "vertically," judging credibility by a site's design, logos, or official-sounding names, and were often misled by polished pages.

Fact-checkers, in contrast, immediately left the original site to research who created it and what others say about it. For example, rather than relying on the Employment Policies Institute's website, they checked a *New York Times* article and a Wikipedia entry identifying the institute as a fiscally conservative think tank opposed to raising the minimum wage, staffed by employees of a firm owned by Richard Berman. A quick search also revealed a *60 Minutes* report calling Berman "Dr. Evil" for running nonprofit front groups for corporate clients. While only 40 percent of Stanford students uncovered this connection, every fact-checker did—often in far less time—because they read laterally.

Horizontal Reading

If we think about evaluating sources based on a y-axis of reliability and an x-axis of political leaning, we want to consume factually correct information (i.e., the top of the y-axis), but in order to consider multiple perspectives, we can read horizontally across the x-axis of political leaning (i.e., left ↔ center ↔ right). For example, in a social studies class, students explore the idea of voting rights by reading news articles about election reform from sources with different leanings. A great resource for Horizontal Reading is All Sides (AllSides.com), a news curation website that shows headlines from left-, center-, and right-leaning sources on the same topic.

As students are locating multiple, reliable sources, we want to support them in analyzing sources through a critical lens. As digital detectives, we encourage students to ask *What am I missing?* From a critical perspective, we can encourage students to ask *Whose voices are present and whose are not? Whose interests are served by this message and whose are not?* By fostering these habits of questioning, we help students move beyond simply gathering information to truly understanding the deeper context, perspectives, and power dynamics shaping what they read.

Synthesis Matrix

The next step in the research process is to synthesize evidence across sources to create claims. Back in my day—when cut and paste involved actual scissors—we used notecards for this step, similar to the List, Group, Label strategy in Chapter 8. We'd read our sources, jot down one idea per card (with proper citation, of course, lest the wrath of a red pen fall upon us), and then shuffle those cards around like a high-stakes game of academic poker. Once grouped by topic, those little paper squares magically became the body paragraphs of our research paper.

The idea of the Synthesis Matrix is to take the notecards from analog to digital. The matrix acts like a digital notecatcher where students organize their sources down the first column of the spreadsheet and their subtopics or key ideas across the top row. Students can insert full citations, helping them keep track of where their ideas came from and making the Works Cited page way less painful in the end. In each cell, students can cut and paste quotes or paraphrase main ideas (still with proper citation, of course). This setup lets students visually compare perspectives across sources, spot agreement or contradiction, and see where more research is needed. Foregrounding synthesis helps students avoid the classic "source-by-source" summary trap—much like the Questions Into Paragraphs strategy illustrated in Figure 4.2. As a digital matrix, students can revise their thinking, add or reorganize ideas, and move columns around without rewriting every card. Additionally, students can collaborate with each other easily and share with the teacher for feedback along the way.

Multimodal Digital Composition

Multimodal composition is creating texts that combine more than just written words. They might include images, audio, video, animations, hyperlinks, graphics, and interactive elements. Memes are quintessential multimodal compositions in that the image alone or the text alone does not communicate the meaning in the same way as the two together. Multimodal composition involves using the full range of digital tools to communicate ideas, arguments, or narratives in layered, engaging ways. It encourages students to use their creative, technical, and collaborative talents to show what they know—whether that's through a podcast, an infographic, or a documentary-style video. Today's students are already swimming in multimodal texts. Teaching them to critically analyze and intentionally create these forms prepares them for real-world communication.

Remix

A hallmark of digital literacy is the concept of remixing, which draws on the language of hip-hop to name and value the practice of creating new compositions from existing texts. Think of how Pnau remixed Elton John songs (e.g., "Rocket Man" and "Sacrifice") and released as "Cold Heart." The remix alters the original in a way that communicates a new feeling. Students can remix texts, songs, images, and videos to communicate new messages, to show understanding about their learning, or to create counternarratives to push back on harmful messages in society.

For example, tenth-grade students in New York City responded to how women of color were portrayed in media through the remix practices of reframing, juxtaposing, mash-up, and collage. DeJaynes and Curmi-Hall (2019) describe the result:

> In a final hallway collage of words, photos, and a link to a film, the youth researchers juxtaposed media tropes with the multiple identities and experiences of young women of color in their school to visually narrate and celebrate their lived realities as scholars, media makers, and civic actors. (p. 299)

The youth reframed popular images as stereotypes and juxtaposed these stereotypes with reality through both visual collage and video mash-up, making powerful multimodal compositions.

Digital Storytelling

Digital Storytelling is the use of digital tools to tell a story or communicate an idea. It combines traditional narrative skills (like structure, voice, and perspective) with digital literacy skills (like sound mixing, video editing, and visual design). In choosing modes (sound, image, text) and tools (slides, podcast app, movie maker), students learn to think rhetorically: What's the best way to reach my audience? How does design influence meaning? These are essential twenty-first-century literacy skills. What's more, digital storytelling gives students a chance to own their stories—whether personal, academic, or creative—and share them in a format that feels authentic. Take a look at digital storytelling in action in the Tried and True Strategy.

Tried and True Strategy by Shea Kerkhoff

Strategy Name: Digital Storytelling

Context: First-Year Composition course in West Lafayette, Indiana

In my class, I have used the *One in 8 Million* project as a mentor text (http://bit.ly/onein8million). The *One in 8 Million* project features fifty portraits of New Yorkers, combining oral storytelling with black-and-white photography to create powerful video personal narratives. We watch a few of the three-minute videos and discuss what we thought made them powerful. Students usually mention the hooks that immediately grab the audience's attention and pull them into the story as particularly compelling. I also have a learning goal that students will be able to use specific details and imagery in their writing, so I make sure to bring up the vivid details in the narratives if students do not. We rewatch the same videos again, taking notes of the different techniques we notice that we want to imitate in our own digital storytelling.

Students then partner with someone they do not know and interview each other with an interview protocol that asks about an inciting event or circumstance that changed the person. The interviews serve as both an idea generator and a community builder, as these videos often end up being both deeply personal and highly collaborative. After the interviews, the pairs choose one story that came up in the interviews to zoom in on. The person who told the story is responsible for drafting the script and recording the audio. The other person is responsible for drafting the storyboard and taking the photos. Although the responsibilities are divided, the two work together on planning, revising, and editing in order to produce the final product as a video.

Here is a free download of the lesson slides (https://bit.ly/onein8millionslides).

Digitization of Teaching

The digitization of literacy teaching and learning means devices are ubiquitous, but that doesn't mean that students know how to use technology for academic purposes or that integrating technology is always the best option. Because any specific technology I mention could be outdated or defunct by the time you pick up this book, I want to instead offer a framework that you can use to consider what digital tools and platforms to infuse in your teaching and learning.

Teachers can use the Affirm, Deepen, Critique framework when integrating technology in the classroom. Starting with the first component, *affirm* validates the literacies students are already using in their daily lives. Instead of creating hierarchies where some literacies are considered superior, teachers affirm that all forms of reading and writing are valid. Prominent researcher Tisha Lewis Ellison (2023) describes the many ways that adolescents engage digital literacy as content creators, sound engineers, video game builders, app coders, podcasters, digital storytellers, and activists. She highlights how adolescents from communities of color are digital literacy leaders, yet, too often, not recognized as such in school spaces. She states that adolescents from communities of color "take, create, and make meaning of evocative images that portray the ways they wish to be represented, while countering social injustices that say otherwise. Their genius, radiance, and creativity … most times, remain unrecognized and unappreciated in schools" (p. 594). She goes on to say that when educators "really 'see' our children, and their families, from non-bias lenses, there will no longer be missed opportunities in the classroom and communities to build on the digital literacies that are salient to today's students and youth" (p. 596). When teachers recognize and value the digital skills that adolescents already possess, they can then integrate students' digital literacies into the curriculum, affirm their identities, and provide space for them to create and share in ways that matter to them.

The second part, *deepen*, refers to deepening students' learning, literacies, and content knowledge. Simply substituting digital for analog may not always be the best instructional decision. An example of this is adopting a digital version of the textbook. The digital text may enhance students' experience because they can see visual collections of sections they've highlighted or access a built-in dictionary to define words that are unfamiliar. Of course, students could take physical notes, highlight a print copy, and use a dictionary to look up challenging words. Plus, reading comprehension and retention of content are better with print texts (Horvath, 2024), so the technology is not necessarily a net gain for their learning.

Instead of using technology for technology's sake, teachers can select technology that augments and redefines learning (Romrell et al., 2014). Augmentation occurs when technology enhances learning beyond what traditional instructional strategies can achieve. For example, the Social Annotation strategy improves understanding and transforms the reading experience. In Social Annotation, students annotate a shared digital text, allowing them to view each other's notes and add links to additional resources. This turns reading from a solitary activity into a collaborative, social practice. Some learning opportunities are even more radically transformed by technology. For instance, a teacher who uses video conferencing to connect students with peers in another country expands learning beyond geographic boundaries.

Remember the game 20 Questions? Massachusetts educator Laura Gardner (2019) gave it an international twist to launch a Collaborative Online International Learning (COIL) project with her students and a partner class in Canada. Here's the catch—they had no idea where the other class was from. Enter Mystery Skype, the high-tech cousin of 20 Questions. Students took turns firing off up to twenty yes-or-no questions, Carmen Sandiego-style, trying to crack the case of "Where in the world are you?" The two classes then read a novel at the same time and discussed the book using the digital tool Padlet (https://padlet.com). The logistical barriers of taking students to another country make this opportunity nearly unfathomable without the use of technology. Technology gives students the opportunity to connect and collaborate across time, across culture, and across space.

Sometimes teachers express hesitation in using technology because they think technology will be a distraction. And, in some ways, this concern is warranted. Technology can be a distraction. While writing this section, my phone pinged with two new messages, an email, and a reminder for a meeting I have in an hour. However, we must also weigh this potential for distraction with the ability for technology to increase **engagement** for our students. Take, for example, the typical style of lecture where one student responds to a question posed by the teacher while other students passively listen. With technology, teachers can have everyone actively engaged by answering the question simultaneously on their devices. The possibility of technology being a distraction is there, but so is the possibility to enhance, or even transform, our students' learning experiences.

The final element, *critique*, challenges us to pause and think critically about technology's role in the classroom. On one hand, it means being intentional—choosing tech tools not because they're shiny and new, but because they truly support our learning goals. On the other hand, it's about zooming out to see the bigger picture—how technology can mirror and even magnify social problems, and how, with thoughtful use, it can also help address those problems and launch meaningful change. As educators, problematizing technology is part of our responsibility as we engage students in digital literacy.

We must also advocate for our students and leverage literacy learning in the expanding digital frontier. This includes advocating for our students to have access to technology and for student-centered digital literacy instruction. Although we may not always know how or what strategy we want to use, we can find ways to critically and thoughtfully leverage technology to support students in making and communicating meaning.

Conclusion

The definition of literacy has expanded, and with it, the way we teach literacy must also expand. Adolescents are already deeply engaged in complex digital practices—creating content, storytelling, and activism—to express themselves and share their ideas. When educators recognize and build on these existing skills, they not only make learning more relevant but inclusive and empowering as well. Teaching digital literacy equips all students with the tools to critically navigate, contribute to, and shape digital spaces. By embracing students' digital lives and teaching the literacy practices they need to thrive, we help cultivate more equitable classrooms and more just futures.

More to Explore

- Here's a media literacy video from NCTE and Renee Hobbs: https://youtu.be/tX23kM9QN9M?si=dzJc1qy4PI32nkey
- Check out this Ted Radio Hour episode on AI chatbots: https://www.npr.org/2025/07/18/1255880063/ted-radio-hour-prophets-of-technology-part-2
- A plethora of resources for teachers and students are available on the News Literacy Project website: https://newslit.org/
- Even more resources for teachers and students curated by ISTE: https://questionnaire.getdigitalskills.org/
- This podcast episode is called Digital literacy in today's classroom with Dr. Shea Kerkhoff: https://creators.spotify.com/pod/profile/teacherprep/episodes/Digital-Literacy-in-Todays-Classroom-with-Dr-Shea-Kerkhoff-eaqrq5

Reflect

Choose one of the Circle of Perspectives at the beginning of the chapter. Reflect on the reading using these Sentence Stems:

- I am thinking of digital literacy from the viewpoint of [the viewpoint you've chosen]

- I think [describe the topic from your viewpoint]. Be an actor—take on the character of your viewpoint.
- A question I have from this viewpoint is [ask a question from this viewpoint]

Discuss

Questions for discussion to learn from and with each other:

- What is digital literacy and why is it important to teach?
- When is it acceptable to use AI—for writing? for class assignments?
- How can you apply the digital literacy strategies in this chapter to your teaching and learning?
- How does the affirm, deepen, critique framework support teachers when integrating technology?

References

Association for Supervision and Curriculum Development (ASCD), International Society for Technology in Education (ISTE), National Association of Elementary School Principals (NAESP) and the National Association of Secondary School Principals (NASSP). (2023). *Bringing AI to school: Tips for school leaders* [Toolkit]. https://www.aasa.org/resources/resource/bringing-ai-to-school-tips-for-school-leaders

Beach, C., Kerkhoff, S. N., & Langer, S. (2026). Digital divides: Illuminating inequities in access, literacies, and opportunities within and across communities. In J. Castek, J. Coiro, M. Hagerman, E. Forzani, C, Kiili, & J. Sparks (Eds.), *International handbook of research in digital literacies*. Routledge.

Bozic, V. (2023). Artificial intelligence as the reason and the solution of digital divide. *Language Education & Technology (LET Journal)*, *3*(2), 96–109. https://langedutech.com/letjournal/index.php/let/article/view/53

DeJaynes, T., & Curmi-Hall, C. (2019). Transforming school hallways through critical inquiry: Multimodal literacies for civic engagement. *Journal of Adolescent & Adult Literacy*, *63*(3), 299–309. https://doi.org/10.1002/jaal.991

Furze, L. (2024). *The AI assessment scale: A tool for genAI assessment.* https://mcusercontent.com/0e4244172472af8210b990aa9/files/c7e2a935-e60c-ba6a-c737-6952b0d36157/Leonfurze.com_The_AI_Assessment_Scale_updated.pdf

Gardner, L. (2019). Global Read Aloud [blog]. *Massachusetts School Library Association Forum Newsletter.* https://www.maschoolibraries.org/newsletter/global-read-aloud

Horvath, J. C. (2024, July 2). 5 ways to help your brain learn better. *Psychology Today.* https://www.psychologytoday.com/us/articles/202407/5-ways-to-help-your-brain-learn-better

Hudgins, D., & LaGarde, J. (2021). *Developing digital detectives: Essential lessons for discerning fact from fiction in the "fake news" era.* International Society for Technology in Education. https://muse.jhu.edu/book/99244

Levine, S., Beck, S. W., Mah, C., Phalen, L., & Pittman, J. (2025). How do students use ChatGPT as a writing support? *Journal of Adolescent & Adult Literacy, 68*(5), 445–57. https://doi.org/10.1002/jaal.1373

Lewis Ellison, T. (2023). Normalizing Black students/youth and their families' digital and STEAM literacies. *The Reading Teacher, 76*(5), 594–600. https://doi.org/10.1002/trtr.2182

Liu, C.-C., Liao, M.-G., Chang, C.-H., & Lin, H.-M. (2022). An analysis of children's interaction with an AI chatbot and its impact on their interest in reading. *Computers & Education, 189*, 104576. https://doi.org/10.1016/j.compedu.2022.104576

Maqsood, S., & Chiasson, S. (2021). Design, development, and evaluation of a cybersecurity, privacy, and digital literacy game for tweens. *ACM Transactions on Privacy and Security, 24*(4), 1–37. https://doi.org/10.1145/3469821

Marr, B. (2025, June 30). How is AI really impacting jobs in 2025? *Forbes.* https://www.forbes.com/sites/bernardmarr/2025/06/30/how-is-ai-really-impacting-jobs-in-2025/

Romrell, D., Kidder, L. C., & Wood, E. (2014). The SAMR model as a framework for evaluating mlearning. *Online Learning, 18*(2). https://doi.org/10.24059/olj.v18i2.435

Schwartz, S. (2025, June 26). Brain activity is lower for writers who use AI. What that means for students. *Education Week.* https://www.edweek.org/technology/brain-activity-is-lower-for-writers-who-use-ai-what-that-means-for-students/2025/06

von Gillern, S., Gleason, B., & Hutchison, A. (2022). Digital citizenship, media literacy, and the ACTS framework. *The Reading Teacher, 76*(2), 145–58. https://doi.org/10.1002/trtr.2120

Watson, A. (2021, February 21). Educator tools for media literacy and how to advocate for truth [Podcast Episode]. *Truth for Teachers*. https://truthforteachers.com/truth-for-teachers-podcast/media-literacy-tools-and-advocating-for-truth/

Wineburg, S., & McGrew, S. (2019). Lateral reading and the nature of expertise: Reading less and learning more when evaluating digital information. *Teachers College Record, 121*(11), 1–40. https://doi.org/10.1177/016146811912101102

Xu, Z., Wijekumar, K. K., Ramirez, G., Hu, X., & Irey, R. (2019). The effectiveness of intelligent tutoring systems on K-12 students' reading comprehension: A meta-analysis. *British Journal of Educational Technology, 50*(6), 3119–37. http://doi.org/10.1111/bjet.12758

Epilogue

Adolescents make meaning not in isolation, but through interaction with peers, teachers, texts, and the broader social and cultural world around them. By drawing on both cognitive processes and social experiences, we can create classrooms where students think critically, collaborate meaningfully, and grow as readers and writers.

Writing this book has been a growing experience for me and has felt like running a marathon. I realized in my own running journey that the foundation I had built in 5Ks and 10Ks hadn't gone away when I began training for a half-marathon. Once I laced up my sneakers and got back on the trails, I used a lot of the skills from those races to begin training for and ultimately running not just one half-marathon but several. The training plan was different. I had to learn new strategies like staying motivated and fueled during longer runs.

Similarly, with a plan and new strategies, our adolescent literacy learners can make new strides as they build on their literacy foundations. Like training for a race, progress in literacy comes step by step—and often with a few surprising turns along the way. And, who knows, maybe one day I'll actually run a marathon, but that's for another book.

Glossary

academic language: the formal language and vocabulary used in schools

academic standards: agreed-upon goals for what students should know and be able to do by the end of each grade level

affect: feelings and emotions

AI literacy: knowledge, skills, and dispositions needed to engage productively with artificial intelligence

artificial intelligence (AI): use of technology to accomplish tasks that typically require human abilities

asset-based: An approach that focuses on the strengths, skills, and resources that individuals or communities possess, rather than concentrating on weaknesses or deficits

autonomy: able to decide for oneself what and how to learn

background knowledge: what a reader knows about a topic, concept, or the world that helps them make sense of a text

cognitive function: mental processes involved in learning and comprehending

cognitive overload: too much information for the brain to process

comprehension: making meaning of written, spoken, or viewed text

comprehension strategy: a tool that assists readers in making meaning

content area literacy: reading, writing, and language strategies that can be used to support literacy in any content classroom

critical media literacy: knowledge, skills, and dispositions needed to engage analytically and critically with social and mass media

decoding: connecting the graphemes (letters) to the phonemes (sounds)

deep learning: shift from rote memorization to the ability to understand, apply, and connect concepts across different contexts

dialogic: an approach to teaching that values open-ended dialogue

digital citizenship: knowledge, skills, and dispositions needed to engage responsibly with the world through the Internet

digital footprint: all information about a person posted online intentionally or unintentionally

disciplinary literacy: the unique ways that disciplinary experts read, write, and use language in the disciplines

encoding: connecting the phonemes (sounds) to the graphemes (letters)

engagement: emotional connection to or active participation in learning

formal assessment: structured assessments, like tests or portfolios, used to measure learning in an official way

formative assessment: assessment during learning to check how well students are understanding

genre: category defined by shared features that shape how a text is crafted and understood

grapheme: letters of written language

informal assessment: less structured assessments, like class discussions or observations, to gauge learning in a low-risk way

learning objective: specific statement of what students should know or be able to do by the end of the lesson

mentor text: an exemplary text that students can use as a model and imitate

meta-analysis: a type of research that analyzes a large body of research to determine the strength and consistency of the results of previous research by calculating effect size

morphemic awareness: understanding how parts of words carry meaning

motivation: will or drive to do something

multimodal: made up of more than one mode: written, visual, and/or audio

multisyllabic: having two or more syllables

orthography: study of how graphemes (letters) and phonemes (sounds) relate to form words

patterns of organization: structures that authors use to organize texts or sections of texts

phoneme: smallest unit of sound in words

phonics: understanding that sounds are connected to graphemes, the name for written letters

phonological awareness: understanding that words are made up of sounds and the ability to recognize spoken parts of words

proficiency scale: assessment tool that delineates levels of a skill or understanding

reciprocal: two-way relationship

retrieval practice: actively recalling information

rhetorical awareness: conception of audience, purpose, and context of writing

rubric: assessment tool that clearly outlines the criteria for evaluating a student's work

schema: mental network of information

self-efficacy: believing that one is capable of succeeding

self-regulation: monitoring and managing a process, such as the writing process

social practices: actions based on the norms of the group

summative assessment: final assessments, like tests or projects, of what students have learned at the end of a unit or course to measure student outcomes

synonym: a word that means the same or almost the same as another word

syntax: how sentences are structured

text: reading material that includes traditional print books as well as multimedia and digital sources, such as podcasts, videos, poetry, articles, and more

worked example: working through a process step-by-step together

Index of Strategies

write their question without their name on a piece of paper, crumple the paper into a snowball, and throw it to the front of the room. A student volunteer—or the teacher—then reads the questions for the class to answer. Digitally, this can be done with an anonymous digital survey or whiteboard tool. The reverse can also work, where the teacher asks a question and students anonymously answer on paper or a digital tool. p. 117

Anticipation Guide: An instructional strategy that helps students make connections with the text. The Anticipation Guide presents statements related to the text, some of which may be true and others may not. Students make their own assessment of each statement with no consequence for being right or wrong. The point is to activate schema around what students already know and to set a purpose for reading in order to see if their answers were correct. pp. 163, 201

Atwoodian Table: An instructional strategy that invites students to visualize academic argument as a conversation—one where each author has a seat at the table. This approach helps students understand that when they join an argument, they're stepping into an ongoing dialogue, not starting from scratch. Students draw a table on their paper and assign each "seat" to a different voice in the conversation. p. 105

B

Because, But, So: A sentence expansion strategy that also supports content learning as a thinking routine. This strategy works well with content about a change or result. The teacher provides a sentence starter (e.g., A solid melts to form a liquid …). The students then expand the sentence using the words because, but, and so. p. 240

Bell-Ringers/Do Nows/Warm-Ups: Work that is ready for students to complete as they enter the class with the expectation that they begin as soon as the bell rings to begin class. The work typically reviews prior learning or serves as an introduction to the lesson of the day. p. 181

Big 3 Questions: A reading and annotation strategy from Beers and Probst (2015) with three questions: What surprised me? (Mark new insights with an !) What does the author think I already knew? (Mark with a ? and write any questions you have in the margins.) What challenged or confirmed what I already knew? (Mark with an * and make connections in the margins.) p. 61

C

Choice Boards: An assessment strategy to offer students multiple options to demonstrate their understanding of specific learning goals, while honoring their individual strengths, interests, and needs. Each task on the board is intentionally designed to meet the same academic standards but provides varied modes of expression, such as writing, drawing, speaking, or using technology. p. 122

Choral Reading: The group reads aloud together, like how a choir sings together. Choral reading gives adolescent readers a chance to actively practice fluency and expression with the support of a group, while allowing them to blend in and build confidence without the pressure of reading aloud alone. pp. 180, 228

Chunking Text: An instructional strategy where teachers break text into smaller, more digestible sections. pp. 154, 219, 229

Circle of Perspectives: A thinking routine from Harvard Project Zero to practice perspective taking. Teachers can provide choices and have students write and discuss from different perspectives. Students can begin by saying: I am thinking of [the topic] from the viewpoint of [the viewpoint chosen]. p. 263

Click or Clunk: A self-monitoring strategy for comprehension. Readers are encouraged to pause regularly and ask themselves: Did that make sense? Was that a click or a clunk? A click means that the reading makes sense. The reader understands what the words are saying and what's going on. A clunk means something doesn't make sense. It could be a tricky word, a confusing sentence, or an unclear idea. Writers can apply this strategy

The detective's job is to collect clues to detect the truth (not prove they are correct). p. 256

Digital Storytelling: Combines writing, images, audio, and video to help students craft and share personal or academic narratives. It builds traditional literacy skills while also fostering creativity, voice, and digital communication competencies. p. 278

Discussion Cube: A strategy that brings an element of fun and chance to answering questions. Teachers can make discussion cubes out of cardstock or buy soft photo cubes with pockets in which to insert the questions. In pairs or small groups, students roll the cube like a die and have to answer the question rolled. They take turns rolling until time runs out. p. 223

DISSECT: A strategy used to decode multisyllabic words. DISSECT stands for: Discover the context, Isolate the prefix, Separate the suffix, Say the stem, Examine the stem, Check with someone, Try the dictionary. pp. 48, 169

E

Exam-Wrapper: A post-exam activity where students reflect on their performance and study habits. It's a short, often ungraded assignment that encourages students to analyze what they did well, what they struggled with, and how they can improve their learning strategies for future assessments. p. 128

Exit Ticket: A quick, low-stakes way to check what students have learned before they head out the door—think of it as their "ticket to leave" the classroom. It's a classic example of formative assessment because it provides timely insight into student understanding *during* the learning process, not after it's too late to course-correct. p. 117

F

Fist to Five: A nonverbal check for understanding strategy. It can be used as a preassessment to gauge students' background knowledge or during a lesson to check for understanding. The teacher poses a question (e.g., *"Have you ever heard of photosynthesis?"* or *"Are we ready to move on?"*) Students respond by holding up a number of fingers from 0 (fist): "I have never heard of this" or "I'm so confused" to 5: "I'm so confident, I could explain this concept to a classmate" or "I completely understand and am ready to move on." p. 117

Fix-Up Strategies: When monitoring comprehension during reading, use these to fix confusion and keep going: reread the sentence more slowly; look ahead or behind for clues in the text; break the word apart (prefix, root, suffix); check a dictionary or glossary; think about what you already know about the topic; summarize the last part you *did* understand; ask for help from a peer or teacher. pp. 177, 226

Frayer Model: The Frayer Model puts the focus word in the center of a graphic organizer and uses four boxes around the focus word for students to add (1) the definition in their own words, (2) characteristics or features of the term to help students identify it, (3) examples of the word, and (4) nonexamples. p. 191

Frontloading with Images: A strategy where teachers introduce key concepts or vocabulary through carefully selected visuals before diving into a text or lesson. p. 202

G

Gallery Walk: An active learning strategy where students rotate around the room to observe, analyze, and respond to peers' work or posted content. It encourages movement, collaboration, and deeper engagement with ideas through discussion and reflection. pp. 105, 202

Genius Hour: Dedicate time each week for students to pursue their own passion through inquiry-based learning (Krebs & Zi, 2020). This strategy originated from Google's 20 percent time, where employees were allowed to work on personal projects. Students design their project based on their personal values, their needs, and their curiosity and are able to make a plan in a self-directed and creative way. p. 147

Gist Statement: capture the essential idea or main point of a text in just a sentence or two to focus on the core message without getting lost in the details. Two guiding questions to get to the gist are: Who or what is the paragraph/section about? What is the most important thing about the who or what? For a more complex gist, the guiding questions are: Who or what is the paragraph/section about? Did what? When/Where? Why/How? p. 224

Glows and Grows: A reflection or feedback tool to prompt identification of what the person did well, as the Glows, and to frame places that need improvement from a growth mindset, as the Grows. p. 125

Gradual Release of Responsibility: Also called I Do, We Do, You Do. An instructional strategy which scaffolds learning through teaching directly, modeling, and practicing collaboratively, before expecting students to apply the skill on their own. pp. 79, 252, 255

Graffiti Wall: On a bulletin board, chart paper, or digital whiteboard, students use words, images, symbols, colors, and their full linguistic repertoire to visually explore a concept or theme from a text. p. 225

H

Harris Moves: A set of rhetorical strategies developed by Joseph Harris (2017) to help students with just that. These "moves" include the techniques of illustrating, authorizing, extending, and countering. p. 248

Horizontal Reading: Horizontal reading is a strategy where students read multiple sources on the same topic side by side to compare perspectives, evaluate credibility, and identify bias. It helps develop critical thinking by encouraging students to synthesize information across texts rather than relying on a single source. p. 273

Hyperdoc: A document with hyperlinks embedded, to walk students through an inquiry or project one step at a time with the resources they need for each step curated and linked. p. 92

I

Identity Web: An identity web is a visual tool that helps students explore and share the many facets of who they are—such as their interests, family, culture, strengths, and experiences. By creating and discussing their webs, students build self-awareness while discovering commonalities and differences with their peers. For teachers, it's a powerful way to foster belonging, empathy, and community in the classroom. p. 140

I Do, We Do, You Do: Also called gradual release of responsibility. An instructional routine that scaffolds learning through teaching directly, modeling, and practicing collaboratively, before expecting students to apply the skill independently. pp. 79, 170, 176

Imitation Writing/Imitating Other Writers: A writing exercise where students study a sample of writing and then imitate its structure or style, but with their own content. p. 245

Inquiry-Based Reading: An instructional approach that encourages students to actively engage with texts in order to answer an essential teacher-generated question or a compelling student-generated question. p. 98

I Learned … I Will … : A thinking routine to prompt learners to reflect and make a commitment. p. 260

I Notice … I Wonder … : A thinking routine to layer thinking with first observing what is there and then questioning what it could mean. p. 102

It Says/I Say: This strategy integrates reading and writing to learn by having students make a T-Chart. On the left side, they label the column "It Says" and they take notes about the important ideas in the reading using the technical terms. On the right side, they label the column "I Say" and respond to what they are reading, interpreting the ideas into their own words, making connections, and drawing conclusions. Students can turn and talk with a partner about what they are writing at checkpoints during the reading or after finishing the text. They can also use the chart as a prewriting activity to generate ideas. pp. 112, 205

**I Used to Think … Now I Think … **: A thinking routine that supports students' metacognition by considering what they thought before reading and then identifying changes in their thinking after reading. p. 32

J

Jigsaw: For a simple version of this activity, each person in the group is assigned a section of the text to read. They then summarize their section for the rest of the group. It's important that the text used is able to be comprehended without reading the full thing. Another option is to have each person in the group read a different text, such as articles written from different perspectives on the same topic, and then share the perspective from the text with the group. pp. 64, 143

Juicy Sentence Protocol: Break down complex, or "juicy," sentences by analyzing their components and reconstructing them to understand the meaning. First, students start with the whole sentence, identifying challenging elements. Then, they analyze the parts in chunks. Finally, they return to the whole sentence again to see if they understand the meaning. See also Sentence Structure Explicit Instruction Routine. p. 218

K

Kernel Essay: A short, structured piece of writing, often used as a prewriting tool, that breaks down an idea or memory into a series of concise sentences. Teachers can provide structure options for students related to the assignment. Over time, students can also make their own structures. It's like a seed that can be expanded into a full essay. p. 252

KWHLAQ: An expansion of the KWL chart where students either individually or as a whole class answer the questions: What do I already *know* about this topic? What do I *want* to know? And then after the lesson return to fill out What did I *learn*. The expanded chart also includes *How* do I

find out? What *action* will I take? and What *questions* do I have now? p. 147

L

Lateral Reading: A method used to assess the credibility of online sources by seeking information about a source from other trusted websites. p. 273

Layered Annotation: This annotation strategy chunks the look-fors so that students focus on coding for one look-for at a time when reading. This promotes repeated readings, which is necessary for close reading and helpful for building fluency. p. 143

Layered Reading and Writing: An integration of reading and writing through the use of a Dialectical Notebook where students use the left side to gather main ideas, record interesting evidence, and respond to what they are reading. Students then use the right side to process their thinking and generate their own ideas about the topic under investigation. p. 102

Layered Social Annotation: For this activity, students work in small groups and simultaneously annotate a passage on a large piece of paper. Each person in the group has a different look-for or role. First, they mark up the text and write their thoughts in the margin. Second, they annotate their peers' annotations. This is also known as collaborative annotation. p. 143

Learning Menu: Learning Menus are similar to choice boards, but they add a bit more structure in that students make a choice within categories, like starters, main course, and dessert. p. 122

List, Group, Label: It's no surprise that this strategy begins by having students collaboratively list all of the important features, characteristics, or ideas about the focus word. The focus word can be a technical term or the main idea of the text. The students then group words from their list to form categories and label each category. The purpose is not to select the "right" words but on the conversations, reasoning, and synthesis of ideas that

states the main idea. The partner can give feedback if anything is incorrect and is impeding comprehension of the text. They keep switching readers every five minutes until they finish the text assigned. Partner reading can be used in the classroom, for peer tutoring, or at home with a parent. p. 247

Peer Conferences: Students interview each other to support reflection and self-awareness on their writing process and product. p. 128

P.I.E.: A mnemonic to remember that author's purpose generally falls into one of three categories: persuade, inform, or entertain. p. 219

Playing Card Method: Peers give each other feedback using playing cards as a metaphor for giving actionable and specific feedback. Hearts symbolize positive but vague, diamonds positive and specific, clubs negative and not actionable, and spades negative but actionable. p. 128

Possible Sentences: With this prereading strategy, the teacher gives students words from the text to make predictions about what they think the text will be about. Students write sentences using the words and share their predictions with a small group using sentence stems, such as *I predict … because …* Students then talk as a whole group, and the teacher can guide the conversation to make sure there are no misconceptions as far as conceptual knowledge. p. 203

Praise Question Polish (PQP): A peer editing protocol where students first praise something specific in a peer's work, then ask questions to clarify the meaning of words or sentences that are unclear, and finally offer a suggestion on what could be polished to improve the writing. It encourages respectful, balanced feedback and helps students develop both their writing and critique skills. p. 259

Preview Vocabulary: Previewing new words before reading and providing multiple opportunities for students to hear, read, speak, and write the words. Beginning of

each chapter, specific examples in pp. 200, 218

Proficiency Scale: An assessment tool used in education to clearly define levels of student understanding or skill in relation to a specific learning goal or standard. It outlines a progression of learning from limited to advanced performance and helps both teachers and students understand what mastery looks like. p. 123

Q

Question Answer Relationship: This reading comprehension strategy helps students understand how to find and think about answers in a text. Right there are questions that students can point to the answer in the text. For think-and-search questions, students have to synthesize information or connect examples from multiple places in the text. Author-and-me is where the students have to think about what they learned from the text or make inferences connecting the words to their own experiences to answer the question. p. 229

Questions Into Paragraphs (Q→P): This strategy takes an overarching topic and breaks it into 2–4 questions. The overarching topic can come from the curricular unit, and then students can work in small groups to identify lines of inquiry that they would like to follow. Students complete an organizer to answer the questions that help them track information across sources, compare perspectives, deepen understanding, and build knowledge across sources. pp. 100, 274

Question the Author: A simple strategy that invites students to discuss the text in a way that disrupts the idea that authors have all the right answers. For example, a teacher might ask, *What was the author's message? What did the author think that you knew that you did not? What was the muddiest point?* p. 223

Quick List: This is a prewriting activity to help students generate ideas. Students simply list as many ideas as they can think of about a specific topic. Later, they can organize the list and focus on one topic or theme. p. 235

Quick Write: In a quick write, students are free to write their initial thoughts about a question or prompt. The idea is not to worry about grammar or spelling, but to activate prior knowledge and make personal connections to what they will be learning. Quick writes usually range from 2 to 5 minutes. Students then turn and talk and share what they wrote. This provides them the opportunity to use vocabulary words in writing and speaking. pp. 107, 201

R

RADaR Revision: a writing strategy that uses the acronym RADaR (Replace, Add, Delete, and Reorder) to help writers improve their drafts. p. 257

RAFT: An acronym that can be used to design a disciplinary literacy project. R stands for the role of the writer (e.g., You are a travel agent). A stands for audience (e.g., I am your client). F stands for format (e.g., You will create and present a slide deck). T stands for topic (e.g., Plan the ultimate vacation). pp. 93, 256

Reading Conference: A short, one-on-one conversation between a teacher and student during independent reading time. It's used to check in on the student's reading progress, mentor with personalized support, and nurture empowered reading. p. 130

Reading Guide: A teacher-created scaffolded reading experience designed to help students engage more deeply and successfully with a text. It provides reading strategies and structured support—such as guiding questions, vocabulary help, prompts for making predictions or connections, and spaces for reflection—to focus students' attention on key ideas. p. 229

Reading Journal: Place to respond to reading through writing. pp. 63, 147

Reading Sideways: Students create mind maps to visualize and track their thinking as they read digitally. Students begin with a single term, which they write in the center of their page. Using a digital encyclopedia such as Wikipedia, they skim the surface of the topic with the goal of identifying connections, exploring the breadth of the subject, and posing questions for deeper inquiry. Each time they click a link, they add another term to their mind map and draw lines to show clustering and connections. p. 272

Relate and Apply: Annotation strategy to look for ideas that the reader relates to and can apply to their life. p. 236

Remix: The remix alters the original in a way that communicates a new feeling or message. Students can remix texts, songs, images, and videos to communicate new understandings about their learning or to create counternarratives to push back on harmful messages in society. pp. 101, 235

Roles for Group Work: A key to collaboration is to clearly identify the roles and responsibilities of each group member. As an example, groups of three can assign a Reader, Recorder, and Reporter. The reader reads the text aloud, the recorder takes notes on the group's discussion, and the reporter shares the group's ideas with the rest of the class. p. 144

Rose, Bud, Thorn: A simple yet insightful reflection routine that helps students pause and think about their reading and writing. The "rose" is something that went well. The "thorn" is a challenge or frustration. The "bud" is something they're still curious about or looking forward to. p. 128

Rubric: An assessment tool that clearly outlines success criteria tied to a learning goal. p. 123

S

Save the Last Word: In this protocol, each participant selects a meaningful quote or passage and shares it with their group. The other group members then take turns responding to the quote, sharing their interpretations, reactions, or connections. After everyone has responded, the original participant synthesizes what others have said and has "the last word." p. 228

the reader what is happening, students must show the reader through descriptive language. For example, a student might be asked to show that a character is mad rather than explicitly naming the emotion. p. 79

Single Paragraph Outline: A prewriting strategy focused on helping students organize their thoughts and develop flow in their writing one paragraph at a time. The single paragraph often includes a topic sentence, some supporting detail sentences, and a summary sentence at the end. p. 257

Single-Point Rubric: A single-point rubric outlines the expected standard for a task in a single column, allowing space on either side for noting areas that are strengths or need improvement. p. 123

Sketch and Label: During reading, students can draw a model to represent the text and then label the drawing using both the vocabulary words from the text and their own understanding. This works well for short texts, like a mathematical word problem, as well as with longer texts, like a science chapter describing the parts of a cell. p. 205

Sketchnotes: Sketchnotes combine drawing and writing to create a visual representation of the reading. Students can use handwriting fonts, arrows, symbols, doodles, colors, and layout in a way that is creative and personalized to them. For students who are multilingual, teachers can encourage them to use multiple languages too. pp. 82, 212

Social Annotations: Social Annotations use computer mediated communication to combine the active reading strategy of annotation with the power of hearing others' perspectives. When students notice a move an author is making, they can highlight the quote and add a comment to name the rhetorical technique and explicate the impact of the move on the reader. After reading, students can discuss which quote they thought was most powerful or convincing. This strategy can be used synchronously or asynchronously. pp. 106, 143, 277

Source-Based Writing: Integrates reading and writing by having students respond to texts through writing or reading texts to gather ideas to use in writing. An example from social studies is Document-Based Questions. pp. 101, 104

SQ3R: SQ3R is a reading strategy for informational texts that stands for Survey, Question, Read, Recite, and Review. The steps guide readers to preview the text (looking at headings, images, and text features), ask a question about what they hope to learn, read to find the answer, summarize the key ideas, and then review the material to reinforce learning. p. 37

Square, Circle, Triangle: Students can use the Square, Circle, Triangle routine to guide their active reading. While annotating, they put a box around the ideas that square with their thinking (i.e., what they agree with), a circle where they have questions (ideas circling in their head), and a triangle next to important points or takeaways that they want to remember. If they are taking notes, they can make three sections on their paper (one each for square, circle, and triangle). p. 14

Storyboards: Visualizing helps reading comprehension because the reader sees the story or information like a movie. Storyboards were originally used by movie directors to plan camera shots for a film but can also be used to make a movie in a reader's mind as they read. p. 225

Synthesis Matrix: An organizing tool that helps students track key ideas across multiple sources, making it easier to compare, contrast, and synthesize information. It supports critical thinking and prepares students to write evidence-based responses or research papers. p. 274

T

Take a Line for a Walk: A writing exercise that helps students engage in deeper exploration. Students are asked to select a single, meaningful line from a larger text, copy it, and then respond to it. p. 238

Textual Lineage: The textual lineage activity invites students to reflect on the texts (books, articles, songs, speeches, etc.) that have shaped their identities, values, and thinking. The idea is to trace a "lineage" of influential texts—much like a family tree—that helps students understand themselves as readers and how texts influence their thinking. Students often share their textual lineage with peers, creating opportunities for connection and discussion. p. 157

Text-Dependent Questions: Text-dependent questions require students to go back to the reading to support their answers with textual evidence. p. 229

Text Rendering: A strategy to help students get to the essence of a text through discussion. As students read, they highlight ideas that they think are important. When they finish reading, they choose what they feel is the most important sentence, phrase, and word of the piece. One of each. In small groups, they do three rounds of discussion, first sharing their sentences, then phrases, then words. It's okay if something is repeated. A scribe records each phrase and word and then the group choral reads this new text, meaning that they all read it aloud together. Text rendering ends with the group discussing what new insights they gained about the text by looking at it in this way. p. 228

Text Roundup: An activity where students gather multiple texts related to a question. The activity is based on the article type used in journalism and marketing to summarize research or curate a group of texts on a common theme. After a lesson on locating reliable information, a Text Roundup can be an assignment for students to practice gathering relevant, credible sources. You can assign this activity with 3–10 texts around a common theme or inquiry question. A graphic organizer may include columns for the title of the source, the year, connection to the question, genre, author's purpose, etc. p. 99

Text Structure Graphic Organizers: A set of visual tools that shows students how texts can be or are organized. Some examples include sequential, cause and effect, problem and solution, etc. p. 256

Teacher Think Aloud: Teachers model how they apply their knowledge by pausing when reading or writing to articulate their thinking process and reasoning. pp. 79, 91, 194, 203, 252

Thinking Hats: This literacy strategy was adapted from De Bono's (1999) book. p. 137

- White Hat: Focuses on facts, information, and data.

- Red Hat: Deals with emotions, feelings, intuition, and connections.

- Black Hat: Identifies potential problems, risks, and challenges.

- Yellow Hat: Explores benefits, positives, and opportunities for application.

- Green Hat: Encourages creative ideas, new possibilities, and innovation.

- Blue Hat: Manages the process, summarizes, and synthesizes.

Thinking Routines: A set of strategies that help take thinking deeper and make thinking visible through writing and can be used routinely because they can apply to many situations. For example, see *I Used to Think ... Now I Think.* p. 101

Tic-Tac-Toe: This assessment is a type of choice board that presents students with a 3×3 grid of assessment tasks aligned to specific learning goals. Students choose three tasks to complete in a row horizontally, vertically, or diagonally. p. 122

Translanguaging: This instructional approach encourages students to use their full linguistic repertoire to support understanding, expression, and learning. It encourages students to draw on all their languages, including their home language(s), when reading, writing, discussing, or making meaning. This approach not only strengthens content learning and literacy development but also affirms students' cultural and linguistic identities. p. 119

Two Dollar Summaries: See $2 Summary

UV

Virtual Scavenger Hunt: An online strategy to support students in inquiry-oriented exploration. Teachers give students some background information as well as a goal for their exploration. Then, students engage with links to find information. Also called a WebQuest. p. 132

Vocabulary Comics: Students create a short comic strip that uses one vocabulary word or a longer comic that uses a required number of vocabulary words. Combining the visuals with using the word in context supports deeper learning of the word. p. 190

Vocabulary Explicit Instruction Routine: Teachers can use a direct instruction routine for individual words where they project the spelling and pronounce the word, provide a student-friendly definition, and use the word in context. p. 191

W

Wonder Wall: Dedicate a space on the wall or a bulletin board for students to add questions that arise from what they are reading and studying. You can have students use sticky notes to add what they are curious about and what they want to know more about. Use the wall to inform planning future lessons. p. 147

Word Journals: Keeping a word journal is an approach to learning vocabulary that invites students to self-select the words that they are interested in learning. Students can identify words from texts in and out of school and collect the words in a personal journal. There are digital templates available or a composition book works just fine. Also could be part of a Writer's Notebook. pp. 181, 204

Word Ladder: Word ladders are a phonics and spelling activity where students change one word into another by altering a single letter or phoneme at each step (e.g., *cat → cot → dot → dog*). This strategy helps students build phonemic awareness, recognize spelling patterns, and reinforce decoding skills through playful word manipulation. pp. 44, 165

Word Tournament: The Word Tournament routine engages vocabulary from a text in an interactive way. Students begin by choosing 15–20 significant words from the text. In small groups, they collaborate to narrow their list down to eight words, which are positioned on the far left side of a tournament-style bracket. Through discussion, they determine which four words will move to the next round, followed by selecting two finalists, and ultimately, a single "winning" word. Each group then shares with the whole class the reasoning behind their final choice. p. 206

Writing into the Day: Setting aside a brief time at the beginning of class for daily writing practice. Teachers can provide prompts to generate student thinking. p. 237

Writer's Notebook: A dedicated space for students to experiment with writing, note new vocabulary, and collect ideas for writing. pp. 22, 151, 272

Writing Buffet: Each writer brings a draft of their work and staples a sheet of colored paper to the back. All the pieces are then laid out on a "buffet table." Group members move through the buffet line, selecting one piece at a time to read and respond to on the colored sheet. When finished, they return the piece to the table and choose another. This cycle continues until everyone has had a chance to respond to several drafts. At the end, each writer collects their piece, now filled with a variety of thoughtful feedback. p. 257

Writing Conference: A short, one-on-one conversation between a teacher and student during the writing process. It's used to check in on the student's writing progress, mentor with personalized support, and encourage agentic writing. p. 130

Written Conversations: Students write a letter to a classmate and then send it by passing it along or posting to an online discussion board. The classmate writes back. Can be completed in partners or small groups, passing the conversation along several times before returning to the original poster. The original poster then reads the entire conversation, starring an idea or two from the written conversation to initiate an oral discussion. pp. 64, 238

XYZ

Zettelkasten Note-Taking: The method provides categories of notes with different protocols based on the purpose of the note-taking and includes a linking system. Useful for research and writing projects. p. 11

Index